How to get a job in a recession

By Denise Taylor

Amazing People

AWARD WINNING CAREER COACHING COMPANY

How to get a job
in a recession

By Denise Taylor

Brook House Press

www.howtogetajobinarecession.com

Printed and bound in Great Britain by Lightning Press

ISBN 978-0-9561755-0-2

Whilst the author has made every effort to provide
accurate web sites at the time of publication, the
author does not assume any responsibility for errors
or for changes that occur after publication.

Contents

Acknowledgments

This book would have remained a task to do some day without Asif Hasan, Producer/Director with ITV who made the suggestion, more than once.

My thanks go to all the many clients I have worked with over the years who came to me unsure about how to get a job and left with increased confidence and a great future. I feel so blessed to have a job I love so much and the chance to work with so many fantastic people.

I'd particularly like to thank Tatyana, Kim, and Lindsay, who were generous in their feedback and willing to give it a go, even when some of the things I asked them to do went against conventional advice.

I also wish to thank my editor, Dale for his guidance, and Lucy for her attention to detail.

Finally to thank my husband Simon and family who were patient with me whilst I withdrew from family life – a book takes so much more time than expected.

Denise Taylor
Tewkesbury, England
February 2009

Foreword

It has always been the case that knowing how to find and secure the right position has been a crucial skill. However, given the current economic climate, such skills are needed far more than ever before. Although the current situation may make the process a little more challenging, what Denise has done is to demonstrate that it is possible to beat the recession with careful planning, thought and creative thinking. The opportunities exist and it is a case of knowing how to find and make the most of such opportunities.

Not only is Denise Taylor an expert in her field, but she has the knack of presenting the information and skills required to get the most from these challenging times in a logical and accessible format. She makes no assumptions about any pre-existing knowledge an individual may have and takes the reader through all the steps required to successfully deal with the various aspects of the job search process such as designing a CV to practical interview skills. In addition, Denise is able to help the reader understand the job market and brings together up-to-date information and the ways that creative thinking and commitment can get you what you want even in these challenging times.

A practical, down-to-earth, comprehensive and easy to read book that will help many people recognise that in every crisis, there is an opportunity if you only know how to go about finding it.

Gladeana McMahon, Vice President, Association for Coaching, Co-Director Centre for Coaching, listed as one of the UK's Top Ten Coaches by the *Independent on Sunday* and the *Sunday Observer*.

For Simon – provider of love,
support and a clean house

For Tom and Nika at the start
of their career journey

Introduction

How to get a job in a recession

Welcome, I'm Denise Taylor, a chartered occupational psychologist and award winning career coach. For over twenty years, I've been helping people discover what they have to offer, working with them to identify a job they'll love, and supporting them in their job search.

As we enter the recession, it's getting more difficult to find employment. There are still jobs available however. And yes, that great job you've always wanted is still out there. But more than ever, you need to look for ways to stand out from the rest and I'm going to show you how.

I was prompted to write this book following my involvement with the ITV Tonight programme, "How Safe is Your Job?" I worked with people who had been unemployed for months, partly because they weren't realistic in their job aspirations, but also because their job search was not very effective. Too many people take a "scatter gun" approach, sending out numerous CVs with general information not tailored to a specific position. It's much more effective to focus on one job at a time and gear all your efforts (and prepare a custom CV) to land that job. This book teaches you how.

I've written this book for you. Maybe you can't stand another day in the position you have now, you've recently left college or university, or your family commitments have changed and you are ready to enter or re-enter the job market. Maybe you lost your job to redundancy during these difficult times. Maybe you're a contractor who's found that there is a gap (which you hadn't experienced before) between your last contract and now – and the gap is getting scarily wider as each day passes.

Whatever the reason, you need help from a qualified professional. Kim had spent four months searching for a job and had not even got to interview, but within a week of me helping her, she was shortlisted for three jobs and two interviews later she got a great offer. Lindsay was made redundant and was unsure about the proper way to apply for a new job. She followed the advice in this book and had a new job within weeks. Paul was unrealistic in his career expectations and adding to that, his CV and letter were too general and not targeted to the vacancy. Needless to say, he didn't find employment.

I could fill this book with many more examples of client success stories, and I have included some as appropriate. However, my main focus here is to provide practical help for you. Within these pages. you'll go through the same process I use with my clients. I've also given you a plan that includes everything you need to do in the first month of your job search.

Denise x

Is it as bad as the press makes out?

If you've been made redundant it's not good for you and your family. You may have minimal redundancy payments and worries about paying the mortgage and other bills. Knowing that many more people will lose their job as well isn't that helpful (because what you are mostly concerned with is how it affects you). In December, 2008, 27,000 people were made redundant from Woolworths, along with job losses at Adams, MFI, and other companies. The outlook is bleak with the Chartered Institute of Personnel and Development predicting a loss of 600,000 jobs in 2009.

The current unemployment rate is 6% but this doesn't take into account the number of people at home taking care of family members or students who would work if jobs were available. Within a year, this figure could rise to 9%.

According to the government there are over 600,000 jobs available. Some of these are low paying or in the wrong part of the country, but good jobs are still being advertised. My clients are still getting job offers but it is taking longer than they anticipated. Part of my job is to keep them motivated, focused, encouraged and patient. They will succeed – persistence is the key.

> *There are more people looking for jobs so you need to be very clear on what you have to offer*

Some work areas are unlikely to result in redundancies – teachers, health care, funeral directors and work involved with care homes for the elderly. Many other companies will stay in business but there will be fewer vacancies as people decide to stay in a "safe" job.

The changing job market

Thirty or more years ago, people expected to stay in a job for life. However changes in the global market make this a rarity. There is a need to accept change and move on. Seven or eight years ago was the dotcom crash and in a couple of years, 700 companies collapsed. But people moved on to new things. A couple of years ago, many people lost their jobs as back office work and call centres moved overseas. Again people found alternative work.

There was also a high loss of jobs back in the 1990s. This mainly affected the manufacturing and construction industries with a loss of 94,000 jobs in these sectors in the three months from June to September, 1990. Office based jobs were still secure with index linked pensions and jobs for life. However, the difference this time is that job losses brought on by the recession are affecting every region, age group and almost every industry. In particular, it will affect managers, professionals and skilled non-manual workers, from the finance industry to estate agents. It will also affect service occupations. For example, will people still pay for personal trainers and massage therapists? Will people wait longer between hair cuts or dye their hair at home?

The writing is on the wall

It's rare that a redundancy comes from nowhere. There are clues and predictors, but often people miss them.

If you are in work, but wondering if your job will be the next to go, here are some things to do:

1. Read the business press

If you buy *The Times, Telegraph* or similar, make sure you read the business pages or look at the business pages online. You can read about potential lost contracts, and profit warnings. Don't just read up on your company, but also your company's competitors. If you notice a competitor is going into receivership, it could mean there is more business coming to your company, but it could also mean that your company, your industry is in little demand. There are often clues on how your company and industry are doing. Look to the specific market your product is sold in.

2. Notice changes in staffing

Too often, we just focus on our job and forget about a broader view of the company. It's easy to think that because our job is in admin or finance, we don't need to focus on the company products or services. But re-member, products and services are the key reasons the company exists and the further away your task is from the core focus of the business, the more difficult it will be to justify your salary in a credit crunch. At times like this advertising, personnel and middle management jobs will often go.

It could be useful to get to know people in the sales department and notice if any sales staff are leaving. If a company is laying off sales people because they can't afford them, manufacturing and support will be next. When sales consultants resign, it's often because they are finding it hard to earn a bonus and they look else-where to sell a product that is in greater demand.

3. Pay close attention to company initiatives

Finally, pay close attention to company initiatives such as a recruitment freeze and seeking voluntary redundancies as they could indicate the company is in trouble. Also if it is taking longer to pay your expenses, and advertising has stopped it might be time to get your CV ready.

If your job is made redundant

There are wide differences between how people will respond to a redundancy notice. For many people losing their job is a stressful time with mortgage payments to make and bills to pay. They need to get a job as soon as possible, regardless of whether this is the right job for them or not. For others, redundancy can be liberating. If you have been unhappy in your work and you are now leaving with a reasonably generous redundancy payment, it can give you the impetus to make a change while you have six months or more salary to keep you afloat as you consider new opportunities. Don't forget to ask about what professional support is available. You may get some money to spend on a career coach.

A redundancy situation may be an emotional time for you

You are highly likely to feel emotional, so take the time to express those feelings – it could be sadness, shock, disappointment, shame, resentment, and anger. You have every right to feel angry, especially if your employer has been reassuring you that all is OK. That's why you must look out for the signs of change in your company.

You can certainly take the time to grieve the loss of your job, but you need to let go relatively soon, otherwise you will drain your resources. It will be difficult to be successful when applying for a job if you feel depressed or embarrassed by the redundancy. Look for ways to let those feelings out or they will fester inside of you. Exercise can help so go to the gym or take a brisk walk. Work in the garden or take a bike ride. You may prefer to find someone to talk with.

Don't take it personally

Redundancy is more likely to be due to budget cuts and a lack of business than poor performance on your part. In this current recession, with an increasing number of people being made redundant, there will unfortunately be many other people in your position.

Think about what you want to do in the short and medium term

Review your CV and think about what jobs are likely to become available. In the current economic climate, no matter how great you are as an estate agent or banker, if there aren't the jobs available you need a new plan. You may need to take a job which pays a lot less than you are used to, but with the current economic climate, future employers (those you will approach) will probably prefer to see you did something than not working at all. The bigger danger when applying for a lower paid job is in convincing people that you actually want the job and that you won't leave as soon as something better comes along. *Chapter Two, What Do You Want to Do?* will help you with this.

Think about how you will spend your day

When you were working, it gave you structure to your day, so how will you spend your time? If you want a new job, you must focus your efforts and devote your time to your job search. Look for jobs on line, but also be proactive. Get out and meet people, do research, get support from a career counsellor, engage friends and family – any and all of these things will help to speed up the process of getting a new job. The *Daily Tasks* pages in this book will help you to structure your day.

Don't retreat

It can be easy to take a step back from the world, and begin to get a bit too introspective. If you are feeling insecure or want to share your concerns, find someone to talk with. There's a tendency to become self-centred when we are unsure of the future. It's helpful to look for ways to be of help to others. Let your family know how you are and keep an eye out for them as well. Remember, family members may also feel stressed, wondering if all the bills are going to be paid.

Think about networking

Research says that 80% of people find jobs via the unadvertised job market. This means they are going out there and talking with people, meeting people at meetings and events, and specifically seeking people that they can talk with to find out more about jobs that interest them. You need to do the same. As you get clearer on the job you want, the more others can help you in your job search. You'll read more on this in *Chapter Five, Get Networking.*

Look after yourself

Redundancy is stressful, and it will take a lot of energy and stamina to keep going. You will also want to make sure you are in good health for when you start your new job. So take some exercise, get out in the fresh air, eat healthy meals, and sleep well.

Think about voluntary work

Volunteering gets you out of the house and adds some structure to your schedule (since you have to commit to a few hours each week). It allows you to meet others (perhaps less fortunate than you) and it looks good on your CV as it shows you to be proactive.

Getting a step ahead

Who could have predicted that Lehman Brothers would fall? But there were clues this was going to happen. The business press had written how Woolworths was finding it hard to find its place in the current market. It had moved away from its core strengths of being a source for products of good value.

There are steps you can take right now to get yourself ready for a job search in case your job becomes redundant. Put your plan into action right away.

- Network – Keeping in touch with people you know and developing relationships with others who may be able to help you in the future (or you being able to help them). You can learn more about this in *Chapter Five, Get Networking*.

- Skills audit - Be clear on your strengths and what you have to offer. Chapter Two will help.

- Create an up to date CV – Clearly outline your key achievements. It's too easy to leave it as is and then when you need it you realise it's out of date. So look at it critically and make sure it includes up to date information. You can read more about this in *Chapter Three, Creating Your CV*.

- Review the job market – Make a note of what jobs are offered and the salaries they pay.

- Review your finances – Look for ways to economise. Now is the time to review where your money goes and find ways to save. Reducing your debt or getting some savings together will make you feel better.

Will it be me or you?

Often, it's not the whole company that closes, but just a percentage of staff that is let go (for example, one person in each store or department). So you need to look for ways to help increase the chances of you staying.

- Make sure that you do a good job so they are more likely to keep you. Go beyond the minimum of what needs to be done, but look for ways to add extra value such as simplifying processes, improving customer service and reducing costs.

- Be visible. It's not just doing a good job but letting other people know you are doing a good job. Don't hide your achievements. It's also about being seen by senior staff, so get involved in meetings and focus groups, you want to be known to the key decision makers. Also get your boss to let their boss know what a good job you are doing.

- Be indispensible. Be willing to volunteer for the jobs others don't want to do and be flexible in helping out.

Create great relationships with your customers or really learn the computer system. Your boss won't want to let you go.

- Make or save the company money. Look for what you can do to help the company's bottom line. Can you save them money? Simplify processes? Negotiate a better deal with suppliers?

- Have a positive attitude. When people are being made redundant, companies will often use this as an excuse to lay off the "difficult ones."

- Keep your skills up to date. Don't just rely on previous experience, but seek out training and other ways to become more skilled. Your company may not pay for your training, but you could keep up to date through reading relevant articles and perhaps increasing your computer skills through practicing at home.

- Be alert but don't worry. You should focus on doing a good job, not worrying about what might happen. But you can prepare your CV and be clear on the sort of work you would like to do should you find yourself made redundant.

So how do I start?

People differ. Following redundancy, some people may decide to take on any job that is offered, other people will hang on for the perfect job. But remember, 100% of something is better than 0% of nothing. Do your research, if the likelihood of getting a similar job or your ideal job is remote, identify what jobs are more likely to use your skills and experience and focus on that.

Waiting might bring you your ideal job, but waiting may also mean that you get into more debt. Think carefully about any opportunity. It might be something with less money, but it might also give you a chance to learn and develop, or get you into a company that may have other jobs advertised internally.

As you look at the available jobs, you might notice that they seek people with a certain skill set or experience. Could you use this free time to develop some new skills?

Do think it through carefully before deciding to sign up for an expensive course, use fact finding interviews to find out more and be very clear on the benefits before you spend your money.

In the short term, you may have skills that a voluntary organisation could use. This would keep you active, help you to meet new people, and let potential employers know that you didn't just sit back and wait for a new job, but used the time to benefit others.

This book is divided into two sections.

The first section provides the structure for what you need to do – it contains your list of daily tasks. The larger second section is reference material which will help you on your journey.

1. Getting ready, being organised
2. What do you want to do
3. Creating your CV
4. The personal commercial
5. Get networking
6. Fact finding interviews
7. Different ways to get a job
8. Replying to job ads
9. The covering letter
10. Stand out from the crowd
11. The hidden job market
12. The phone interview
13. Interview preparation
14. The interview – you're shortlisted!

Before you get started, listen to Kim's story.

Kim's story

Kim had been made redundant from her job as a Legal Executive in July, 2008. She had applied for over 100 jobs and had not been shortlisted. She visited the job centre and had undertaken an employability course to help her with her CV and interview skills, but no offers came her way. She got in touch with me after seeing me on ITV where she saw I had helped Paul to get a job. She needed a new approach.

Kim and I followed the steps in this book. We talked about her experience, strengths and what she wanted to do. Kim then started revising her CV with guidance from my notes. You can see her before and after CVs in Chapter Three. Here's what Kim did to give her a great chance to become employed:

25th November - Tuesday

I decided to redesign my CV. I worked through the CV Chapter and looked at the sample CV. I then began to draft a new version of my CV. I also sent my CV to my brother for him to look at as suggested by Denise.

Once Kim had revised her CV, she concentrated on rewriting her covering letter, again following the advice in this book.

Kim found this new approach incredibly helpful.

"I am enjoying learning very important skills which will not only help me now but for the rest of my life. I am feeling more confident about my abilities each day."

26th November - Wednesday

In the morning, I went along to the local shopping centre and filled out a temporary Christmas job application for Next. I also asked some of the other shops whether they had any vacancies.

I was very pleased with my new CV, it looks very professional and stylish. I then proceeded to draft a cover-ing letter to send to an agency applying for a job I had already applied for and been rejected. I then went to the job centre to sign on.

Kim had got an immediate rejection from one job. As practice, she applied again, this time sending a revised CV and covering letter. Whilst the job had gone, she had a much more positive rejection letter.

Dear Kim, Thank you for your application for the above position. Whilst your CV and skills do look relevant my client has now made an offer to a candidate who is due to start next week. If the opportunity becomes vacant again I will of course be in touch. Thank you again and good luck with your job search.

Kim was now ready to really go for it!

27th November - Thursday

Re-sent new CV to agencies

I read the Chapter on responding to job ads to help me complete an application form. I did have one job that I wanted to apply for by application form as a Resources Manager at Manchester University, the only problem be-ing that the deadline was the 27th November and this didn't really give me enough time to complete the form. However, I decided that I should have a go and using the Personal Specification dealt with each of the points. I would have liked more time to improve my answers and chance of being shortlisted but had to send it off before the deadline expired.

I bought both the local paper and *Manchester Evening News* today to hunt for jobs.

I have selected four jobs to apply for. I have tried to select these carefully on the basis that I could do the job but I feel very nervous about only applying for four jobs! I am trying to remember that it's not quantity but quality of my applications that's important.

28th November - Friday

Having read the papers, I found a job for a pharmacy assistant and was thinking about applying for it more as a temporary job than a permanent one. I was concerned that I would be rejected for being overqualified and e-mailed Denise to ask what I should do and whether I should amend my CV.

Denise advised me to leave the CV as it was but that I would have to explain my reasons in my covering letter. I decided to search on the Internet for a more suitable position.

I was having difficulty psychologically dealing with the number of jobs I was applying for. In the past, I got some comfort from the fact that I had put in a lot of applications thinking that gave me a better chance of getting a job. Denise had told me this was the wrong approach and I should select jobs more carefully, applying for fewer positions and taking the time to make sure my applications were the best they could be.

I searched on the Internet for jobs and found one at a firm of Solicitors and drafted a covering letter.

I found another position on the Internet as a General Coordinator through Office Angels. I didn't feel that the advert gave enough information about the job so I called to find out more but they wouldn't really give me any more details so I decided to draft a covering letter and send it off in any event.

I also received a rejection e-mail from Cheshire County Council. I asked them for some feedback and they said they could see that I have some excellent work experience but that I had not explained in sufficient detail or given enough examples of my experience. I think for now I am going to cease applying for Council jobs as I believe they prefer to recruit internally.

Monday - 1st December

Denise liked the draft covering letter and thought I was a good match for the job. She made a couple of amendments and I then sent off my application for the job at the Solicitors.

I cut out other job adverts from the paper re-reading them to decide whether I was in fact a suitable candidate and also checking the job description and personal specification. I decided that I would only apply for jobs where I felt I was a strong candidate and where I had a good chance of being shortlisted. I found two more jobs to apply for, one as an Administrator for Manchester University and one as Administrative Officer for Salford University.

The closing date for the latter was the 4th December and as an application form had to be completed I decided to print off all the details and read them carefully before starting to complete the form.

Tuesday 2nd December

I carefully started to complete my application form taking my time to ensure that I had completed it to my best ability.

Wednesday 3rd December

I continued completing the form.

Thursday 4th December

Finally satisfied that I had done my best completing the form having reviewed it a number of times. I had written two pages relating to the personal specification (which is the most I have ever been able to write) so I sent the form off.

Drafted a letter to go with my CV applying for the other university position (still to send).

Bought both the local paper and Manchester Evening News to hunt for more jobs.

Friday 5th December

Met up with old colleagues from work for lunch including one girl that had been made redundant before me in May. She had moved back to her parents in Malvern but had got a job after four months with a defence company reviewing their sales contracts. She had just sent out a huge number of applications!

Went through the papers deciding which jobs to apply for next week.

Just had the agency on the phone for the second job I applied for as a General Coordinator and they want to see me tomorrow morning so they can put me forward for this job and also search for other jobs for me both temporary and permanent! The advice in this book is really helping; these are the first two jobs I applied for after going through this programme.

This evening I'm going to a Virgin Vie party at a friends tonight and will do some networking at the same time.

Monday 8th December

Happy Days! Received a letter from Salford University inviting me for an interview - Hooray! 16th December at 9.30am.

Read letter and sent an e-mail response to confirm attendance and request parking space reserved. Completed the forms enclosed with the letter ready for my interview.

Researched another position on-line that I want to apply for as Administrator at Manchester Metropolitan University.

Received a phone call from Office Angels. Keen to see me ASAP to put me forward for the position I had applied for and also to look at other positions both temp and permanent. Made an appointment for next day 11.00am Tuesday 9th December.

Sorted out paperwork and continued to read through the book. Arranged to get new pair of reading glasses!!

Tuesday 9th December

Had my appointment with Emily at Office Angels. I wore a suit to give a good impression. I was there for two hours filling in forms and doing three tests on the computer. I was very disappointed to hear at the end of it all that the job I had applied for was in fact "on hold." She did appear however to be proactive referring to me as a top candidate and was going to contact all her clients, the only other concern was salary. She didn't hold out any hope of getting a good salary. I will have to see what develops.

Applied for a job at Salford University but had awful problems with the on-line application (so don't think that will be successful).

Wednesday 10th December

Had my appointment with the Job Centre. I tried to explain what I was doing but they really do not understand anything you say – their focus is on the number of applications, not concerned with quality at all! They haven't given me any help or support in finding a job. In the beginning they told me they would not help me because I was highly skilled when I knew that I needed some professional guidance. I tried phoning them once and was told that I could have careers advice in a room with a whole load of other people and the girl also said that lots of people had complained it wasn't suitable as they were expecting a one to one session!

In the afternoon I helped to organise a talk at the nursing home. The manager of the nursing home sat me down and said the staff had told her how caring I was with the patients and did I want a job!

Thursday 11th December

Went to visit my newborn nephew.

Bought the local paper and Manchester Evening News to search for jobs.

Also did an Internet search.

Friday 12th December

Collected recent Maths Certificate from Georgina at the Training Centre.

Collected suit from the dry cleaners and shoes from the cobblers for my interview.

Re-sent application to Salford Uni as HR wanted me to submit through the website.

Did final research on last weeks job adverts to eliminate ones not suitable.

Saturday 13th December

Had a break for the day. I went to the hairdressers to ask what I could do to improve my hair ready for my interview.

Sunday 14th December

Read through the interview chapters and carefully planned answers to the questions.

Had an e-mail from friend whose Virgin Vie party I had gone to say she knew of a company that had vacancies and she was going to let me know if suitable for me.

Monday 15th December

Went to the Salford University office pretending to go on a course and picked up two copies of the prospectus which I read to give me as much knowledge of the organisation as possible.

Copied my Maths Certificate for my portfolio.

Called HR to confirm they had my e-mail confirming attendance.

Read the interview chapter ready for my interview and did an interview coaching session with Denise. Redrafted answers and tried to remember them.

Tuesday 16th December

Got up at 6.15am and prepared for my interview at 9.30am which finished at 10.00am. Sent a thank you e-mail to Jackie who interviewed me. Completed the Interview Evaluation Form.

Arranged to meet up with one of my referees Julie and also my friend Kerry (made redundant with me).

Had an e-mail from Hays to say that they were still considering my application for a job I applied for in October in Dubai so sent them the updated CV and asked them to pass it on to the recruiter doing the short listing.

Had an unsuccessful e-mail from Cheshire County Council and e-mailed them to ask them to give me some feedback.

Started applying for an Administrator position at South Manchester College.

Completed the application form for South Manchester College and sent it off.

Wednesday 17th December

9.30am Jackie from Manchester University called to say that I had not been successful following my interview and they had decided to offer the job to a candidate who had experience of working at the University. She did say that I had interviewed well and I couldn't help but think that it had been a done deal because I had only been given half an hour to be interviewed which wasn't long enough and also the questions were fired very quickly, it was all too fast paced!

I was a bit disappointed with the news and found it difficult to think about getting back to job searching so met up with my friend Kerry for a coffee and had a good chat and a giggle for a couple of hours. Then decided to do a bit of Christmas shopping I had been putting it off because I could only afford small gifts this year. Felt a bit better.

Thursday 18th December

Woke up feeling a bit more determined to get on with my job search.

Bought the local papers and started searching for jobs and also looked on the internet. Found a job advertised by an agency for a temporary position and even though the pay rate was low, I thought I would enjoy the work and phoned the agency. I spoke to Adam and he advised that the position was working at the Tribunal Office attending all the tribunals. We chatted about my experience and I asked if I could come along to see him in Manchester and we arranged an appointment for 11.00am the next day.

I also decided to chase up some of my other applications. I called XYZ law firm as I had not heard back from them for a job I applied for at the beginning of December and they had not put a closing date on the job advertisement. The HR lady Kirsty advised that my application had arrived after they had shortlisted. I had noted on the website that there was another vacancy for an Administration Assistant and I asked if I could apply for that position and she said yes so I sent my application off straight away.

Also applied for a position as a Customer Service Assistant with an events insurance company.

Friday 19th December

8.40 am Kirsty from XYZ law firm called to ask me to attend an interview on Monday at 11.30am.

11.00am Dressed smartly for my meeting with Adam and we got on well. We filled out a lot of forms together and he explained that his agency did all the work for the

Tribunal Office. He wanted me to go along straight away to meet his client for an interview. Their office was just a few minutes walk around the corner so I went off to meet Tanya.

They were delighted to see me ... they talked to me about the job and we agreed that I would start in Manchester on the 5th Jan. Tanya said all the judges would absolutely love me because of my legal knowledge and experience!

At last some progress although I have to keep focused on the next step of my interview and prepare properly for the day by doing some research on the internet over the weekend.

Monday 22nd December

Attended the interview which I was very much looking forward to as I had done a lot of research on their website and they seemed such a professional firm with impressive offices.

I met the personnel manager who I liked. Then she called in the partner from the Debt Recoveries Department and from then on, things went from bad to worse. I found his interview style aggressive and sexist and I felt he asked personal questions not relevant to the job.

"Do you actually need to work?" I said yes. Would he ask that question of a man I wonder.

"There are partners here that I wouldn't walk within a five mile radius of" his comment when I said I wanted to work for a professional firm.

"Whilst your CV looks good there are some bad points for example you have had a lot of jobs and how do I know that you won't leave after the housing market picks up."

He had not read my CV properly. I informed him that I had only worked for two employers and that I had different roles working for those employers.

After the awful interview, he said "well I have finished beating you up now" and handed me back to the personnel manager who apologised for his interview style saying that they had a number of staff leave after a short time - I'm not surprised!! The interview had lasted an hour and a quarter and I had the headache from hell and wished Denise could have been there. I hope and pray they don't offer me the job. They said they would let me know the next day.

Tuesday 23rd December

I had a phone call from Salford University (who had advised that I was unsuccessful) saying that they had in fact change their minds (after I asked them for feedback as to why I wasn't shortlisted) and they were now having a two stage process of interviews and I would need to go and do a test for the first round of interviews.

The Personnel Manager from the law firm called to say that they hadn't made a decision regarding my interview but they hoped to get back to me at the beginning of January and I told them that I had accepted another job offer. I just could not take a job with them as it would have made me miserable.

Signed off at the job centre.

I've introduced you to Kim so you can share someone else's experiences. It didn't come easy to Kim, she struggled alone with poor advice from those she thought could help her. Following this structured process has given Kim the confidence to present herself well and to get a new job. In the rest of this book you will be able to follow the same steps Kim took until you too gain success in a new job. Should you need a more personal service, do get in touch.

Part One

Daily tasks

Introduction

I want you to follow a structured and organised approach to your job search, to make best use of your time and keep you focused. You need to treat your job search like a marketing campaign where the product is you and everything you do gets you closer to your desired result, a job.

Each day you will undertake certain activities – it's important that you do these, and **review your progress at the end of each day**. It may take some time before you get a job offer, but as you complete each action you can celebrate a mini success, completing the tasks means you haven't just sat back and given up.

The review stage is important. If, when you talk with people, they aren't clear on what sort of job you are looking for, revise what you say. If you are not getting shortlisted, review your CV and the way you complete application forms. As part of your review you should ask yourself:

Have I followed the advice in this book?

Do I need to discuss my approach with a job search buddy or a job search coach/ career counsellor?

Am I actually **doing the steps I should do each day and not just reading what to do?**

It's not enough to just read this book, you need to do the activities and **keep** doing them.

Even in a booming economy some people give up on looking for a new job because it's hard work. But if you are committed, and follow the steps … Kim and Lindsay were highly determined and both started new jobs within 2 months of working through this programme.

Others take longer and I've worked with people who didn't follow my advice and aren't getting interviews. When I review what's going wrong, it's usually for a number of reasons – their CV needs a rewrite, they don't have a structure to the covering letter, they are sending out generic letters to jobs they are clearly unlikely to get and take far too long to do anything.

Just last week Paul asked me to review his covering letter for a job, I gave comprehensive feedback, all explained in *Chapter Eight, Replying To Job Ads,* but his second letter, which came a week later still didn't address the points in this chapter. Follow the steps and put your effort into the jobs you are a reasonably good match for rather than a general application to many jobs.

This workbook includes a full month of tasks which will be helpful, informative and fun – that's what my clients tell me. Some days you may not have the time to compete a task so either catch up on the next day or slow down your approach. Other days you may find it easy to move ahead. Work at a "stretch" pace, you can't afford to take too leisurely a journey if you want to find a job in a recession.

Expect there to be some setbacks, but if you continue to nudge ahead, you will get there

It's going to take time

Please be realistic about how long your job search will take. It generally takes three months in a good economy from first looking to starting work in a new job. In a recession it could easily take twice this. It all depends on the type of job you are seeking, the higher your salary requirement, the longer it is likely to take you. It's obviously easier to get a lower paid job (more quickly) as there are so many more of them. I've allocated you the first couple of weeks for preparation. It could take less if you are already "job search ready" and/or you are working full time on job search. That's why it's important to have an up to date CV should you need to get a job fast.

Notes and review

I've included some space for you to make notes as you go along, but you may prefer to use a notebook or A4 pad. **I've also included all the forms in an eBook which you can access at low cost from the website.**

Keeping a daily log and monitoring your progress will help in your job search. Noting down what you have done each day, what you have learnt from it and what you are going to do next day will keep you on track.

Day 1: How are you feeling?

It can be quite scary looking for a new job, particularly if it's a long time since you last looked for one or you have yet to get a first job.

Let's start with how you are feeling right now?

Action: Take 5 minutes to make a note of how you are feeling:

You may have used words describing your concern over the future, and how you feel right now – angry, resentful, bitter etc. but also, whilst perhaps a bit concerned and unsure, you may be excited, this might be the prod you need to start working for yourself or to do something new.

Many of us are in jobs that we don't really like – we find them boring, we have a boss who creates too many problems, we don't feel we are paid enough for what we do. So, particularly if you have got a reasonable redundancy payout, this may give you the impetus to do something you actually want to do.

We can't ignore our feelings and of course it's ok to become disappointed, concerned, etc. But to be successful in our job search, we also need to set these feelings to one side. If not, these feelings will keep popping up as we apply for jobs and at interview, and still feeling bitter about what's happened, won't help us perform well and an interviewer will pick up on them.

So aim to concentrate on the positive. Start by listing three things you are grateful for. You can then refer back to this when things appear difficult.

Action: List 3 things you are grateful for:

1.

2.

3.

You may have included your family, your health, friendships and your ability to learn new things. These positive things will help you as you progress in your job search.

Practical steps

You also need to take practical actions. If you are not in work you need to get on with relevant activities each day. This includes spending a minimum of 4 hours a day (on average) with effective job search activity. Other things you could do during the remainder of the day include: voluntary work, exercise (could be a brisk walk each day) and developing your skills, such as learning to use Excel.

You do need a reason to get out of bed each day and if you are feeling a bit low and despondent, having a preset schedule will be helpful.

Offering your skills to a voluntary organisation for a day a week can allow you to have meaning and structure to a day, work in a team environment, use and develop skills and will be useful to include on your CV and to discuss at interview. You won't have just sat back and waited for a job. You might make some useful contacts as well! Tomorrow you will be looking at how to be organised and will get together everything needed for your job search.

Register at the job centre

If you are unemployed register at the job centre – you can do this on line at www.jobcentreplus.gov.uk or through phoning 0800 055 66 88. When you call you will need to have your national insurance number, and details of your rent/mortgage payments; employment history and savings. They will arrange for you to meet with an advisor and let you know if you are entitled to any financial assistance or free training programmes.

Note: You may have the time to get ahead, so feel free to start on day 2 if you have the time.

Day 2: Getting organised

Read *Chapter One, Getting Ready - Being Organised*

Systems! You love them or hate them, but for job search you are going to need to be organised.

1: Create a filing system

You need to be able to easily access everything that will make job search easy. Chapter One lists what you need to have ready.

2: Plan your days

Plan how much time you will spend each day on job search and how committed you are to it. The amount of time you spend will depend on if you are currently in work or if you have all the day free.

3: Personal support system

This chapter also gets you to look into the need for a personal support system. Who or what can provide the support you need? Decide which method will work best for you.

4: References

Before you are offered a job, you will need to provide references. This section will help you decide who to choose and how to get the best out of your referees.

Summary: Have you read Chapter One and completed the activities?

Do you have the forms ready to use? Use the forms in the book or use the accompanying eWorkbook available at low cost from the web site.

Have you decided when you will do your job search?

Do you know what you will do when you need some support?

Have you arranged to contact the people you will use for your references?

Day 3: What do you want to do

Read *Chapter Two, What Do You Want to Do?*

It's not enough to want a new job. You need to be clear on the **specific** job you want. That means you can market yourself properly.

In today's chapter you can complete various exercises to get you focused on who you are and what you ideally want to do. You'll then do a reality check. It can help to come up with two jobs, your ideal and a job that will do in the short term, so you have money to pay the bills.

If you have money available you may chose to take some assessments to help you get clearer. The ones I recommend are:

- *Highlands Ability Battery* to identify your natural abilities and talents
- *Myers Briggs Type Indicator* to understand personality style
- *Strong Interest Inventory* to gain a list of how well your interests measure up to a database of jobs

You can read more on these at the end of *Chapter Two, What Do You Want to Do?*

Having Fun

If you are out of work, treat job search like your full time job, but still make time for things you enjoy doing – music, reading, sport, wood work, whatever it may be. Ensure you take time to do something you will really enjoy each day.

Summary: Have you read Chapter Two and completed the activities?

Are you now clearer on what you want to do? If not you may want to stay longer on this step or get some external coaching support or careers guidance.

Days 4 and 5: Create your CV

Read *Chapter Three, Creating your CV*

Your CV is the foundation of your job search campaign. Whilst many jobs will involve completing an online form your CV will mean you have most of the information you need for this and lots of jobs actually want a CV.

You have two days set aside so you can create your best possible CV.

Action: Follow this chapter for a step-by-step guide to creating your CV. Part 1 is to collect the information you need and Part 2 is to put it together. The chapter is written like a coaching session with Denise so you should find it easy to follow. You have 2 days to create your CV so make it as good as you can.

Remember, you can arrange for an independent review of your CV. For more details visit the web site. You can also share your CV with friends/family or people in work to get their views.

Summary: Have you read Chapter Three and completed the activities?

Two days are set aside for this and you should now have one version of your CV but will still adapt it to suit different jobs.

Day 6: Register with employment agencies and identify the best web sites for you

Would today be a good day to register with **local employment agencies**? Dependent on your background you may want to register with some of the national agencies as well.

Would today be a good day to **review different newspapers and job sites** and make sure you know which ones are the ones to review regularly? You should be able to set up alerts, but it is also worth taking some time to browse. If not today, when?

Summary: Have you registered with employment agencies and identified relevant web sites?

Day 7: Relaxation day

Have some fun! I don't want you to get bored with your job search so today spend time with your family, have a pamper day or get on with your passionate interests. Of course you could keep going, but sometimes it's good to have a change of focus and we should all take time to relax.

Feel great; reflect back on what you have already done

- Got your paperwork together.
- Planned how you will spend your time.
- Got clear on what job(s) interest you.
- Created your CV.
- Registered with employment agencies and shortlisted web sites to visit regularly.

Day 8: Create a personal commercial

Read *Chapter Four, The Personal Commercial*

Today you will read this chapter and create your personal commercial. This will mean that when you meet people and they ask you what you are looking for, you will have created a reply.

Summary: Have you read Chapter Four and created your personal commercial?

Day 9: Networking

Read *Chapter Five, Get Networking*

Most people get a job through networking, talking with people they know and building relationships with people who may be able to help. This chapter talks you through how to develop your network and the steps you need to take when you meet someone.

This can be quite a scary stage. A lot of people don't want to get out there and talk to others as they fear rejection, so take it in baby steps and start with people you know.

When you talk with people they are likely to ask you questions about your current position. You must focus on your positive qualities and set aside any feelings of bitterness or self pity.

You could hand out your CV to people you meet, or you could create a one page biography. This moves away from the different jobs you have had to an overview of your strengths with specific examples.

Action: Read the chapter and decide who are you going to talk to.

Summary: Have you read Chapter Five and completed the activities?

Do you now have a list of people you can contact? Remember you can start with people you know so it isn't too scary.

Day 10: Fact finding interviews

Read *Chapter Six, Fact Finding Interviews*

To find out more about a particular job you can do fact finding interviews and this chapter tells you how. You probably won't start doing these today, but you will understand what you need to do and are ready to get started on these when it will help in your job search.

If you are unemployed

One of the things we miss when we lose our jobs is the companionship of our colleagues and it can be hard motivating ourselves to work alone. You probably know someone else who is also unemployed so why not arrange to meet at least once a week to offer mutual support. Also, even though you can do most of the research you need using your home computer you might like to visit the library as a means of meeting new people. There may even be a job search club you can join.

Summary: Have you read Chapter Seven and completed the activities?

You now know what to do once you need some specific help from people, your networking skills will help you to find people to talk with.

Day 11 – Different ways to find a job

Today is a reading day. To open you to different ways to get a job, be ready for applying for jobs and to know how to write an effective covering letter.

Read *Chapter Seven, Different Ways to Get a Job*

Read *Chapter Eight, Replying to Job Ads*

Read *Chapter Nine, The Covering Letter*

You can go back and read these chapters again once you are ready to apply for jobs.

Summary: Have you read Chapters Seven, Eight and Nine?

Do you now understand about the different ways to get a job, how to take a structured approach to replying to a job ad and how to write an effective covering letter?

Day 12: Start looking for jobs

The first 11 days have been getting you ready – it's now time to start looking for a job. From today onwards you need to create a plan of what you are going to do each day and then do the things you say you will.

It can increase your commitment if you let someone else know what you plan to do and then you are more likely to get things done, so who are you going to tell?

Job search plan

Plan in advance what you will do each day – many of the tasks will be done every day.

At the end of each day review your activity, what has moved you forward on job search and what hasn't helped.

Make a note of the tasks you **intend** to do today, and which ones you **actually** do.

- Research jobs on web sites and upload CV (and covering letter) as appropriate.
- Read newspapers and journals (many are online) to identify jobs.
- If you are interested in retail, walk around to notice any jobs that might be advertised outside the store.
- Research to find out more about a company and industry.
- Write covering letters highly focused on a job.
- Practice and use your "personal commercial."
- Talk to people.
- Undertake fact finding interviews.
- Knock on doors with copies of your CV.
- Arrange to contact companies direct.

- Get some exercise each day.
- Eat healthy.

Chapter One, Getting Ready - Being Organised, has lots of forms to help you keep track so plan what you are going to do for the week, and also for today.

In the introduction you read Kim's diary. It can really help keep you focused if you keep a log. You can also plan what to do in advance and then review at the end of the day what worked and what was less effective.

Action: Complete your daily activity log, there's a form in Chapter One for you to copy and use.

Daily Review

- What did you do today?
- What was helpful?
- What hindered?
- What could you do tomorrow to help you reach your goal of a new job?

Day 13: Job hunting

You are going to continue to follow your job search plan. You already have read how to reply to jobs you see advertised and how to write a covering letter so you can now put what you have read into action.

Action: Complete your daily activity log, there's a form in Chapter One for you to copy and use.

Daily Review

- What did you do today?
- What was helpful?
- What hindered?
- What could you do tomorrow to help you reach your goal of a new job?

Day 14: Relaxation day

Have some fun! I don't want you to get bored with your job search so today spend time with your family, have a pamper day or get on with your passionate interests. Of course you could keep going, but sometimes it's good to have a change of focus.

Feel great; reflect back on what you have done over the past 7 days:

- Created a personal commercial.
- Sorted out your referees.
- Read about networking and created your networking list.
- Checked your online presence.
- Got clearer on how to apply for jobs you see advertised.

Day 15: Job hunting

You will be continuing with job hunting.

Have you posted your CV on relevant sites, ensuring you read the privacy policy first? You may want to create more than one version if your are looking for different types of jobs.

Why not have a go at creating a covering letter so you are happy with how to do this for when it really counts? You may have a great CV but it is wasted if you don't also do a covering letter which matches up with the requirements of the job.

At the end of the day take time to do your daily review.

Action: Complete your daily activity log.

Daily Review

- What did you do today?
- What was helpful?
- What hindered?
- What could you do tomorrow to help you reach your goal of a new job?

Day 16: How to stand out from the crowd – develop your online presence

Read *Chapter Ten, Your On Line Presence*

One way to make yourself stand out from the crowd is to have a strong on line presence so if people search on line for your name they can read positive comments on you.

Summary: Have you read Chapter Ten?

Do you want to develop your on line presence?

Is this something you want to do? If so, what can you do to develop this?

Are you already there? What action do you need to take?

Day 17: The hidden job market

Read *Chapter Eleven, The Hidden Job Market*

More people find a job through the hidden route than through applying to advertisements. It can appear a mysterious secret, but **this chapter will show you exactly what you need to do**. You will learn why you should undertake a proactive approach to job hunting, begin to identify companies and know how to make speculative enquiries to potential employers, agencies and consultants. You'll learn to sidestep the gatekeeper to talk with the relevant person. What more could you want?

Summary: Have you read Chapter Eleven and completed the activities?

Are you going to include this approach in your job hunting plan?

Day 18: Job hunting

You are going to continue to follow your job search plan. You already have read how to reply to jobs you see advertised and how to write a covering letter so you can now put what you have read into action.

Action: Complete your daily activity log.

Daily Review

What did you do today?

What was helpful?

What hindered?

What could you do tomorrow to help you reach your goal of a new job?

Day 19: Job hunting

A couple of days ago you read *Chapter Eleven, The Hidden Job Market.*

If you are going to follow this approach you need to identify companies that are likely to want someone with your skills and background.

Today spend time creating a list of companies you want to contact and draft out an initial letter which you can then adapt to each particular company.

At the end of the day take time to do your daily review.

Action: Complete your daily activity log.

Daily Review

What did you do today?

What was helpful?

What hindered?

What could you do tomorrow to help you reach your goal of a new job?

Day 20: Job hunting

You are going to continue to follow your job search plan. You already have read how to reply to jobs you see advertised and how to write a covering letter so you can now put what you have read into action.

Action: Complete your daily activity log.

Daily Review

What did you do today?

What was helpful?

What hindered?

What could you do tomorrow to help you reach your goal of a new job?

Day 21: Relaxation day

Have some fun! I don't want you to get bored with your job search so today spend time with your family, have a pamper day or get on with your passionate interests. Of course you could keep going, but sometimes it's good to have a change of focus.

Feel great; reflect back on what you have already done:

- Created a covering letter.
- Read about the hidden job market and identified companies to contact.
- Read about interviews and scheduled a practice interview.
- Actively worked on job hunting.

Day 22: Phone interview prep and job hunting

Read *Chapter Twelve, The Phone Interview*

You've spent the past week looking for jobs to apply for now is the time to get ready for interviews. Today we will start with the phone interview.

Now you are applying for jobs you may need to undertake a phone interview. *Chapter Twelve, The Phone Interview*, provides all the guidance you need to perform at your best. You may also like to practice a phone interview with a friend.

You will also continue with your job hunting activity.

Summary: Have you read Chapter Twelve and completed the activities?

You should now understand how to get the best out of a phone interview. At the end of the day take time to do your daily review.

Action: Complete your daily activity log.

Daily Review

What did you do today?

What was helpful?

What hindered?

What could you do tomorrow to help you reach your goal of a new job?

Day 23: Interview preparation and job hunting

Read *Chapter Thirteen, Interview Preparation*

The Interview is often the scariest part of applying for a new job, so find out some of the secrets and be well prepared! This chapter helps you to prepare. It may be a few weeks before you get to interview but you can practice now.

You will also continue with your job hunting activity.

Summary: Have you read Chapter Thirteen and completed the activities?

You should now feel more comfortable about a forthcoming interview.

At the end of the day take time to do your daily review.

Action: Complete your daily activity log.

Daily Review

What did you do today?

What was helpful?

What hindered?

What could you do tomorrow to help you reach your goal of a new job?

Day 24: Job hunting including a practice interview

Read *Chapter Fourteen, The Interview – You've Been Shortlisted*

This explains everything you need to do once you are short listed for a job.

Summary: Have you read Chapter Fourteen and completed the activities?

You should now feel even more comfortable about a forthcoming interview.

At the end of the day take time to do your daily review.

Action: Complete your daily activity log.

Daily Review

What did you do today?

What was helpful?

What hindered?

What could you do tomorrow to help you reach your goal of a new job?

Day 25: Psychometric testing and assessment centres and job hunting

Read *Chapter 15, Psychometric Testing* and *Chapter 16, Assessment Centres*

Psychometric testing, assessment centres and job hunting

When you apply for a job it's often more than an interview. You might need to do psychometric tests as part of the first stage of selection and for many professional and managerial jobs you may need to participate in an assessment centre. *Chapter Fifteen, Psychometric Testing,* tells you how to get the best out of psychometric tests and *Chapter Sixteen, How To Pass Assessment Centres,* tells you how to pass assessment centres.

You may find it helpful to do some practice tests and there are web sites and books to help you. (See the *Useful Resources* section.)

Summary: Have you read Chapters Fifteen and Sixteen?

You should now feel more comfortable should you need to undertake psychometric tests or have to attend an assessment centre.

At the end of the day take time to do your daily review.

Action: Complete your daily activity log.

Daily Review

What did you do today?

What was helpful?

What hindered?

What could you do tomorrow to help you reach your goal of a new job?

Day 26: More job hunting

You are going to continue to follow your job search plan. You already have read how to reply to jobs you see advertised and how to write a covering letter so you can now put what you have read into action. You can also continue to talk with others (*Chapter Five, Networking*) and seek out companies to take a direct approach with (*Chapter Eleven, The Hidden Job Market*).

Action: Complete your daily activity log.

Daily Review

What did you do today?

What was helpful?

What hindered?

What could you do tomorrow to help you reach your goal of a new job?

Day 27: Staying motivated

As we reach the end of the first month you may have already had an interview or are still in the application stage. You've probably realised that it is tough, the recession is making job search more difficult than even a year ago. You need to stay motivated, but don't beat yourself up if you are having a bad day or even month.

Chapter Seventeen, Staying Motivated, will help you to think about ways to review your progress and stay motivated.

Day 28: Relaxation day

Have some fun – I don't want you to get bored with your job search so today spend time with your family, have a pamper day or get on with your passionate interests. Of course you could keep going, but sometimes it's good to have a change of focus.

I have taken you through 28 days of preparing for and getting focused on job search. You now know what to do and need to do what you know.

So set up your plan for next week and keep focused!

After four weeks you now know what you should be doing so from now on I want you to create and follow a daily plan.

And finally ...

You will get a job offer and when you do you want to make sure it's the right job for you and you get the best salary and benefit package you can. There are three more chapters which will be helpful for you:

Chapter Eighteen, Before You Say Yes

Chapter Nineteen, Salary Negotiation

Chapter Twenty, The First 90 Days

Once you get a new job, go back to **all** the sites where you uploaded your CV and details and delete or inactivate your CV so you can no longer be contacted. You don't want your new boss thinking you are already looking for a new job. Also note which sites were most helpful for you and which CV was most effective as you may, unfortunately be in this position again.

No job is for life, so remember the lessons learned from this and keep your CV up to date just in case.

All my very best in your job search success.

Part Two

Chapter One

Getting ready - being organised

This chapter helps you put a system in place that is efficient, productive, and eventually leads to that great job you've always wanted. Getting organised includes finding a quiet, comfortable place to work, setting up a filing system for all your important papers and forms, and establishing a method that gets the best possible results.

By the end of this chapter you will have:

- A system in place to manage papers and forms.
- Made a commitment to the task of finding work.
- Decided how you will allocate your time.
- A support system in place.
- The ability to effectively track your job search.
- The forms needed for an effective, well-planned job search.

1: Introduction

Although some have the luxury of a personal home office, most of us live in the real world and share our computer and work areas with family members. It's important that you talk to your family and let them know you need a space that's large enough to work comfortably in, and one that is quiet and without interruptions. Also, make them aware of the importance of your paper work including letters, forms, posh paper, research materials, and job postings.

2: Create a filing system

You will need easy access to a number of documents. An early task will be to find a place to store the following:

1. **Master copies of your CVs:** You will need different versions of your CV for different applications – have both printed and electronic versions available. Keep a master copy of each so you can review it for future applications. You may also want a copy handy for review when making phone calls.
   Action: You don't need to do anything with your CV today, but do get any versions you have handy ready to review on day five.

2. **Certificates, letters of recognition, etc.:** You may need to let a future employer see your certificates and diplomas. You may also want to show letters of recognition from customers, so get them all ready now.
   Action: Find these now and get them in a display wallet so you can take them along to interview to support what you say.

3. **Applications and covering letters:** Each time you apply for a job, keep all the information together – the advert, additional information, copy of application form, CV version, etc. In addition to storing your letters and applications on your computer, have printed

copies easily accessible. **Action:** Have some plastic wallets ready to file away your different applications.

4. **Speculative approaches to organisations, consultancies and agencies:** Detailed information of each company, letters sent, and next steps to take. **Action:** Get some copies of the form printed from the form library in this chapter.

5. **Diary or personal organiser:** To keep track of your appointments. **Action:** Make sure you have a great method of keeping track, one that's easy for you to keep updated. Either in written form or you may be comfortable using the calendar on MS Outlook.

6. **Stationery:** Not photocopying paper, but good quality 100gsm paper with matching envelopes. **Action:** Buy some decent stationery soon. Having stamps on hand would help too!

7. **To do list:** So you are clear on daily and weekly tasks. **Action:** Start a "to do" list and review it each day.

8. **Contact list:** Details of whom you contacted, the reason for the contact and any follow up action. **Action:** Get started on your contact list today.

3: Commitment to the task

"When you look to a date in the future, remember: if you had started today, you would already have achieved success." -- Denise Taylor

Looking for a job is a full-time job. If you are out of work due to the recession, you can devote many hours a day to your search efforts. However, if you are in a full-time job, you are going to want to plan your time carefully so you have the time and energy to devote to this task. You must be sure to continue to work effectively in your job no matter how much you may not like the work you do. There will be plenty of other people eager to take on your job and if your boss thinks you are not really interested in your job, it could be you who is the one to lose their job.

How will you find a couple of hours a day to spend on job search? This needs to be high priority, and having a routine can help. Could you stop watching as much TV or get up at least an hour earlier each day? How about working on weekends or taking a day's holiday to focus solely on your job search?

If you begin any task in a half-hearted way, you are unlikely to succeed. You will stumble and be hesitant at the first sign of difficulty and that bold decision to get a new job will fade away.

Think about your level of commitment. Make a note of how committed you are to your job search. 10 is totally committed, and 1 means you are not at all committed:

1	2	3	4	5	6	7	8	9	10

With a level of commitment of 7 or below, you are unlikely to reach your goal of getting that great new job. If you find one excuse after another for why you don't get started, it represents lack of commitment. There is also the danger of having too many other commitments and not enough time for your job search.

4: Plan your time

Have an established routine – make sure you do some work each day

If you are in full-time work, will you complete your job search and applications before or after work?

Make a note of how many hours you will spend on your job search each week. This needs to be a minimum of eight hours, and ideally more. If you have limited time available, decide whether to give up other commitments, or take a slower approach to your search.

I will spend ___ hours a week on job search.

What is your commitment level now?

1   2   3   4   5   6   7   8   9   10

Make a note of how you will divide this time. You might prefer to do one hour a day, or to divide your time into three periods. Remember, you will be making phone calls as part of this process so you need to have some time available during working hours. Fill in the details below.

I will spend ___ hours on Monday on job search.

My commitment to this is:

1   2   3   4   5   6   7   8   9   10

I will spend ___ hours on Tuesday on job search.

My commitment to this is:

1   2   3   4   5   6   7   8   9   10

I will spend ___ hours on Wednesday on job search.

My commitment to this is:

1   2   3   4   5   6   7   8   9   10

I will spend ___ hours on Thursday on job search.

My commitment to this is:

1   2   3   4   5   6   7   8   9   10

I will spend ___ hours on Friday on job search.

My commitment to this is:

1   2   3   4   5   6   7   8   9   10

I will spend ___ hours over the weekend on job search.

My commitment to this is:

1   2   3   4   5   6   7   8   9   10

Now look at your commitment level. If it is low for the weekend, can you fit in more hours in the week? Or vice versa?

5: Get a support system in place

Personal support system

Job hunting can be one of the most challenging times of our lives. We are likely to experience rejection not only once, but again and again. With the current recession, it's going to be even tougher, with sometimes very large numbers of people for every job vacancy, so you need people and things to keep you motivated when you feel like giving up.

It's imperative to have support and motivation from others. Of course, you'll want your friends and family on your side. But what will you do if they aren't supportive and encouraging?

Knowing how to find support in difficult times means we have a plan ready when the need arises, but don't forget to support yourself from within. Most of your job hunting will be done alone.

Answering these questions can help to build your resilience for the future. Look at the list of supportive system activities below and make a note of those you might turn to when things get tough:

- ☐ Hard physical exercise
- ☐ Talking with a friend
- ☐ Yoga / meditation
- ☐ Relaxation exercises
- ☐ 'Treating' myself (e.g., buying a new shirt or book)
- ☐ Talking positively to myself
- ☐ Writing out a plan of action
- ☐ Writing down my feelings
- ☐ Involving myself in a hobby

☐ Enjoying outdoors and fresh air
☐ A change of scene
☐ Listening to music
☐ Going to the pub / club
☐ Reading fiction
☐ Reading a self-help book
☐ Making a list of things to do
☐ Finding time to reflect
☐ Joining a Job Club to talk to people in same situation
☐ Work with a counsellor or coach
☐ A bottle of wine (but not every night!)

Write below your top three ways of dealing with the negative aspects and frustrations of looking for a job:

Top three ways

   1.

   2.

   3.

   Have a talk with a friend or colleague about how you can make sure you turn to these supportive activities when needed. Do you need more information, for example, where can you learn yoga or the address of a local fitness club? Could you arrange regular meetings with someone to 'keep you going' during a difficult period? This is important because not only will you have positive activities, but a friend as well to help you get through the rough spots.

6: References

You will need to contact people to provide references

Who to choose?

You will want to choose people who know you. Often you are asked for both work and personal referees. It's a good idea not to choose relatives, they don't carry much authority. Ideally, choose people who are professionals with a good reputation. Former employers carry the most weight, also key suppliers and customers who can vouch for the work you do. Referees are sometimes phoned and if they can clearly give examples of your achievements, it will definitely improve your chances.

Get their permission

Ask general permission before you start your job hunt. You don't need to contact them each time, but you may want to remind them you are still looking if your job search drags on. By asking permission, you show respect for them and their busy schedules. Although most of the time many will be happy to help you in your career search, some previous employers or university academics may not wish to participate. Respect their wishes: a half-hearted testimonial is worse than no reference at all!

Letters of recommendation

It might be helpful to get a letter of recommendation that you can show when you go to interview.

Brief them

Do they know what you have been doing in your current and previous jobs? Do they know what you are applying for? It can help to let them have a copy of your CV plus details on the job(s) you are applying for. Give each referee a copy of the CV and covering letter that you sent to the employer. Also, supply each referee with a copy of the description of the job you are applying for and a list of the specific features you would like them to mention to the employer. Make it easy for the referee to help you.

Have correct contact information

Make sure you have all details correct, especially phone numbers and email address. Also be sure you have their correct job title. It may have changed since you were last in touch. It's more official to include the person's work rather than home contact details.

Keep them informed

When you know that a referee has been contacted, give them a call to say thank you. Later, let them know if you did or didn't get the job. Periodically during your career search, send a letter of thanks to your referees, along with an update of how your career search is going. Developing your relationship with them can only enhance what they write about you. This will be a positive reinforcement of your interpersonal skills.

Remember to thank them

When you finally get the job, you can let your referees know how much you appreciated their involvement. This will help them feel good about themselves and make them more likely to help others in the future.

Activity: Decide who will make your best references and get in touch.

7: Form library

Having worked with hundreds of clients, I know the forms that will help you in your job search. I've included them all below, and if you visit the website, you can access them via a low cost eBook.

CV Preparation (Chapter 3)

For each job make a note of:

Dates, including month as well as year.

Organisation name

Address

Job title

Brief description of the organisation (unless a national brand)

Your department's purpose and objectives?

Main responsibilities? Include numbers of people managed and size of budget where appropriate.

List your achievements - quantify wherever possible.

Why you left

Who will give you references?

Leaving salary and benefits

Networking (Chapter 5)

How many people do you know?

Family

Friends

Work (present colleagues)

Other people where I currently work, including clients, suppliers

Past bosses and past colleagues

Neighbours (present)

Clubs and organisations (church, professional societies, trade associations, chambers of commerce):

School / College / University / Friends / Teachers:

Contacts from seminars and conferences:

People where I have worked in the past:

Bank Managers, Accountants, local professional people:

Friends of your parents (or children):

Neighbours (past):

Professional organisations / memberships:

Networking record sheet

This form helps you keep track of whom you have contacted and helps you follow up.

Name	Position – job title
Assistants name	**Company name**
Address	
Telephone	**Email**
Source of information (who referred you)	
CV included?	**Which version?**
How contacted	**Date contacted**
What discussed	
Personal insights	
Referrals	
Follow up 1 date	**How followed up**
Follow up 2 date	**How followed up**
Follow up result	

Fact finding interviews (Chapter 6)

What do you do during a typical workday or week?

How much of your day do you spend working with ...
(people, computers, sports cars etc.)?

What kind of challenges or problems do you have to deal with
in this job?

What skills make you good at what you do?

What do you find most satisfying and most frustrating about
your job and field?

Is it important to be able to pay attention to detail?

What administrative duties are required of you? How much
time do these take?

What do you see as the future for this kind of work?

What preparation, training and/or experience would you
suggest for someone entering this field?

Knowing what you know now, how would you have
approached this career differently?

If people say you need to have an MSc, ask if they know
anyone who works in this field who doesn't have one.

What would I need to do to become an attractive candidate for
a job in this field?

Can you suggest any relevant professional associations,
journals or publications that I should be using?

Who else would you recommend or suggest I talk to, to learn
more about this career?

Do you have any other advice for me?

May I contact you if other questions arise?

Fact finding interviews (Chapter 6)

Career / Job title:

Source of Contact:

Name:

Company:

Position:

Phone/fax/extension numbers and best times to call:

Address:

Meeting summary:

Reading list:

Best preparation (experience and education):

How to start in this field:

Further contact (name, phone, company, position, how do you know each other, can I use your name? etc.):

Job search: My weekly targets

Keep track of priority action for the forthcoming week so you can plan your activities and decide the best day to carry out certain tasks. Each day's tasks should contribute to each week's targets.

Week commencing:

Priorities				
	Priority 1	**Priority 2**	**Priority 3**	**Priority 4**
Monday				
Tuesday				
Wednesday				
Thursday				
Friday				

List all your tasks here, so you have the satisfaction of striking them through once completed.

Job Search: My daily tasks

Use this list as a reminder of what you need to do each day. Remember, each day's tasks should achieve part of the week's targets.

You can review your activities to identify:

- What was useful?
- What was a waste of time?
- How you can make better use of your time?

Activity	Tick when completed
Deal with incoming mail	
Check and telephone previous contacts	
Check your application has arrived	
Begin preparation for any adverts from yesterdays job search	
Prepare speculative letters to companies	
Prepare speculative letters to agencies	
Visit library	
Research for speculative letters	
Read newspapers – in print and online	
Write up notes of recent interviews	
Prepare for next interviews	
Write follow up letters for interviews	
Make phone calls	
Check route for interviews (use www.multimap.com) or similar	

Job Search: daily activity log

List the objectives for the start of each day and then make note of how you use your time. A review will ensure you are making good use of time and not getting bogged down or distracted!

- Try to just do one thing at a time and follow it through.
- It can be most productive to do telephone calls in a block. Often lunchtime is good.
- As you plan your day, make sure to leave some time for the unexpected.
- Your activity log helps you recall what you have done, whom you have contacted and makes sure you follow through on each activity.
- List every activity you do alongside your comments on how well you are doing.
- Record information about the people you meet. Make sure you have their contact details correct. You may need to follow up on what they agreed to do.
- Note names of any secretaries or assistants you speak with – they can be flattered you remember their name.

Today's objectives are:

Time	Item	Outcome	Follow up on
8 am			
9 am			
10 am			
11 am			
12 am			
1pm			
2pm			
3pm			
4pm			
5pm			
6 pm			
7 pm			
8 pm			
9 pm			

Learning points

Don't forget to include lunch breaks and relaxation

Example of a daily activity log:

13th February

I collected a national paper to scan for any jobs. I put a cross through those that were clearly unsuitable and used my highlighter to ring any that would be of interest.

Visit to library to read *Financial Times* to keep up on industry changes.

Chatted to another job hunter and went for a coffee. We swapped cards and will meet in the library next week to pass on any useful information. Glad I have her email details.

Saw that XXX services are expanding. They may have some upcoming vacancies in my area of expertise, I've noted to follow up.

Spent all afternoon on my application form to ABC Ltd, it was a complicated form so I was glad I had photocopied it yesterday so I could use it to create a draft copy.

Looked at my circular letter and tweaked it so I could send it to XXX. I rang first to find out who was going to be the most appropriate person to send it to.

Received a phone call from Colin Pemberton (01684 XXXXXX). He is a friend of Andrew Wilson and said there may be something coming up and he would like to meet. We have arranged to meet at the Old Swan, Cirencester at 11.45 this Friday. Forgot to ask for some info on the company but have noted to do an Internet search.

Made a note to follow up on the 10 circular letters I sent out last week, this will be my first task of the morning.

Response to adverts record sheet

Producing a copy of this for each application helps you be clear what you sent and avoids any possible confusion.

Advertisement replied to		
Position	**Newspaper**	
Salary	**Date**	**Page**
Contact	**Employer/Company**	
Address		
Telephone	**Email**	
Letter number	**Date sent**	
CV included?	**Which version?**	
Response	**Response date**	
Further action		

Keep this with a copy of the job ad.

Personal contacts action

To keep track of contacts and make a note of follow up.

Date of contact	Name and address	Telephone number	Position	Manner of approach				Result	10 day date	Result
				Email	Letter	Tel	Visit			

Weekly summary of job search

This helps you keep track on the breadth of your job search and reminds you that you can't just follow one method.

Week commencing: (insert date)

Who have I registered with?

National agencies	
Local agencies	
Online agencies	

Where have I looked for jobs?

Daily papers	
Local papers	
Sunday papers	
Local Radio?	
Internet site 1	
Internet site 2	
Internet site 3	
Internet site 4	
Internet site 5	
Journal 1	
Journal 2	
Journal 3	
Other	
Other	
Other	

Keep track of your on line job search

Keep a record of:

The name of the job site and the date you set up an account.

Your account name and password.

The date you posted your CV and the version you used. For example, emphasising technical skills and management skills.

What job services you signed up for.

Phone calls and emails that directly relate to this site, and the amount of spam as well.

The levels of privacy you have chosen.

The privacy policy of the site.

The terms of use for this site.

Keep track of all your applications:

The job title, reference number and location.

Date you applied.

Version of CV and which covering letter.

Details of your contact within the company.

Any notes you took when you phoned for an informal chat.

Response to job ad form

Read the detail in the Replying to Job Ads chapter.

Job Title:

Job advertised in:

Closing date:

Your requirements	My skills

Telephone message form

This provides a means of friends and family taking down phone calls you may receive. Do also remind them to answer the phone in a professional manner!

Telephone calls:	
If someone calls when I am out, please make a note of the following information:	
Name	Company
Date	Time
Caller's telephone number	
When is it convenient to call back?	
Message	
I will be back home at (insert time) Give them my mobile number (insert number)	

Job adverts summary

This helps you to keep track of job adverts. You can then chase up if you haven't heard anything from them by the 10th day.

My ref:

Name of newspaper:

Date of paper:

Job title in advert:

Date CV/letter sent:

Date acknowledged by company:

No acknowledgement – 10 day date:

Name of person to be seen:

Result:

Interview date:

Mail shot follow up

You may choose to send out a similar letter to a number of people. This form enables you to keep track of what you receive back and the next step to take.

Name	Position
Company/consultancy	
Telephone	**Email**
Date received	**Follow up type**
Information obtained	
Action required	
Date action taken	
Further action	

Interview self debrief

After each interview you will want to review your performance. This form will help you.

Position applied for	Company	
Date of interview	Interview type	
1st Interviewers name	Position	
2nd interviewers name	Position	
Give yourself a score out of 10		**Rating**
Was I in the right frame of mind?		
Was my physical presentation all right?		
Eye contact and did I smile?		
Did I display initiative?		
How did I deal with awkward questions? Which questions did I get asked – which did I answer well or not so well – why?		
Did I manage to put my achievements across?		
Who controlled the interview?		
Had I done sufficient homework?		
What were my questions like?		
In general did I come across as myself?		
How did the interview end. When will I know the outcome?		
Total rating:		
Follow up letter required Y/N	Date sent	
Positive things I did	Learning points	

Post initial follow up

To keep track of where you are up to with each contact:

Post initial follow up _____

Contact number _____

Client name _____

Telephone home _____

Telephone business _____

Date	Action	Result	Next action

Track your job search

This chapter has emphasised the importance of being organised and shown you a number of ways to get prepared for your job search. Using the forms provided will help you capture the kind of information needed to find a job even during the toughest of times.

Job sites

Keep a separate note on each job site you use and track the success you have had with each. Where was the best source of jobs? Which were a waste of your time? Which sites promote interest and respond to your efforts and which result in unanswered emails? Being able to answer these and other questions will help you be more effective in the future.

Chapter Two

What do you want to do?

What do you want to do? To some this may seem like a silly question. You bought this book because you want to get a job, right? But what job exactly? In a recession, not all jobs are attainable. Even worse, many are eliminated. Marie was expecting to get promoted to Land Director, but instead was made redundant when the building company she worked for lost 90% of its value. Kim was made redundant as fewer people were buying houses and she was no longer needed as a legal executive. Roger was made redundant as a sales manager for a car dealership when car sales dropped.

They all loved their jobs and wouldn't have sought a change in position, but their redundancy gave them time to reflect on what they actually wanted to do. It didn't take long for Roger as he was a natural sales person with an excellent track record and found a job quickly, but Marie and Kim took time to consider alternatives and take a fresh look at the job market.

Marie was able to refocus and adjust her skill set and is now working as a project manager in sustainable development. It doesn't pay as much as she earned before but she has a better quality of life and is now home by dinner time.

Kim looked for work that would make good use of her high level of organisational skills and her legal background. She was fortunate to get two job offers and has now gained employment making great use of her particular skills and background. Her new job allows her to meet staff from law firms, enabling her to build contacts in case she wants to make a change when the economic climate improves.

Roger used the proactive approach and took another sales position, earning even more than before. Kim found her job in the newspaper and Marie was approached after uploading her CV onto a jobs site.

Too often people choose a new job by looking at job sites for something they think they can already do, utilising skills they already have. But in a recession, these jobs may not be available. You may not be able to stay on the same career path – no matter how good you are. So you need to think about what else you can and want to do. If you have (or had) a job you hated, this might be the best time to consider doing something different.

In a recession it's even more important to be clear on what you do want to do. With the increase in people looking for a job, knowing yourself, knowing more about the job you seek, and being clear how you match up will dramatically increase your chance of success.

People differ. Being made redundant with a mortgage to meet and debts to pay means that many people must get a job as soon as possible, regardless of whether it's a job they want to do. But for others, they are able to take some time to get clearer on their options. This is not necessarily a radical change involving a high level of retraining, but being clear on who you are and why you want a particular job will help you to stand out from the rest. In a recession, there is greater competition for jobs, so you need to separate yourself from all the other candidates through your CV, application letter, covering letter, and what you say at interview.

Making a choice - what do I want to do?

Are you being constrained by your CV?

You may look at your CV, which describes your experience as an engineer for example, and think you "need" to be an engineer. That's what you trained for and what you've been successful at, right? Are you a teacher who wants to do something else, but can't see beyond another job involving children? Are you a PA and up until now only considered similar roles? What does a chef do who wants a different career?

Step away from your CV and take a broader view of who you are and what you want to do.

Have a clear vision of your future work environment

Think about your ideal working environment. What sort of environment would enable you to work at your best? This includes the company, culture, salary, location and anything else you can think of. Don't be shy, let your imagination go to work! The following questions should help:

- What does your ideal work day look like?
- What salary would you like?
- How far are you willing to commute?
- What sort of manager do you want to have?

- What type of people would be your ideal colleagues?
- What do you want this next role to lead to?
- Work/life balance and flexible working practices – how important/necessary are they to you?
- Consider the size of organisation. For example, you could be a catering supervisor in a large company and move to be a catering manager in a smaller company. Or be a general manager in a smaller company and change to an operations manager in a medium size company, etc.
- Do you want to be at the launch of a start up, or an established company with stability? How about a small company without bureaucracy but few resources, or are you happy with red tape but plentiful resources?
- What about dress code or perks?

You may not get exactly what you want, but answering these questions can help you focus your job search efforts on the right job (and organisation) for you.

Example: Samira

Samira was a financial analyst and a fully qualified accountant. She realised that despite her initial concern over being made redundant from a high paid job she was working on a product she didn't believe in, with a not very supportive manager and working for a large city firm with a long commute each day didn't give her time for any hobbies. By the time she got home from work each day she was ready to slump in front of the TV.

Her ideal working day would be working within a 30 minute journey from home and with the freedom to work from home at least one day a week. She was willing to earn less if it meant she could work with a company she believed in. Working in the voluntary sector would match many of her needs.

What do you love to do?

There are various tasks we perform at work, some we can do really well and love to do. And others that we may be good at but don't enjoy. There may also be some skills we have developed in our personal lives that we would love to use as part of our job.

Samira loved helping others and was already working, on a voluntary basis, as an accountant for a charity. She also loved art and used to make hand-made cards for family and friends when she had time for hobbies.

Action: make a note of all the things you love to do.

Either use the space below or use your notebook to capture your thoughts.

How would you describe your personal style?

The following questions can help you understand yourself. (For a more in-depth understanding, you will want to use a personality measure such as the Myers Briggs Type Indicator.)

- Think about when you are being positive. How would you describe yourself?
- Think about when you are being negative. How would you describe yourself?
- Think about when you've been in a difficult situation at work, how was it resolved and what was your part in this?
- Write down the key words that describe you, and then ask close friends or relatives to see if they agree. For

each word, give an example of when you used your strengths in a positive way. For example:

o Cooperative: I work well with other people. For example, my colleague had a problem with a project and several things needed completing at short notice. I reprioritised what I was doing to help her out, including staying late so that she met her deadline.

o Customer focused: I pride myself on doing all I can to achieve customer satisfaction. When I overheard a customer complaining at a till, I took them to one side (so it did not impact on other customers), listened to their problems and dealt with the situation swiftly. This resulted in a letter of thanks to my manager, and a larger order from the customer.

Your responses can help in thinking about the role you want to undertake with a company and how you can best relate to others.

Samira said: *"I'm quite an outgoing person who has been forced to work alone for so much of the time. I'm assertive and not afraid to stand up for things I believe in. I am trusting and wonder if at times I can be a bit too trusting. I love change and am not constrained by traditional ways of working. I'm a perfectionist so I do a really good job but it does mean I can be a bit critical of others. I sometimes find it hard to meet deadlines as I can get distracted by other people."*

Action: list your top personal characteristics.

Skills

Skills are the things we have learned to do. We gain skills through both paid and unpaid activities. As you think about your skills, don't just think about the work you do in your day job. You may have gained relevant skills via hobbies (organised a wedding, or a group holiday?) or perhaps voluntary work (leader of the Brownies?). Perhaps you have entrepreurial skills and have been selling things online or via market stalls.

Samira said: *"My top skills are paying attention to detail, being quick and accurate with numbers and in being organised. I've got good listening skills and I'm the sort of person that others confide in, I'm creative and like developing new solutions."*

Make a note of the skills you have gained.

Some of these skills you will want to keep on using, but there will be many that you don't enjoy. So cross them out!

With the ones that remain, make sure you are specific. For example, are your communication skills best written or verbal? One to one or in large groups? Providing an example of this skill will be very useful when you are ready to make a change in your job or career. For example:

Organisation: I can organise people, information and things. For example, I planned a conference entertainment programme, negotiated with suppliers and produced publicity materials. (This can then lead to a separate heading of communication.)

Identifying your skills reveals all you can do, and editing them determines which truly interest you. Doing this not only keeps you from focusing solely on using the skills you have, but shows you which skills you truly enjoy using.

Action: make a note of your top skills, with a specific example.

Know your values

Our values are the guiding principles that drive our behaviour. When we live a life in line with our values, we concentrate on what is most important to us. This helps in decision making. For example, if health is our number one priority, it will affect what we eat, how much we exercise and how we spend our leisure time. When we do work that is in line with our values, it is more of a calling than a job. When our values are incongruent with our career, it can lead to stress, discomfort and unhappiness.

Decide what is truly important to you! What motivates you? Success, helping others, belonging, money, security? Start a list and keep adding to it over a period of days. Why is each one important to you? Getting results? Making a difference? An opportunity to display your creativity? Take each in turn and think about them deeply.

When you look at your list, you may see there is some conflict. If both family and success at work is important to you, what will you do when you get offered a promotion that means working much longer hours? Or have to travel a lot? Or have little or no vacation time?

Action: make a note of your top values.

For Samira, her top 5 values are:

- Helping others.
- Making friendly contacts.
- Creativity.
- Challenge.
- Learning.

Samira identified her values using an extensive card sort exercise and you can buy your own set via the web site. Alternatively, you can access a list of values from the web site.

As you identify possible jobs and find out more about them, your list will help you see how each prospective job aligns with your values.

Abilities

"Our abilities are perhaps the most fundamental piece of the career puzzle."
                    -- Hutchinson and McDonald

What are your natural talents? You may already know. You may be an accomplished musician, athlete, or artist, but it's likely your abilities go much further. Ability testing defines your natural abilities based on timed work samples, and covers a wide range of abilities including problem solving, spatial relations, verbal memory, observation, idea productivity and visual speed and accuracy.

The very best way to identify these is via a test, and I highly recommend the *Highlands Ability Battery,* read more at the end of this chapter. An alternative is to think about what you do and list your strengths and skills. It's important to ask others to help you with this as they may see hidden talents in you that you are not aware of.

Action: make a note of your key strengths and abilities

If all jobs paid the same what would you do? Write it down!

Putting this together

Below, please summarise your answers to these questions and then ask yourself, and other people, what other careers are possible for you.

What do I want to do?

(see table next page)

As you discuss this with others, make sure to tell them that you don't want advice, but rather their creative input.

I love to ...	My top personal characteristics are:
My top skills are:	My top values are:
My key strengths and abilities are:	

Can you now draw up an ideal job description, outlining what it is that you want to spend your day doing? Also, give thought to what would be the ideal industry or sector for you. A particular job from Accountant to Writer can differ depending on whether you work in manufacturing, charity sector, high tech or education, etc.

What jobs are you considering?

You may also be interested in finding out more of the jobs that are more likely to be available in a recession. Jobs you might like to consider are teaching, health care and care for the elderly. Children will still need to go to school, people get ill and with an aging population there is likely to be more jobs available in the care sector. It's worth keeping abreast with the news to see where the government is likely to invest money. For example, if it is in construction or green energy, these are areas you may like to consider. Companies may be cutting back on training and possibly advertising but certain back room functions stay in demand such as IT and Finance. It could be worth looking into what you need to do to become a credible candidate in these areas.

Looking on line

You can now find out more about these different jobs via my two favourite web sites.

1. Prospects: http://tinyurl.com/217kn. This is from a graduate recruitment portal. Jobs are listed in alphabetical order.

2. Learn Direct: http://tinyurl.com/22uege. With this site, you can follow through and find out about many different types of careers, what they are all about, the training requirements, etc.

Both sites have links to job categories such as "administration and clerical" or "medical technology." You can also use the search box to type in the name of job that interests you.

Read up on job profiles when you want to find out if a job interests you, if you match the criteria needed and if the pay scale and prospects meet your needs.

From this you can decide that a type of job is worth applying for or that you need to gain experience/qualifications before you are likely to be successful. Each site provides links so you can find out more. For example, if you are interested in being an events manager, you can follow up with seven organisations including:

- Association of British Professional Conference Organisers (ABPCO).
- Association for Conferences and Events (ACE) and
- Association of Exhibition Organisers, with details provided.

The sites also suggest similar jobs, for example:

- Wedding Planner.
- Charity Fundraiser.
- Marketing Manager.
- Conference and Exhibition Organiser.

These web sites are very informative and provide plenty of detail on what the job involves including common salaries and tips on how to find out even more details. Review your options and produce a shortlist.

Once you've found out more about particular jobs and careers, you can move on to the reality check.

What jobs are on your shortlist?

List the jobs and then indicate how happy you are with them on a 1-5 scale, with 5 being I'd be really happy and 1 if you don't think you will be happy at all (but the job will at least pay some of the bills).

What to do when you want to be a … (fill in the blank) and lack the relevant experience?

You may have identified the career you want but lack the skills and experience to be a credible applicant. Also, in a recession, it may be much harder to get taken on in a trainee capacity.

To increase your chance of success, you may need to look beyond paid work to consider unpaid/voluntary work. You can gain many transferable skills this way. You can also increase your chance of success via attending relevant business seminars, training courses and you can also ask people if you can shadow them through doing unpaid work for a week.

What jobs are you realistically likely to get?

It's now time for a reality check. Are the jobs likely to be available in our current recession? If you have the right training or experience are you likely to be a credible candidate?

Important: There are a number of ways to increase your chances of getting a job you will truly be happy with. Some of the following chapters include topics such as undertaking training, unpaid work experience, the assistance of friends, family, and colleagues, writing an effective covering letter, a personal "commercial" and a great deal more.

What are you going to look for?

It may be a specific job, or it may be a broader area, but the clearer you are on the sort of job you want the easier it will be when other people ask you what you are looking for. So write it down.

My preferred job is

Does this answer the question of the type of job you are seeking, the sort of company etc? Read it out loud and fine tune it till it sounds natural. You will find more detail on how to be clear on what you want in *Chapter Four, The Personal Commercial.*

Career Assessments

Details of the three most popular assessments are included here. Not because it is essential to take them, but they can be very useful to help you to make a career choice. Do you need more help in making a choice? Further details and prices are available via the web site.

The Highlands Ability Battery

The Highlands Ability Battery (tHAB) comprises 19 separate validated objective tests. The HAB isolates natural abilities and analyses combinations of aptitudes in addition to individual aptitudes. It is an objective measure of your relative ability to do specific things from solving problems to remembering what you read. It tells you what you'll find easy, what will be difficult, and is a good foundation to effective career choice.

Real career success rarely comes down to money and status. It's much more to do with finding a job which ties in with what you can do easily.

We all have talents and abilities we are born with. These give us a special ability to do things easily and a reason why we find other things difficult. We develop this ability through heredity and in childhood and our abilities can be measured from age 14.

Because they are hard wired, abilities do not change. Practice won't make them stronger and ignoring them won't mean we lose them. They differ from skills, which we can develop, but which we can also lose, and interests which can change. However, both skills and interests can enhance our abilities.

We are happiest and most satisfied when we make maximum use of our abilities. An individual may develop the skills to practice law, for example, but if she doesn't have the inborn talents which make the practice of law easy and satisfying, she will find her work unrewarding (and, even, as in the case of many lawyers, frustrating). When we apply our abilities to our study or work, we do our tasks better.

Knowing your abilities and natural talents can help you to:

- Understand where you are naturally talented.
- Know how you solve problems and make decisions most effectively.
- Understand clearly why you would be happy in some fields and not happy in others.
- Choose the best option from a group of study / career/ job / business choices.
- Know how to study most effectively.
- Know what other jobs within your organisation you would be more fulfilled with.
- Use your true strengths more effectively and more consistently.

Why I suggest the Highlands Ability Battery

Since 1922, hundreds of thousands of people have used aptitude testing to learn more about themselves and to derive more satisfaction from their lives. The Highlands

Ability Battery is based on over 80 years of research, beginning with Johnson O'Connor. It is psychometrically valid and reliable. The information and suggestions that it makes are highly accurate. The minimum reliability standard for the 19 tests that make up the Highland Ability Battery is $r = .80$ and the reliability range is to .93, with 1.0 being perfect. It has been described as the equivalent of getting a CAT Scan for a painful injury instead of a traditional X-ray. As an Associate Fellow of the British Psychological Society, I would not use any test that doesn't match what it sets out to measure.

Thousands of people have taken the Highlands Ability Battery and I've personally guided over 300 clients using it. People seek out objective data so they know more about themselves and can use this to identify careers to which they would be well suited. Some people are hesitant to take ability tests because they are afraid their scores will indicate that they lack intelligence. However, aptitudes do not correlate with IQ tests, and aptitude tests are not based on knowledge or experience. You can't pass or fail the Highlands Ability Battery.

The Highlands Ability Battery does not measure or determine IQ. However, most experts agree that IQ tests are not inherently helpful when trying to decide on a career path. Two people can have identical IQ scores but very different aptitudes.

The main reason to take The Highlands Ability Battery is to find out where you have natural ability. Research from the Johnson O'Connor Research Foundation says that people tend to be more satisfied and successful in occupations that use their aptitudes and do not demand aptitudes they lack.

You might think the worst option is to work in a job where you don't have the natural abilities, but research has found that people experience greater problems when they have strong abilities that they are not able to use in their job. These can distract you from your ability to do the job and you would need to find an outlet for them through an activity outside of work.

Every occupation, for example, engineering, medicine, law or management, uses certain aptitudes. The work you are most likely to enjoy and be successful in is work that uses your aptitudes. For example, if you are an engineer but possess aptitudes **not** used in engineering, your work might seem unrewarding. If you **lack** the engineer's aptitudes, your work may be difficult or unpleasant.

"The individual, who knows his own aptitudes, and their relative strengths, chooses more intelligently among the world's host of opportunities." -- Johnson O'Connor, 1940 p134

For further information including sample reports or to arrange to take the questionnaire: http://www.amazing-people.co.uk/highlandsabilitybattery.htm

The Myers Briggs Type Indicator

The MBTI® assessment is a self-reporting personality inventory, designed to help individuals understand themselves. It helps people understand their natural preferences, motivations and potential areas for growth. It aids in understanding others, particularly those with different types.

The MBTI® instrument is my favourite assessment for helping individuals learn about themselves. It helps to identify preferences in four areas:

- How am I around people?
- How do I prefer to gather information?
- How do I make decisions?
- What sort of lifestyle is best for me?

There is a strong research background to this assessment. As a Chartered Psychologist, I wouldn't use anything that had not been well researched. The MBTI® assessment is based on the work of mother and daughter Katherine Briggs and Elizabeth Briggs-Myers. **Today, the MBTI® assessment is one of the most widely used tools for self-awareness**. It has been translated into several languages and is used to help people in career choices, in relationship and family counselling, in team development and executive coaching.

The MBTI® assessment describes an individual's personality preferences on four dimensions:

- **Extraversion** - prefers to gain energy from the outside world of activity, people and things OR **Introversion** - prefers to gain energy from the inner world of reflections, feelings and ideas.
- **Sensing** - Prefers to focus on information gained from the senses and on practical applications OR **Intuition** - prefers to focus on patterns, connections and possible meanings.
- **Thinking** - prefers to make judgements on logic and objective analysis OR **Feeling** - prefers to base decisions on values and what is important to people.
- **Judging** - likes a planned and organised approach to life and to make decisions OR **Perceiving** - likes a flexible, spontaneous approach and prefers to keep options open.

The MBTI® assessment doesn't measure, but sorts. It sorts people into 16 types based on how they fall on the four scales, for example ISTJ and ENFP.

Taking the MBTI® assessment will help you to understand your natural preferences, motivations and potential for growth. You will find out why you get on well with some people, but with others things don't go smoothly; learn how to enhance relationship; and improve your leadership and communication skills. It helps you understand how you make decisions and assists in creating a personal development plan.

For further information including sample reports or to arrange to take the questionnaire: http://www.amazingpeople.co.uk/myersbriggstypeindicator.htm

The Strong Interest Inventory

The Strong Interest Inventory® is the most sensitive and widely used interest inventory available and designed to help you identify your pattern of vocational interests. It was developed at Stanford University in the late 1920s by Professor Edward K Strong with Jo-Ida Hansen, and David Campbell and was based on the work of John Holland. Holland defined six basic occupational themes (called Holland Codes) that can be used to categorise occupations as well as individuals.

The "Strong" measures your interests using 291 different questions to explore your likes and dislikes with regard to careers, leisure activities, school subjects and other categories.

- 107 questions about careers you would be interested in doing.
- 46 questions about interest in different subject areas.
- 84 questions about interest in activities.
- 29 questions about interest in different leisure activities.
- 25 questions on the people you would like to work with and their personal characteristics.

Your responses are compared to a representative sample of people who:

- Enjoy their work.
- Have worked in that area for at least three years.
- Who do typical work for the field.

People tend to search out those environments that match their interests, and an environment attracts people who share similar interests.

The "Strong" is based on the idea that people who enjoy their work will, in all likelihood, share similar interests. The theory states that individuals with similar interests are often attracted to the same kind of work, feel comfortable with others who share their interests, and are likely to be successful in a work environment that reflects those interests.

Also, the "Strong" is a quick way to get a snapshot of career interests, but the highest interests may not be the most appropriate career for a client. That's why I recommend that you use it in conjunction with other assessments.

For further information including sample reports or to arrange to take the questionnaire: http://www.amazingpeople. co.uk/stronginterestinventory.htm.

Chapter Three

Creating your CV

1. Introduction

When I work with a new client, one of the first things I do is review their CV. Unfortunately, I see too many that are ineffective, even those written or reviewed by people who proclaim they are experts.

There are many books on the market focused solely on writing a CV, so to cover this topic in one chapter is encouraging me to be succinct, just like your CV needs to be!

Your CV is a key element of your job search. You will use it not only for job applications but also for speculative enquiries. One version is not enough. It's best if your CV is tailored specifically for each job (or type of job) you apply for. This chapter will help you prepare the most effective CV possible and thus, make your job search a successful one.

Generally, CVs will be up to two sides in length, and every statement on the CV must be relevant. You don't need to include everything, but it should highlight your achievements, skills and what you have to offer. If it gets you to interview, it has done its job well.

Many CVs have a poor appearance. They are too lengthy, have too many typos, or have a layout that is hard to follow. There are many different layouts used and I tend to use different styles to suit different jobs and individuals. Font and layout can be left to personal choice although I suggest to avoid the templates found on word processing packages as they will make your CV look too rudimentary and it will stand out for all the wrong reasons.

How to help the recruiter

Less than a minute is spent short listing each CV so you need to highlight the key points, through layout, judicious use of bold and underlining, and careful use of white space. The goal is to get your CV in the pile that gets a second review.

It's hard work but worth it!

You can easily spend £300 or more on getting your CV professionally created and for many, it is money well spent. To do it yourself, you will need to invest time in collecting the information you need, then writing it as clearly and effectively as possible. The applicants that get shortlisted are those having CVs that are effective and focused on the job.

2: What type of CV will you use?

The three main categories of CV are:

- Chronological.
- Skills-based.
- Combination.

The Chronological CV

The chronological CV is most effective for individuals who have a steady record of employment in an industry or functional area and want to stay in the same line of work. It is not recommended when:

- You are changing careers or have changed employers frequently.
- You want to de-emphasise age.
- You have been absent from the job market for some time.

The Skills-based CV

Choose a skills-based CV if you want your next job to be in an area where you will have a significant shift in responsibilities or to move to a different sector. Highlight skills and achievements rather than the chronology of events. A skills-based CV is useful when you:

- Are making a career transition.
- Want to return to a professional area you worked in earlier in your career.
- Want to disguise a previous career path.
- Have large time gaps in your CV and/or other biographical materials.
- Have extensive accomplishments in volunteer work or hobbies.

For example, John worked for many years as a church minister but wanted to pursue a career into human resources. Rosie had been on a career break for several years and needed a way of including all the skills and experience she had gained via voluntary activities. For both John and Rosie, a skills-based CV significantly increased the number of interviews they gained.

Why you need a skills-based CV

Too many potentially suitable applicants fail to get short listed due to the fact that they do not fit the expected applicant profile. A skills-based CV can help you to overcome this problem.

For the skills-based CV, details of your transferable skills constitute your strong selling points.

However, the deviation from the chronological format can cause confusion or suspicion, (HR people may wonder what you are trying to hide) and the CV has to change significantly according to the positions applied for.

You must ensure that your covering letter sounds positive about your previous work experience and keenness for a new challenge.

3: Preparation Phase

Before you decorate a room, you get the walls and paint-work prepared and make sure the brushes are clean. When producing your CV, take the same approach, you will make faster progress if you collect all the details in advance.

Step 1: Work History

The first task is to collect the details on each of the jobs you have had so far. If your work history goes beyond 15 years, you may not need to go further back, unless there is something relevant to the current job you are applying for. For example, Kate was a legal secretary before following a career in hotel and catering. When she decided to apply for work as a legal executive, her previous work experience was relevant, despite it being 20 years previous.

If you are a recent graduate, you need to ensure that you include details on all your vacation work and perhaps also include details on your other interests (passions, hobbies, voluntary activities) particularly if they reflect attributes such as leadership and organisational skills.

You may not be using all of this information in your CV, but it will be useful to be able to refer to it in the future. Sometimes when you complete an application form, they request further information and it's helpful to have the details to hand.

Don't forget about volunteer work. It can be helpful to include, for example, coaching a junior football team if you are seeking a teaching job. It will have more impact if it appears here, rather than under General Interests.

For each job make a note of:

- Dates (including month and year).
- Organisation name.
- Address.
- Job title.
- Brief description of the organisation.
- Your department's purpose and objectives.
- Main responsibilities. Include numbers of people managed and size of budget where appropriate.
- List your achievements - quantify wherever possible.
- What strengths/skills or attributes do these achievements reveal?
- What do you most enjoy about your job?
- What do you least enjoy?
- Why are you leaving?
- Who will give you a reference?
- Leaving salary and benefits

You can download a template to help you collate this via the web site.

This may seem like a lot of extra work, but the aim of your CV is to get you to interview, and the thinking and reflection to answer these questions will enhance your performance at interview.

Step 2: Education and short courses

Think back over each job and make a note of all courses, both internal and external, which you have completed. Some employers will ask to see your certificates, so find them and put them in a folder. Don't be tempted to fabricate your results. If you are found out, you will likely be dismissed.

For each course, make a note of:

- Title of course.
- Date of course.
- Length of training course.
- Training provider.
- Benefits gained.

Computer Experience

Almost all employers want people who are comfortable using a word processing package, email, etc. How confident and competent are you? Make a note of the software you can use and for each, list:

1. Frequency.
2. Examples of use.
3. Level of comfort in using it.

Languages

Make a note of any languages you can speak and the level of fluency, e.g., French (fluent); German (basic).

Don't fib! I've interviewed someone who said they could speak Polish, but was unable to answer a simple question. As a recruiter we think that if they have fibbed here, where else may they?

Step 3: Personal interests / leisure activities

I'm cautious about including personal interests on a CV. Although some interviewers like to see it as it provides details on the whole person, it can also fuel their prejudices. Some people take a dislike to people with a certain hobby for example. There is no way to know what the readers prejudice may be so it's best to be cautious.

Sometimes, people will write down things to make them look good. If you do, you need to be able to discuss them. If you put down reading for example, be able to discuss your favourite author or what you are reading at the moment.

If you have an unusual hobby you may want to include it as you could get short-listed because a potential employer might be intrigued and want to know more. When I used to apply for jobs, interviewers would always ask me about my hobby of English Civil War re-enactment. On one occasion, this lead on to a discussion of how the war could have been avoided and I was glad I could speak with some authority on the subject.

When listing interests, it can help to expand a little. For example, saying not just running, but training to complete a half marathon in the Spring. If you are a history buff, you might expand it to reading historical biographies. No matter the subject, be prepared to discuss it.

Organisational memberships

You may have gained skills and competence through a membership organisation. If these skills are relevant to an employer, include them. Were you on a committee at university? Do you take part in environmental projects? Are you involved in a community action group, etc? If it could be relevant make a note.

Memberships might reveal some personal information (e.g., you are gay, a member of a particular religious or political group, etc.) but most people will not use this against you. (If they do, would you really want to work for them?)

4: Creation phase

There are a number of styles of CV, but for now, let's take your initial work and create effectively written text. You can then play around with the layout later.

It is important to be in a positive frame of mind when you produce your CV. No matter what your situation, you need to look for the high points of what you have achieved, not get side tracked into worry over, for example, how long it may take you to get another job.

The whole point of the CV is to get you an interview, so put yourself in the position of the interviewer. For whatever job you are applying for, what are the most important things for the interviewer to know?

Section 1: The top of your CV will contain your personal details

All personal details except name, address and phone numbers should be at the end of your CV. Do include your email address, particularly if you are "more mature" as it shows you are competent with new technology.

Females need to think about whether to include Ms, Miss, or Mrs. I prefer to use my name without a title.

Make sure there is a professional answer phone message on each phone number you provide. Just use your mobile number if there is a chance a family member could answer the phone in a less than professional way. Never include your work number.

Section 2: Profile or career summary

The Profile can be seen as an optional element of the CV. It gives the reader a concise overview of your skills, experience and aptitudes. Like with all CVs, you will customise it for every job you apply for.

The biggest mistake people make is to focus on themselves and their needs. Think about it from the employers' point of view. They want someone to solve problems, so think about what it is that you can do for them, not the other way around. If you say:

"Seeking a position where I can utilise my skills and with potential for career advancement"

This may sound fine to the person writing the CV, but it isn't focused on what the employer wants or needs. They will more than likely tell themselves, "So what, that's what you want, but I want someone who can use their skills to solve my current problems." So make sure you focus on the job, its requirements, and what you have to offer. Anything super-fluous should be removed.

This was used by one of my clients and it resulted in an interview.

"Award-winning, highly accomplished Operations Manager with successful track records of consistently increasing revenue and slashing operating costs now seeking a new challenge where my skills and track record can be utilised in the facilities sector."

Section 3: Work History

This section, and the following one on education, may be interchangeable to suit individual circumstances. For example, if you are a recent graduate with a thin employ-ment record, put Education and Training before Work History.

It is customary to set out your details in reverse chronological order covering the last 10-15 years of em-ployment. Unless you are considering a complete career change, emphasis should be placed on your current or last position. That is what the reader will be particularly inter-ested in. If you had a large number of jobs earlier in your career, or if your career goes back over many years, sum-marise this information as an "earlier career" paragraph.

Include the minimum detail on your previous companies, as the CV is about **you**, not what the previ-ous company did! However, one line with a succinct de-scription of the company might be helpful.

If you have had a lot of jobs, put the dates on the right hand side. We read left to right, so the dates in this case, come across as less important.

Should your existing or past job titles be peculiar to your company or industry, express them in terms that are recognisable to the outside world.

If you have worked as a temp, your employer is the temping agency, not the company where you worked. Don't be tempted to state otherwise, it could be seen as a reason for dismissal.

As you look at your jobs, have a look at the job title. Some companies give people fantastic job titles (look at all the Vice Presidents in American companies). So, if the job titles seem "high," review what you write down. In some companies, every one is a manager, as they manage themselves, whereas in the Civil Service, the word officer as part of a job title can refer to a quite senior role.

For example, Sally worked as a HR Manager, and her next job was HR Director. (This was with a much smaller company, and she was not a director in the true sense, the work was less involved than in her previous job and she left after a year due to frustration and boredom). She then joined the council as Personnel Officer, and was now earning more than in the previous jobs. But the job titles make this look like a *backward* step. She amended her CV to show HR Manager, HR Director and Government Personnel Officer, which flagged a reason for a perceived lower status job.

The Work History section should emphasise and quantify key achievements. Think back to your daily duties. What good things were achieved because of what you did? Write them down, and the more specific the better. Using a bullet format makes it easier for the reader to notice the key points.

For example, instead of writing:

"Responsibilities included implementation of policies and procedures, training new employees, interfacing with subordinates and associates"

Which is a bit of a mouthful. It is much more effective to say:

"I worked with staff and associates to increase product turnover by 15 percent and sales by 23 percent. Also trained 14 new employees, five of who were rapidly promoted."

You may want to add more to the achievements you listed earlier:

- What was your achievement?
- What was the problem, situation or opportunity?
- What core skills, strengths or technical expertise did you use?
- What was the benefit of the action you took?
- Can you quantify any of these benefits in terms of money saved, time saved, reduction in staffing costs, etc?

As you review your job history, you may notice that several appointments have been held at similar levels in a relatively short space of time. It is important not to be perceived as a "job hopper." The problem can be overcome by incorporating several positions into one paragraph, for example:

1985-89   Quantity Surveyor

During this period, key positions were held with several multinational companies on fixed term contracts including major development projects for Amec, Wimpey, Balfour Beatty etc.

Followed by a summary of responsibilities and achievements throughout the period.

Achievement Statements

Too often, people fill their CV with description of the tasks they do. But employers don't want to know the detail of your job description, but rather what you have achieved and how you have stood out from the majority.

As you put your bullet points under each job, avoid starting a statement with a qualification such as "part of …"

If you write:

"My role involves dealing with customer enquiries, responding to orders and helping to produce end of month reports"

a recruiter may think, "So what if that's how you spend your time, but what did you actually achieve?"

Here are some poor examples of what to include under career history. Paul had been advised to include the sorts of phrases and words that people would be looking for, but what do they mean?

- *"Allowing prospective employers to make use of my exemplary interpersonal and communication skills and diverse working environment experience."*
- *"Providing employers with the assurance of my intuitive, interpersonal and self management skills and the development of my business acumen."*

Make your achievements specific. Instead of "duties included the supervision of staff," replace that with "successfully supervised and led a team and staff." Instead of "responsible for departmental budget." Replace with "personally controlled a budget in excess of £xxx." Instead of "excellent verbal skills," replace with, "trained 24 new employees on customer service procedures."

Now review the achievements you listed in **step 1 of the preparation phase.** As a prompt, you might like to ask yourself if you can think of examples where you:

- Achieved a major objective.
- Contributed to a major decision.
- Handled an emergency situation.
- Re-organised administration systems.
- Increased efficiencies.
- Reduced overheads, came in under budget.

- Saved time, money, equipment, facilities.
- Improved a product, services, or procedure.
- Consistently met deadlines.
- Solved a seemingly intractable problem.
- Brought a project to a successful conclusion.
- Created, invented, built or improved something.
- Developed and implemented ideas.
- Received a reward or special commendation.
- Achieved sporting or social recognition.
- Received a letter of thanks or congratulation.
- Led a team to meet a deadline/target.
- Achieved more with fewer deadlines.
- Improved team morale.

Examples of achievement statements

You have now identified a number of statements, excellent! Now it's time to tighten the language and compare them to your various appointments.

Before you do this, have a look at the following examples to give you some ideas. Note that wherever possible, there is a numerical result, improvement or outcome of some type.

When referring to money, use k to express thousands, e.g., £25k not 25,000 or 25 thousand. Use M to express millions, e.g., £10M

You can also tighten words by, for example, replacing "more than" with "+." For example, change managed more than 50 staff to managed 50+ staff.

- **Developed** a more integrated working relationship with the American parent company leading to significant economies of scale.
- **Introduced** a computerised Credit Control and Debt Collection system. This reduced debtor days from 55 to 44 within 6 months from introduction.

- **Cut inventory levels** by £1m over two years by introducing new inventory control procedures, at the same time improving stock availability by 10%.
- Successfully **set up** and ran a community centre for three years.
- Ensured ISO9001 **quality standards were met or exceeded** and conducted regular quality audits leading to enhanced efficiencies which saved the company £0.5m.
- **Learned** new graphics package and used this to improve presentations for sales force. This was well received by clients and contributed to the company achieving a 20% increase in sales in my area.
- **Devised and implemented** a new sales training programme which resulted in a 37% increase in new business.
- Relocated business, systems and administration functions from London to Leeds, **saving** £4.6m over two years.
- **Introduced** a photocopy logging procedure, which was adopted throughout the company, saving £750 per month. Together with the Marketing Manager, designed and produced the company's quarterly catalogue.
- **Fostered good relationships** with new suppliers. Negotiated and improved terms and quality of supply, which reduced manufacturing costs by 60%.
- **Developed** a new system for generating sales leads which was adopted throughout the group, resulting in a 30% improvement in sales performance with the same number of sales executives.
- **Project managed** each individual business system and personally designed, developed and implemented the financial accounting, grain trading and seed systems.
- On the strength of reputation as a firm yet caring leader, put in charge of low morale team of 30 medical and support personnel and **improved effectiveness** and

discipline through developing good team spirit which help motivate and bond the group.

- **Reduced** inventory by 25% within a year after installing a material control and forward planning system.

Each of your bullets should start with a positive action word. Use this list as a prompt for other words to use:

Accelerated, Accessed, Accomplished, Achieved, Acquainted, Acquired, Acted, Activated, Adapted, Added, Addressed, Adjusted, Administered, Advanced, Advertised, Advised, Aided, Allocated, Altered, Amended, Analysed, Answered, Anticipated, Applied, Appointed, Appraised, Approved, Arbitrated, Arranged, Ascertained, Asked, Assembled, Assessed, Assigned, Assisted, Attained, Attended, Audited, Augmented, Authored, Authorised, Automated, Averted, Awarded.

Balanced, Boosted, Briefed, Broadened, Brought, Budgeted, Built.

Calculated, Calmed, Canvassed, Captured, Catalogued, Categorised, Chaired, Challenged, Charted, Checked, Choreographed, Clarified, Classified, Coached, Collaborated, Collected, Combined, Comforted, Communicated, Compared, Competed, Compiled, Completed, Composed, Compounded, Computed, Conceived, Conceptualised, Condensed, Conducted, Conserved, Considered, Consolidated, Constructed, Consulted, Contacted, Contracted, Contributed, Controlled, Conveyed, Convinced, Corrected, Correlated, Corresponded, Counselled, Crafted, Created, Criticised, Critiqued, Cultivated, Customised, Cut.

Debated, Debugged, Decided, Decreased, Deduced, Defined, Defused, Delegated, Delighted, Delivered, Demonstrated, Depreciated, Described, Designated, Designed, Detailed, Detected, Determined, Developed, Devised, Devoted, Diagnosed, Diagrammed, Directed, Disciplined, Disclosed, Discovered, Dispatched, Dispensed, Displayed, Disproved, Dissected, Disseminated, Dissuaded, Distributed, Diversified, Diverted, Documented, Doubled, Drafted, Dramatised, Drew, Drove.

Earned, Edited, Educated, Effected, Elaborated, Elected, Elevated, Elicited, Eliminated, Emphasised, Employed, Enabled, Encouraged, Endorsed, Enforced, Engineered, Enhanced, Enlisted, Enriched, Ensured, Established, Estimated, Evaluated, Examined, Exceeded, Excelled, Excited, Executed, Exhibited,

Expanded, Expedited, Experimented, Exploited, Explored, Expressed, Extended, Extracted, Extrapolated.

Fabricated, Facilitated, Familiarised, Fashioned, Filed, Finalised, Financed, Fixed, Focused, Followed, Forecasted, Formalised, Formed, Formulated, Fostered, Found, Framed, Fulfilled.

Gained, Gathered, Generated, Governed, Grew, Guarded, Guided.

Handled, Harnessed, Hastened, Headed, Helped, Highlighted, Hired.

Identified, Illustrated, Imagined, Implemented, Improvised, Incorporated, Increased, Inferred, Influenced, Informed, Initiated, Innovated, Inspected, Inspired, Installed, Instated, Instigated, Instilled, Instituted, Instructed, Insured, Integrated, Interested, Interpreted, Interviewed, Introduced, Invented, Investigated, Issued.

Joined, Judged, Justified.

Kept.

Launched, Learnt, Lectured, Led, Leveraged, Licensed, Lifted, Lightened, Linked, Liquidated, Listened, Lobbied, Logged.

Made, Maintained, Managed, Manipulated, Marketed, Mastered, Maximised, Mediated, Memorised, Mentored, Merged, Met, Minimised, Mobilised, Modelled, Moderated, Modernised, Modified, Monitored, Motivated.

Named, Narrated, Navigated, Negotiated, Nurtured.

Observed, Obtained, Offset, Opened, Operated, Orchestrated, Ordered, Organised, Oriented, Originated, Oversaw.

Participated, Perceived, Performed, Persuaded, Pinpointed, Pioneered, Planed, Practiced, Praised, Predicted, Prepared, Prescribed, Presented, Preserved, Presided, Prevailed, Prevented, Prioritised, Probed, Processed, Procured, Produced, Programmed, Projected, Promoted, Proposed, Protected, Proved, Provided, Provoked, Publicised, Published, Purchased.

Quadrupled, Quantified, Questioned.

Raised, Read, Realised, Reasoned, Received, Recognised, Recommended, Reconciled, Recorded, Recruited, Redesigned, Reduced, Reengineered, Referred, Refined, Registered, Regulated, Rehabilitated, Related, Remembered, Remodelled, Rendered, Reorganised, Repaired, Replaced, Reported, Represented,

Requested, Researched, Resolved, Responded, Restored, Restructured, Retrieved, Revamped, Reversed, Reviewed, Revised, Revitalised, Revolutionised, Rewarded, Routed.

Saved, Scheduled, Screened, Searched, Secured, Segmented, Selected, Sensed, Separated, Served, Serviced, Set, Settled, Sewed, Shaped, Shared, Shopped, Showed, Simplified, Sketched, Sold, Solicited, Solved, Sorted, Sparked, Specified, Spoke, Sponsor, Stabilised, Staffed, Staged, Started, Stimulated, Streamlined, Strengthened, Stretched, Structured, Studied, Submitted, Succeeded, Summarised, Sung, Superseded, Supervised, Supplemented, Supplied, Supported, Surpassed, Surveyed, Symbolised, Synthesised, Systemised.

Tailored, Talked, Targeted, Tended, Terminated, Tested, Thanked, Thought, Thrived, Told, Took, Traced, Tracked, Traded, Trained, Transacted, Transcribed, Transferred, Translated, Travelled, Treated, Trimmed, Tripled, Troubleshot, Turned, Tutored, Typed.

Umpired, Uncovered, Understood, Understudied, Unified, Unravelled, Updated, Upgraded, Used, Utilised.

Validated, Verbalised, Verified, Viewed, Volunteered.

Widened, Withdrew, Won, Write.

Section 4: Education and training

You have already collected details on your education and training courses. Now you will review this to choose what is most appropriate for each particular job you seek.

Don't overload this section with lists of dates, schools and colleges, etc. Include what's appropriate for the job. Also include specialist training and professional qualifications. As you get older, you don't need to include details of your earlier education.

List the courses in order of significance. If you have attended a large number of courses, only list those that are relevant to the post that you are applying for to ensure that they are noted and considered.

Are you a member of any professional organisation? Perhaps you do not have full membership yet, but are an associate or affiliate. Include this information here.

Section 5: Interests

If there is space, you can include any interests that are relevant or might serve as a comfortable topic for discussion at interview. Think about which of your interests can be used to demonstrate qualities of leadership, fitness, intellectual capacity etc. Also include committee memberships, including those you have held in the past. When including interests, try to select an interest that falls into one of the following categories: active or sport, group or team, creative. Make sure they are real interests you can describe if challenged.

Section 6: Optional personal details

It is in the last section that you can include other relevant information such as a full, clean driving license or willingness to relocate (if you are). Some people include details on marital status, children, nationality, etc. My personal view is not to include them unless you believe it will give you an "edge" for a particular job vacancy.

Your Career Summary, version 2

Earlier you completed your first attempt. You can now review what you wrote and amend it to suit each job you apply for. **Make sure you have focused on what you can offer and your enthusiasm for the job, rather than what you can get from the job.**

Read through these examples, to see what others have done.

- An experienced, very adaptable Manufacturing Manager with professional training and a good understanding of Total Productive Maintenance. An able communicator at all levels who is both objective and pragmatic. Works well under pressure and remains calm in difficult situations. Used to working with little or no supervision and on own initiative.

- An experienced and innovative manager who has led a multi-skilled team through difficult and changing times with inspirational and influential leadership.

- Excellent people management and problem solving abilities, coupled with a strong desire to work in a "get things right" environment and the aptitude to motivate others, are the strengths which have been called on most in the past three years.

- A responsible and mature business manager with substantial experience of retail and wholesale banking with a major UK Clearing Bank. Highly developed aptitude for customer liaison, most recently used as a Financial Consultant and previously as a Client Service Manager. Strong interpersonal communication skills, supported by a high degree of commitment and integrity. Fluent German.

5: The Skills-based CV

In a skills-based CV, the main focus will be on the skills, activities and achievements which best represent your suitability for new employment, with no account of where the experience was gained. This is followed by a summary of your career history, then education and training relevant to the position sought.

1: Skills-based headings

Provide highly-focused paragraphs on specific skills and abilities as **this CV encourages the reader to initially focus on your abilities and skills.** This helps a recruiter to clearly see how you measure up to the requirements of the job.

With a skills-based CV, you list your experience under a number of headings chosen to be relevant to the job you are applying for. For example, administration, communications, consulting, counselling, design, engineering, human resources, management, planning, research, sales, training, and writing.

As you review the job you are applying for, pick out the key elements of the job, and provide examples under each heading. Put these headings in descending order of importance with the number of headings to six maximum.

Having created your headings, place 2–5 bullets with specific examples of what you have achieved relating to each heading. These examples can be drawn from both your work and personal life.

2: Brief employment history

An organisation will want to know who you have worked for, but as this is not the main focus, it comes after the skills-based headings. I would keep this brief but would include employer, job title and dates. Some people will decide to leave out this section but doing so makes it look like you have something to hide and you may not get short listed.

3: Education/Qualifications/Training

As with any style of CV, include details on secondary schooling and university alongside qualifications, including relevant short courses you have attended.

Interests and positions of responsibility

Include them if they will enhance your application.

6: Example CVs

Too many CVs are based on templates and look like it. You can see from Kim's initial CV that there is a lot of room for improvement:

- The tiny print for contact details.
- The lack of dates for education and training.
- Professional skills mixing up catering and business skills (unless she wants to work in catering, this detracts from the relevant qualification).
- The way a number of jobs are listed within just two job titles.
- The lack of her achievements.

13b Mill Lane
Macclesfield
Cheshire
SK11 5TG

Phone 07931 567xxx
E-mail kim75@yahoo.co.uk

Kim Richardson

Profile

I am a reliable and hardworking property lawyer with the ability to work on my own initiative. I work with enthusiasm and enjoy a challenge. I am committed and flexible with good interpersonal and communication skills. I can deal professionally with a diverse range of people and motivate colleagues. I prioritise my workload and work effectively under pressure.

Education/Training

Loretto Convent 1979 – O'Levels Achieved

English Language, English Literature, Human Biology, Food and Nutrition, French and Religious Studies

St Peters School 1981 – A' Levels Achieved

English and Food and Nutrition

Manchester Polytechnic 1981- 1984

HND in Hotel Catering and Institutional Management

South Manchester college and distance learning from the Institute of Legal Executives.   2001 - 2006

Level 3 passed

Level 4 passed Probate and Succession, Land Law, Conveyancing Practice and Landlord and Tenant

Qualified as a Fellow of the Institute in June 2008

Professional Skills

Salon Culinaire silver award

Proficient in use of computer software accountancy packages

Royal Institute of Public Health and Hygiene Certificate with Merit

Hotel and Catering Industry Training Board certificates in Organisational Training and Assessment, Group Training Techniques and Trainer Skills 1

Proficient in use of DPS and Eclipse legal case management systems

Member of the local branch of the Institute of Legal Executives

Director of Winston Management Ltd the company managing the freehold of the flats where I live

European Computer Driving Licence (ECDL) commenced course and studying Modules 1 and 2

Employment Experience

2002 – 2008   Wilson and Foster Solicitors. Stockport

Legal Executive

Conveyancing work from instruction to completion consisting of sales and purchases for both freehold and leasehold properties. Equity Release, re-mortgages and transfers of equity.

Preparing contract reports, financial completion statements and arranging client meetings in the office.

Achieved and exceeded fee targets

I deputised in Solicitors and Partners absence

Plan and implement marketing strategies for the firm

Represent the firm at corporate and client entertaining events.

Excellent client survey responses received post completion.

Effectively communicating with estate agents, mortgage brokers, surveyors and other Solicitors

1988 – 2002   Gardner Merchant Management Services North West Division

District Support Manager

Responsible for the implementation and review of company control systems

Ensure that financial targets exceeded and costs controlled

Responsible for training and developing Catering Managers

Team manager

Liasing with clients and senior executives of the company.

Successfully marketing additional services to increase profits and ensure contract retention

Deputising for the District Manager in the highest earning area of the business

References

Supplied on request

Kim's Revised CV

Now look at Kim's revised CV and see the difference!

- Contact details are much clearer.
- Employment includes specific examples of what she had achieved in two different roles.
- The catering experience is divided into three different jobs.

- The education includes dates, and the business elements of the hotel and catering HND are highlighted.
- Professional skills are divided between hotel and catering and business.

Kim Richardson
13b Mill Lane, Macclesfield, Cheshire SK11 5TG
Home 01625   277456   Mobile 07931 567 xxx E-mail kim75@yahoo.co.uk

Key areas of Experience

A Legal Executive with experience of acting for high profile clients in a professional manner. Kim works with enthusiasm, enjoys a challenge and prioritises work effectively under pressure. Excellent communication skills together with a high level of commitment and integrity resulting in excellent client care survey comments. Confident at problem solving, with attention to detail and good organisational skills, Kim has successfully completed complicated transactions working on own initiative.

Employment
Legal Executive, Wilson and Foster Solicitors
July 2004 – July 2008

- Residential conveyancer working on a varied caseload consisting of freehold and leasehold sales and purchases including new builds, equity release, remortgages and transfers of equity including both probate and matrimonial matters
- Exceeded fee target by £30,000 in first year working as a fee earner
- Deputised in Solicitors and partners absence across all 3 branches, demonstrating flexibility
- Saved the firm money on expensive locum costs by assisting locums who were only employed part-time
- Planned and implemented marketing strategies for the firm, successfully establishing good relationships with local Estate Agents to increase number of referrals and improve level of fees
- Achieved objective of completing the Legal Executive course, passing all exams required to qualify as a Fellow whilst working full time
- Responsible for the people management of two secretaries, working well as a team even during exceptionally busy periods
- Providing a high level of Customer Service with excellent post completion client survey responses together with many letters of thanks

Paralegal, Wilson and Foster Solicitors
January 2002 – July 2004

- Assisted three fee earners consisting of two Legal Executives and one Partner with the administration and correspondence on all their files
- Responsible for completing contracts, deeds, transfers and property information forms
- Carried out research both on line and in the firm's library to obtain copies of Acts of Parliament and case notes
- Resolved outstanding issues to close backlog of files ready for archiving, resulting in additional revenue to the company through finalising unpaid invoices.

Support Manager, Gardner Merchant Management Services, Northern Division
January 1996 – January 2002

Responsible for training and developing a team of 15 Catering Managers In the following areas:

- o **Budgets** – planning and ensuring financial targets were exceeded and costs controlled
- o **Food hygiene and safety standards** – monitoring practice to ensure compliance with company and legislative requirements
- o **Recruitment** – assisting with the interview and selection process for various roles
- Management of large, complex catering events such as Gourmet dinners
- Achieved a bonus of £250 for improving standards at a new site and ensuring staff were both motivated and enthusiastic

- Actively increasing revenue by providing sales leads which were successfully converted into contracts for both cleaning and vending services and receiving a selection of gifts as a reward
- Deputised for the District Manager where appropriate in the highest earning area of the business sector and receiving a letter of thanks from the Operations Director
- Carryied out audits throughout the District on all Personnel and Training records and successfully achieving the Investors in People Award for the division
- Project managed and co-ordinated the opening of a prestigious contract at large multiple sites

Assistant Manager, Gardner Merchant, Barclays Bank (Radbrook Hall)
August 1992 – January 1996

Responsible for the smooth and efficient transfer of the Catering Operations from in-house to Gardner Merchant at a time when existing staff resisted change. Implementing all the company procedures

- Deputising for the manager during periods of absence
- Training, developing and managing a team of 25
- Organised special functions for VIPs and received a handwritten thank you letter from the Chief Accountant for Barclays

Area Relief Manager, Gardner Merchant, North West Division
September 1988 – August 1992

- Provided both chef and management cover for all Catering Managers during periods of absence.
- Assisted the Area Support Manager and Area Manager with the opening of new contracts during a period of rapid growth.
- During hurricanes in 1990 provide emergency cover at the weekend providing hot meals for Electricians at short notice

Education:

1973 – 1979 Loretto Convent   6 O'Levels, grades B – C including English
1979 – 1981 St Peters School   A'Levels in English D and Home Economics C

1981 – 1984 **Manchester Polyetchnic - HND in Hotel Catering and Institutional Management**
Covered: Business Administration I (Accounts), Management and Business Administration II, Marketing Accommodation and House Services, Food and Beverage Management

2001 – 2006 **South Manchester College and distance learning - Legal Executive Course from the Institute of Legal Executives**
Passed Levels 3 and 4 in Probate and Succession, Land Law, Conveyancing Practice and Landlord. **Qualified as a Fellow of the Institute in June 2008**

2008 - Learn Direct **City and Guilds in Maths Passed**

Professional Skills

- Hotel and Catering Training Board Certificate in Trainer Skills 1 1985
- Hotel and Catering Training Board Certificate in Organising Training and Assessment
- and Craft Trainer Award 1992
- Royal Institute of Public Health and Hygiene Certificate in Food Hygiene with Credit 1996
- Proficient in DPS and Eclipse legal case management systems   2002 -2008
- European Computer Driving Licence (ECDL) commenced course and passed Module 2 2008

Travel – I have recently returned from a round the world trip stopping in Los Angeles, Fiji, Sydney and Hong Kong.

Nationality: British | Full clean driving licence

And here's a skills-based CV:

Vicky Hudson
62 Benson Street, Northwich, Cheshire CW9 5KK
T: 01606 556 788| M: 07931 344 562 | E: vhudson@gmail.com

Key areas of Experience

High level team administration
- Taking minutes of team meetings using excellent short hand
- Taking notes at grievance meetings, e.g. pay disputes, and staff stepping "out of line", maintaining confidentiality
- Coordinating and minuting the Northwich Tackling Drug and Alcohol Together Group
- Preparing duty manager rotas

Computer Skills
- **Word:** including mail merge, tracking changes, creating forms and templates Completed advanced course (2003)
- **Sage HR:** database for personnel – created reports for sickness and holidays for different teams
- **Power Point:** creating presentations
- **Excel:** can produce spread sheets and formulas

General administration
- Ordering stationery, photocopying, monitoring petty cash, faxing, scanning and dealing with mail
- Facilities management – arranging for repairs to be undertaken, new carpets fitted etc.

Support to the company secretary and chief executive
- Various tasks including preparing and circulating board papers
- Sensitive note taking at senior management business meetings

HR Administration – Recruitment *Extensive experience*
- **Preparation:** drafting the ad, liaison with agency, producing information packs, collecting names and distribution, receiving application and collating ready for short listing
- **Interview:** sending out letters, preparing paper work and exercises, arranging schedules, looking after candidates
- **Post Interview:** Sending out letter to successful and unsuccessful, requesting references, creating and setting out contracts

HR Administration – Payroll and sickness monitoring
- Collating information on a monthly basis related to annual leave
- Preparing monthly spreadsheets related to sickness monitoring

Training administration (*Working with the Work Force Development Manager*)
- Administrator for core training for all staff - sourced a venue and trainer, set up venue, informed staff of date, collected names and allocated to courses. Collated evaluation forms onto spread sheets.

Legal Secretary
- Typing letters, legal documents and statements, general admin duties
- Experienced in probate, conveyancing and litigation, attending court and taking notes
- Producing detailed bills; contact with clients – in person or by telephone

Employment

xxxx Trust –Drug Addictions Agency
Counsel people with drug addiction – 4 offices with 150 staff across the North West
HR Administrator: 2006-2008
Senior Administrator: 2004-2006
The detailed aspects of these two roles are shown on page 1

Senior Administrator: 1996-2006
Supporting the community alcohol team and volunteers
- Reception duties, Sourcing rehabs, Mentoring volunteers, Producing display stands
- Mentoring volunteer staff to obtain NVQ qualifications
- Office management including managing a tenant company
- Running reception for weekly specialist clinics for consultant and CPN
- Inputting and updating database of service users, using a tailor made package
- Covering admin in other offices – Warrington, Widnes, Crewe

Word Processing Operative, Technical Services Department, Vale Royal Council
The technical services department covered planning permissions, estimates for resurfacing, trees etc
April – December 1995 (Maternity cover)

Secretary, Treemont Consultants
Recruitment agency where I supported the 4 partners
Typing and administration, produced mail shots, sourced suitable candidates.
1993 - 1995

Legal Secretary, 1970 – 1983
Secretary, Hayes and Simpson: 1970-1972
Secretary to partner, Robinson-Chase: 1972-1980
Secretary to litigation partner, Judith Morrison: 1981-1983

Education

Relevant education includes
- RSA: Typing Levels 1, 2 and 3, Shorthand to 80 wpm, Secretarial duties, Audio-typing, English Language – Level 1 and 2; Pitman: Shorthand to 90 wpm
- NVQ D32/33 – Business admin (1998)
- London Chamber of Commerce – French to intermediate level (1993/94)
- CLAIT Level 1 (1994)
- RSA: Word Processing (1989-1991)
- GCE 'O' level – English and Commerce (1970)

A variety of short courses including: Diversity, Equal opportunities, Customer Care, Dealing with difficult situations, Master class - Absence monitoring conference in London, Master class seminar in HR admin in London, Display techniques, Minute taking course, advanced training in Word and Excel

Nationality: British | Full clean driving licence

Photographs

Some people include a photograph as part of their CV, included in the layout. I've discussed this with fellow recruiters and we agree that if a photograph is needed, it should be sent separately and should only be included when personal image is an important job element. Then it must be of high quality and not a holiday snap.

The text-based CV

Most internet job sites and on line application forms will want you to paste your CV into boxes. Starting with a plain text version means you won't get unusual symbols as their software strips out your formatting.

How to create a text-based CV

Don't play about with your word document, instead save it as a text file or copy it into a text editing programme such as notepad. Once you open it, you will see you have lost all formatting such as underlines, bold, fonts, etc.

You can improve the layout by using a hard return. It might look OK in a word processing programme, but can be very difficult to read via a text package without hard returns. Try it out if you want to see for yourself. You can make improvements to the style if you use CAPITAL LETTERS as headers.

Make sure you include all contact details on their own line, with a hard return in between.

Key words

When a CV is uploaded to a jobs database, companies will search for relevant candidates using key words. So you want to choose **as many key words as possible** to increase your opportunity to match your suitability for jobs and to increase the number of "hits" you can attract. You can **identify words by reviewing advertisements for**

similar vacancies and using them in your CV. For example, for an IT job, include Java, relational databases, etc. For a job in accounting, use financial statement, inventory, etc.

Use enough key words to define your skills, experience, education, professional affiliations, etc. Increase your list of key words by including specifics. For example, list the names of software programes you use such as Microsoft Word. You can enhance your chance for success by linking each key word with a specific achievement which expands on the key word, e.g., how you have been using the software, for how long, and on what projects.

When searching for specific experience, the **company will search by entering key words (usually nouns)** such as writer, MBA, marketing manager, engineer, Japanese (in the case of language fluency), London, etc. So the more attention you pay to choosing the right key words, the better.

7: Style, layout and review

Layout and format

The work you have done so far is to help you produce an effective CV. You will next take your draft and assess it against the following:

- Keep your CV tight. Two sides should generally be the maximum. Make sure it sounds positive, strong, and to the point. Be concise, and clear, and make sure every word helps make the pitch. If you are, for example, an academic, use an addendum for research papers.
- If your CV covers a page and a half, do not be tempted to fill the space.
- Will it grab the reader's attention in the first 10 seconds?

- Avoid lists of responsibilities and job functions, it becomes boring and lengthy. Only highlight achievements that will benefit the employer.
- Keep to a logical pattern following conventions. With a chronological CV, always start with the most recent job and work backward.
- To ensure there are no gaps in dates, use years only since leaving school, or be prepared to explain the gap. If you were self-employed or at home to bring up a family, say so!
- Include a clear summary or objective.
- Have you used action statements not vague terms? For example, saying not excellent written communication skills but more specifically, "Wrote jargon free user guide for 10,000 readers."
- Take the focus off you, and move it to the company. Make sure they know how you can help them.
- Explain your current role. Do not assume people will know what your responsibilities are.
- Describe how your work has led to measurable outcomes benefiting your organisation.
- Have you used the word I? If you have, change the phrase to an action word.
- Don't undersell your achievements. Your CV is a marketing tool, so use it as one. Don't oversell either.
- Put the dates on the right hand side if you want to de-emphasise them.
- Margins should be at least one inch. Don't make smaller margins so you can fill in more words. Less is more and decent sized margins will help your CV to stand out.
- For layout, use the tab key to make sure columns line up.
- To fit more on a page, you can use an 8pt font for the space lines or change the heading.

- You can also reduce the character spacing on the font by 0.2 points. If you do this, do it throughout the document.

- What font will you use? Apparently Times New Roman is proven to generate more responses (Tony Antin, Create print advertising, creative approaches, strategies and tactics, New York: John Wiley & Sons 1993 pp125-6).

- Use bold for your name and section headings and to emphasise key words.

- Use *italics* for the names of publications and foreign phrases, if any.

- Use just two font sizes, and avoid ALL CAPS and too much <u>underlining</u>.

- Use present tense verbs for your current job, and past tense verbs for all previous jobs.

- Do not justify the text. A ragged right edge is much easier to read.

- Are all the words used in their simplest form? You don't want to make the person doing the short listing feel inferior as they don't understand your superabundance of polysyllabic terminology, (your use of too many big words!). As another example, don't "interface" with people; "work" with them.

- Don't rely on your spell-checker. It's not enough as it will not catch misused, yet properly-spelled words (like sun or son, site or sight, etc.)

- You must read through your CV, once for accuracy (numbers, city names, etc.), once for missing/extra words, and once more for spelling. Use a dictionary to be certain. Then, show your CV to several friends and ask them to read it out loud. Listen to where they put the emphasis as it might reveal that you've written something confusing or inaccurate. After you get their feedback, read through your CV once more and make any changes until it's 100% error-free.

- Put your **name on each sheet of the CV**. It may become separated when it is being photocopied. You can put your name in the footer.
- **If posting, don't staple pages**. When the staple is removed for copying, the pages may tear. With high quality paper, you could use both sides of the paper. Do not put your CV in a folder, it can slow down photocopying.
- **The ink should be black**. When you type your email address and it gets turned to blue, it will draw the reader's attention away from your name. Make sure you change the font to black and remove the underlining of your email address.
- If your CV is going to be successful in getting you a job, it will probably be seen and sifted through by several different people. Recruitment agencies, HR departments, and line managers will be reading it and looking for different qualities in it. You want it to appeal to all of them.
- Check to see if it is free of jargon. Often we use abbreviations and anachronisms in our everyday language (TQM, BPI) or internal descriptions for job roles which have little meaning for others. Also make sure everything is easy to follow and ask the people who read your CV if they understand it.
- Make sure you are comfortable with your CV. Can you defend it at interview if required? Use my advice as a guide, but add your own ideas and touches to make it personalised and unique.

Finalising your Curriculum Vitae

You are now reaching the completion of your CV. Please check against the following *(see next page)*. If you cannot answer yes to every question, go back and make changes and revisions until you can.

Is my CV focused on the needs of the particular job?	Yes/No
Is it achievement-orientated?	Yes/No
Are the verbs in the "active" tense?	Yes/No
Is it structured in my favour? Do I really want to tell them I am an unqualified 60-year-old before they read about my chief executive experience?	Yes/No
Does it emphasise my special skills?	Yes/No
Does it emphasise special achievements outside work?	Yes/No
Have I avoided any "gaps" which would cause interviewer anxieties?	Yes/No
Is what I have done quantified where appropriate?	Yes/No
Have I used significant or emphasising adjectives? (**Excellent** experience, **sole** responsibility)	Yes/No
Am I saying what I can do for the employer? Focusing on benefits?	Yes/No
Am I only telling them what they need to know?	Yes/No
Is my CV laid out elegantly with plenty of white space and not too many fonts?	Yes/No

Your CV is ready for sending. If you email it, ask for a receipt so you know it has arrived. If you post it:

- Print it using a high quality print setting and on good quality paper (not photocopy quality but 100gsm). Choose a pale colour, ideally either bright white or cream. Pastel blue or pale grey is a possible option. Your CV may be photocopied and dark coloured paper doesn't photocopy well. **Using cream will make sure it stands out from the rest.**

- Place your CV **unfolded** in a good quality envelope.

- Either write neatly or type the envelope. If you claim computer expertise, use your computer to address the envelope as it makes your software claims more credible.

Do I really need more than one CV?

If you have followed all the steps, you will now have a CV that will get results.

If you are clear on the type of job you are looking for, you will only need one CV. However, if you are looking for different types of jobs you will need a CV to address each. For example, earlier in my career, my background made me suitable for roles as counsellor, trainer, project manager or psychologist. Thus, I would have emphasised different achievements depending on the job I was looking for.

The key points I want you to remember from this chapter are:

- Review your CV for each application. It may just need a tweak, it may be fine, or you may need to include more elements that are relevant to the job.
- You may need to use your CV again, either for promotion or due to company changes. Review it on a regular basis.

CV distribution services

I sometimes get asked if a client should use a CV distribution service. My answer is always no!

First of all, you don't know who will receive it, so it may be sent for a job you would prefer not to apply for. Or in some cases, you would have preferred to have sent a more customised application.

If you will be applying via an agency, it will cost the employer a lot more to employ you than if you had contacted them directly. For this reason, companies would rather deal with you directly than through an agency.

One last thought: what happens when you have finished your job search? How do you get the CVs removed and destroyed?

You should now have a CV that will get results and is ready to use this when applying to job ads and when networking. If you still lack confidence in your CV or need additional support or guidance, do as much as you can then contact a job search specialist such as Denise to arrange a personal review.

Chapter Four

The Personal Commercial

If you are going to be seeking help from others in your job search, you need to be able to succinctly describe who you are and what you can do.

This chapter will help you to:

- Understand why you need a personal commercial.
- Create your own personal commercial.
- Be ready to start using it in your job search.

Introduce yourself with a personal commercial

"Hello, my name is Denise Taylor. I am a specialist career psychologist, working with individuals to help them understand themselves, and identify a job that will match their skills, interests and talents. I then support

them throughout their job search – from developing a CV, planning their campaign and helping them develop interview techniques. This is enhanced through my ongoing assignments as an assessment specialist helping to recruit graduates and professionals though assessment centre selection procedures."

This is my personal commercial. It's what I can say when people ask me what I do. I call it a personal commercial, as there are similarities with TV and radio commercials that (in 30 seconds) make you aware of a product. A personal commercial needs to be short and concise enough to make an impression in all sorts of situations.

When do I use this?

You can use your commercial in all sorts of occasions such as when you meet new people, while networking, at interview, or any time when people may ask you what you do.

The format needs to be in clear, specific stages such as:

Example 1
- Who am I?
- What do I do?
- How do I help?
- What do I need?

Example 2
- Name and job title.
- Desired position.
- Something unique.

Here is an example:

The "Who am I" stage

The first step is to say who you are and what you do:

My name is Denise Taylor. I am a specialist career psychologist.

You want to introduce yourself as an expert in a particular area. Why not have a go?

I'm, _____ ,
and my expertise is in _____

My name is _____.
I am a specialist _____

I'm _____.
I am specially trained _____

My name is _____.
I am a qualified _____

Your commercial needs to be upbeat and positive. You don't want to come across as negative. So don't say things such as:

"I'm Fred Jones and I've been made redundant."

"I'm Christine Lewis and I'm an unemployed graduate."

The "What I do" and the "how you can help" phase

The second step is to say what you do, or how you can help. This helps people to understand the details of your work. A job title is too distant. Will people really know what it means? If not, I will say:

"I work with individuals to help them understand themselves, and identify a job that will match their skills, interests and talents. I then support them throughout their job search – from developing a CV, planning their campaign and help them develop interview techniques."

Some other examples:

"I create warm relationships with customers so they come back and buy from me again and again."

"I am careful with my deliveries and make it a smooth and pleasant transaction for customers."

"I can create passion for history with students by helping them go beyond the text to really get a feel for the past, through getting to really know the key characters."

Activity: Now you try:

I help _____

I create _____

I work with _____

The "what you need" phase

The final step is to either say something unique (if you are looking for clients) or what you need from them. If you are looking for people to help on your career quest, you need to be specific. Saying: "I am looking for a well paid job," or "I need security for the future," is far too broad. Similarly, to say "I was a child care worker," is too narrow. It's best to expand your statement to say you are looking for a job working with children in places like nurseries, hospitals or infant schools. Give examples.

In my example, a lot of people offer job search support but it is rare for the same person to also be involved in the recruitment side. So my unique statement is:

"This is enhanced through my ongoing assignments as an assessment specialist helping to recruit graduates and professionals though assessment centre selection procedures."

My job search clients may say:

"I'm looking to talk with people who can help me get a better understanding of the role of technical author."

"I would like to explore the possibility of working as a TV researcher. Would you know someone who I could talk with?"

"I'm looking for accountants to discuss how to make the transition from marketing to finance. Could you suggest someone for me to talk to?"

Now you try. What do you need from others?

Now put it all together. Write it down here.

Say it aloud. Does it flow? Does it sound right for you? When we draft things out, they often come across as stilted, so use less formal language. Now say your commercial aloud to family and friends and be receptive to feedback. Make any changes you need to make and capture them below.

Congratulations, you now have your own personal commercial! Now that it's complete, you can use it in different ways:

- At an interview to answer the question: "Tell me about yourself."
- In a covering letter to highlight your background and key abilities.
- When talking to other people to help you get contacts for information gathering interviews.
- During any professional, social or organisational meeting when you are asked to introduce yourself.
- Cold calling companies to explain how you may be of service.

Now that you have learned how to create this, you can keep your personal commercial up to date as you develop new roles.

Chapter Five

Get networking

This chapter is all about using personal contacts to support you in your job search.

By the end, you will:

- Have identified members of your network.
- Have expanded your network through meeting with people.
- Have devised a way of keeping a record of your contacts and keeping them informed.
- Know what to do at a networking event.
- Prepared thoroughly before your first networking call.
- Have followed up with leads.
- Know why you should keep in touch with your network even after you get a job.

Networking

1. Introduction

Looking for a job can be frustrating, time consuming and disappointing. It's even more difficult when you conduct your search alone. Left to our own devices, we can easily lose our momentum, convince ourselves that there are no jobs, and worse, give up!

So what can you do?

Involve as many people as you can in your job search. It is highly likely that you will find about your next job from someone you know. That's why networking is so vital to a successful job search.

What is networking?

Networking is a means of making connections and is part of business life. It is an essential element of job search where you use relationships and contacts to help you to identify work opportunities.

Networking is not something separate from the four generally recognised ways of getting a job – adverts, agencies, contacts, and cold calls, but a very powerful way of maximising them. It doesn't mean making a nuisance of yourself to the point that none of your contacts will ever speak to you again. Nor should it involve embarrassing people and making them feel morally obliged to help you.

Networking involves self-marketing, telephone skills and letter-writing techniques. The approach may feel a bit unusual at times but you will develop the relevant skills as you do more networking. You will ask people for advice and make it clear that you are not seeking a job. You will find most people are flattered and can be of great help to you.

Do I have a network?

We all have a network – it's the people we know. There's the close network of family, friends and business colleagues, and the loose network of university friends and social acquaintances.

Why a network is important

Building up your network of contacts is very important as it's a way of sharing ideas, gaining leads, following ideas and practising interviews.

Networking works! Research by the *Chartered Institute of Accountants* shows networking is very effective. Of those surveyed under the age of 35, a quarter got a job through networking; between the ages of 35 and 50 it was half, and for those over 50, 80% found their job through networking.

In a recession, where there are less jobs available it's even more important to get as many people as you can helping you with your job search – from letting you know of jobs that might be coming up, getting you introductions to people that can help and keeping you motivated through being there to both listen to you and keep you updated on new initiatives etc.

Job offers don't always come through a direct contact, but through someone who knew a friend or colleague of a friend.

Activity: who is in your network?

The first step in building on your network is to prepare a comprehensive list of people you know.

Your friends and relatives are the people most willing to help you find a job. To see how networking can work for you, begin by writing down the names of three friends or relatives.

1.

2.

3.

If you asked the first person on this list for the names of two people, you immediately have two new contacts. Your network will begin to grow as quickly as that! Networking is a simple idea and it can help you meet potential employers you would not know about otherwise. These potential employers may be a friend of a friend of a friend, and therefore may be open to see you. The first step in building your network is to prepare a comprehensive list of people you know.

How many people do you know?

In just five minutes, see how many names you can write down of people who could give you advice. The following headings should help. Jot these down in your notebook or use the form in *Chapter One, Getting Ready - Being Organised.*

- Family.
- Friends.
- Work (present colleagues).
- Other people where I currently work, including clients and suppliers.
- Past bosses and past colleagues.
- Neighbours (present).
- Clubs and organisations (church, professional societies, trade associations, chamber of commerce).
- School/ College/ University/ Friends/ Teachers.
- Contacts from seminars and conferences.
- People I have worked with in the past.
- Bank Managers, Accountants, local professional people.
- Friends of your parents (or children).
- Neighbours (past).
- Other.

As you go, add more names then start to make contact with them. You will find it useful to make a new list, including addresses and telephone numbers of those people who are likely to be most helpful to you.

Have a look through your address book, Christmas card list, etc. Don't forget you can also network with people you meet in the week, perhaps in the queues at the petrol station, supermarket, etc. I have personally made useful contacts through chatting at the gym and at a supermarket check out.

Review your list

You can't contact everyone on your list, so prioritise your top ones. Your top contacts are anyone who:

- Has the power to offer you a job or can tell you about real opportunities and refer you to someone who has.
- Can refer you to someone who can arrange an interview and review your CV.
- Can give you information about job vacancies.
- Is knowledgeable about the industries in which you are interested and may have key contacts who can help you with advice or information.
- Can provide you with other contacts who may be able to do any of the above.
- May be unlikely to have immediate contacts, but may be a source of useful ideas.

From the above, you are now in a position to rearrange and prioritise your contacts.

Activity: Choose your top 10 contacts and write them down in your notebook.

Let's look for ways to increase your network

There are many places where you can increase your networking such as professional and industry associations and societies. You can attend meetings and get involved in the online community. It's not just about what you can get from others, but also seeing how you can help them.

If you have recently been made redundant, you are likely to have free time so ask yourself what might be a good organisation to join.

You can also meet people at conferences and formal networking clubs. If you think a particular club would be a useful one to join, call and ask who is in charge of new memberships. They will likely meet and introduce you to others, so you will already have your first contact. At these events, collect business cards and write the event name and date on the back of the card. Then be ready to respond within the next couple of days.

You could also get involved with on line networking communities such as www.linkedin.com, www.ryze.com or www.ecademy.com. These are places that recruiters will look for potential recruits.

Keeping records

Networking is a business activity and you should do it professionally. Keep good records of everyone you are in contact with – when you meet them, what was said and who they referred you to. You can then follow up later to thank them for their referral. Also keep some more personal details of your contacts so you can look for ways to help them, such as forwarding a relevant article.

A card box system is a low tech way of dealing with the data – one side of the card can contain contact details (names, email and phone numbers), who referred you, etc. The other side can detail the date of each phone call, and/or meeting, topics discussed, and any personal insights.

Keeping in touch

It's important that you keep your contacts informed of your progress with the companies and people to whom you have been introduced. This will maintain their interest and keep you in mind as they come across further useful information or people.

Write a short letter of thanks as soon as possible after each meeting and keep a brief record of the meeting: date, time, place, discussion points, etc.

Remember to say thank you anytime someone helps you out, even if it doesn't result in an interview or job offer.

Is it relevant to me?

Many people tell me that networking isn't relevant to them, only to "high flyers." However, once they understand the importance of talking to others to find jobs, they begin to network. For example, Vicki, who had just been made redundant from her job as a training administrator, found out about a small company who needed admin help and found herself on a shortlist of one. Alison's partner spoke to a chief executive of a company and found out about a job that would be perfect for Alison. This contact meant that Alison got seen and shortlisted.

Be clear what you want and clearly describe it

Before you make contact, get clear on what you want. If you are vague, it's much harder to get help from others. Not just, "I'm looking for something in the training field," but "I'm a technical trainer looking for opportunities to teach end-users how to use business applications software in a Windows environment." Certainly you need to go beyond the vague, "I'm looking for anything."

- I've worked as a legal executive and now want to move into public relations.
- I've been an occupational therapist, but am now looking for something in writing, such as on a newspaper, a magazine, or company newsletter.
- I've had experience in managing an English department at grammar school, and I make a very good manager.
- I'm a highly experienced accountant and want to work for a small company that wants an ethical and pragmatic accountant.

Be specific. The more information you give, the easier it is for the other person to think of possible job opportunities and contacts that can help you.

It can also help if you suggest the types of companies that would be interested in you. For example, instead of saying, "I was a nursery nurse," you could say, "I'm looking for a job working with children in places like a nursery school, day care, hospital or primary school."

Activity: What would you say? Write a first draft here.

Now reread it. Is it clear? Do you understand what you are looking for? Will others? Can you explain this in 30 seconds or less? If no one understands what you are looking for, they will not be able to refer you to the people you need to speak to.

You are now ready to network!

When you meet people, the initial emphasis must be on getting to know them and developing a relationship rather than being too direct on what you want.

First contact

It is essential to prepare thoroughly. You may like to practice making phone calls before the first contact if you feel unsure.

A vital feature of the process is for you to use your existing contacts to give you the names of other contacts and thus, widen your network.

Although the top category on your list contains the names of people who have the power to give you work, there may be no position available at the time you make contact. So **don't ask for a job**. You will embarrass your contact and will have reached a dead end. If, on the other hand, you ask for advice, it will be easy for him or her to do just that.

Activity: How about calling and scheduling a few appointments today?

List here who you will call:

| |
| |

Wait

Make sure you know enough about the company to ask a qualified question. There are plenty of examples as you work your way through this chapter. You can now contact people on your list. Aim to get two names from everyone you talk with and then follow up on those names.

Make a diary note for how many people you will contact each day over the next two weeks:

	Week 1	Week 2
Monday		
Tuesday		
Wednesday		
Thursday		
Friday		

Ways of making contact

The three ways of making contact are:

- Personal meeting.
- Telephone.
- Letter.

Meetings are by far the most effective method of contact.

Reminder: you are asking for advice, not a job. Do not see this as a job interview. If you try to sell yourself as a potential employee, you'll lose the important contact!

You can then ask for the names of other people to contact. You could also ask whether she or he sees the current needs of their company changing in the near future. You may, from this, receive advice to contact him or her again at a specified time in the future.

Also consider how you can help them. Perhaps through providing a relevant article?

The networking approach. A step-by-step guide of what to do.

1 – Initial contact

Start with your top 10 list

Call or write to each person on your list. You can't just send a brief letter or email. You must include detailed and specific ideas about what you are looking for, and remind your contact of some of your key achievements.

Typical structure of the letter

Short introduction:

"Despite the recession I'm determined to get a job and I'm researching to find out as much as I can so when I do apply I'll be a strong candidate."

In the next paragraph, include what you are seeking and what you want:

"I am looking for a project management position within the following companies (list the names of the companies here). Do you know anything about these companies, or know anybody who works for them? I've looked on line but would love to know more about the management style, business plans, or anything you think may be useful for me."

In the next paragraph, remind them of your skills and achievements. Make it simple for those who may not understand the specifics of your skills base.

In the paragraph, you could include a quote from one of your bosses/clients.

You can conclude with:

"I'm really excited with the prospects of working in this area and would love to talk to anyone who might be able to help me."

"Thanks so much for your help, and I'd be very happy to send my CV to any of your contacts."

This can be a better approach than sending your CV straightaway and gets you a chance to follow up with your contact.

Ask each of them if they know of anyone who might know of job opportunities in your field. If they give you a name, ask if you can mention their name when you contact the person they've recommended.

You will have to decide whether your initial contact is by telephone, email or letter. A phone call will work well with someone you know but with busy people, you may not be able to get through. I suggest sending out a short letter and following it up with a phone call. That way, the person is expecting your call and may have left a message with their secretary.

I don't recommend emailing someone you don't know as it's too easy for them to hit the delete key. You have a better chance of something being read if you post it.

2 - Schedule a face-to-face meeting

Make an appointment and arrange to meet your contact. You could suggest meeting before or after work. Some people can be hard to contact, but do persevere. Relationships build much quicker when you meet face-to face.

Primary contacts

Primary contacts are people you already know. If you haven't been in touch for a while, they will want an update on what you have been doing, so prepare some brief notes, covering:

- The reason for contact – you are or will be looking for a job.
- What you have done since you last met, in case it is needed.
- Details of your recent achievements at work.
- The areas or industries in which you are particularly interested.
- A prepared list of what you want from this contact with space to write answers, against each item. This could include:
  - o General advice about business opportunities.
  - o Information about any possible leads or information in the area or industries in which you are interested. Your contact may know, for instance, that a company is expanding or moving into the area, etc.
  - o Information about specific requirements.
  - o Names, addresses and phone numbers of any contacts who can give further help along the lines of the above.

o The best means and times for contacting them.

o Whether or not it is possible to use your prime contacts name.

Referred contacts

The approach will vary and could include your contact:

- Being prepared to set up a meeting or even take you along and introduce you.
- Suggesting that you speak to someone, and passing on your CV which he or she will hand over personally to the referred contact.
- Suggesting you get in touch with someone but to not mention their name. This becomes more like a cold call and needs careful preparation.

Do prepare as thoroughly as for your primary contact.

The more people who join your network, the faster you will find a job

Networking Questions

As you make contact with people the following questions may be helpful:

- Can I use your name as a referee when I apply for positions?
- Could you write me an open letter of recommendation?
- Have you heard of any vacancies?
- Can you let me know if you do hear of any job openings?
- Do you know of anyone leaving their job?
- Do you know of any companies that might have a vacancy?
- Could you ask some people you know if they know of any vacancies?
- Will there be job openings coming available in the near future?

- Can you think of any other companies that may be recruiting people with my skills?
- When I contact that company, may I say that you suggested I contact them?

Ask for specific information. For example, if you want a job in the computer gaming industry, you could ask:

- What do you know about the computer gaming industry?
- Tell me about the business culture in Dundee?
- What companies would you suggest I contact?
- What are your thoughts about the proposed merger of A and B?
- Do you know anyone who works for Clink Productions?

You may also find some of the questions from the fact finding interviews chapter useful here.

Jo had worked as a marketing executive in the telecoms industry. She was no longer happy in this work and there were talks of redundancy, so she was keen to make a move. Jo followed the exercises in this book, identified her skills and values, and this made her realise that it was the right job – she loved marketing but the wrong product. She was very keen to use her skills in the charity sector but wasn't sure how she would make the move.

She didn't know any one who worked in the charity sector, but used her contacts to find people to approach. Within a week, she had the names and contact details of six people who worked for charities, including Charles. Charles was an operations director with a national charity, and had previously worked in marketing with a children's charity.

Let's follow Jo in her job hunt and look at some of the letters she actually used.

This is a typical letter. You can use it to form the basis of your own letter.

Dear Charles,

I would welcome input regarding the next phase of my career.

Having developed my skills and experience as a marketing executive in the telecommunications industry, I am considering transferring my skills to the not-for-profit sector.

You know a lot about the charity sector and I would appreciate hearing about it's current conditions. I have enclosed my CV to bring you up to date with what I have been doing over the last few years and would appreciate meeting up with you soon.

I will telephone you in the next few days to find out when you are free.

Yours sincerely,

Jo Harvey

Jo sends out the letter so that it will arrive on a Tuesday (to avoid the Monday rush) and telephones on Thursday to make an appointment. The recipient of the letter, Charles is pleased and flattered to be asked for advice.

The phone call

As indicated in the letter, Jo follows this up with a phone call. She stands up to make her call as she will sound more alert.

"Hello, Bill Jones suggested I call you. I am doing research into charity marketing (name the company's business) and you are a well regarded professional who really understands this sector. Could you spare 20 minutes at the end of the day to answer some questions?"

On the other end, the person asks "Are you looking for a job?"

"Not yet. First I need to be sure that my skills will be needed in the charity sector and I am sure you can help me to understand this. Could we meet on Tuesday next week?"

Be prepared when networking by telephone for questions about yourself, perhaps from a receptionist wanting to pass on a message to the person you want to contact.

Activity: What would you say if having given your name and telephone number, you were asked "and where are you from?"

Space for your notes:

3 - Conducting the meeting

You have requested the meeting so you must decide on the agenda and lead the discussion. Advance preparation is therefore essential, as it is for any kind of interview.

Start by establishing some rapport:

- If you are talking to a primary contact, remind him or her of the circumstances in which you became acquainted or have worked together.
- In the case of a referred contact, get him or her to talk about their business and the issues they currently face. Your homework can be very useful here.
- Make it clear that you don't expect a job offer.
- Keep the meeting short, a maximum of 30 minutes.
- Be clear on what you want.
- Summarise your own background and situation and outline your job search strategy.

- Ask for comments on its viability within their sector and invite suggestions. If you have a target list of companies, she or he may be prepared to evaluate them or may know some senior people to whom they can provide an introduction.

- Get your contact to comment on your CV in relation to your job search, either during your meeting or by leaving/sending a copy. Ask them how your CV looks. What they would change about it and if it makes sense. Ask them if they know anyone you could talk to.

- The more she or he knows and understands about your background, the more she or he will be able to help, either in terms of additional contacts or the direction of your search. There is always the possibility that during your meeting, your contact may begin to consider you for a position within his or her own organisation – one clue being that he or she starts to take control and asks you questions.

Listen carefully to what they have to say. They may tell you about problems in their company or industry and you can then think about ways to solve them and get back in touch.

Be careful not to talk too much
Listen 80%, Talk 20%

Yes, you have a goal in mind. However, do not forget that the other person took time out of their day to meet with you and help you. Listening shows your interest in them. When they have finished speaking, you can tell them about your situation.

Let's see how Jo is getting on

At the meeting, Jo repeats the substance of the letter. Charles tells her useful facts about the present state of the industry. Jo doesn't ask for a job, but tentatively asks if any consultancy work is needed in Charles's organisation. Whether paid or initially unpaid, this might lead to a permanent job, full or part-time. Finally, at the end, Jo thanks Charles and makes one further request – to ask for referrals. These could be for future fact finding interviews or job leads. She remembers to ask for a business card so she doesn't have to guess their job title.

"That has been most useful. From what you have said, I would like to meet with some environmental charities. Can you let me have the names of two people who I can talk with in order to get more details about requirements there?"

From this, you will get more referrals.

4 - Follow up

For Jo, the meeting has been positive and when she returns home, she produces a thank you letter. She could send it by email, but prefers to send a handwritten note. Taking the personal touch helps create greater impact. She uses correspondence cards (size of a postcard) pre-printed with her name and contact details so it is quick to produce.

Dear Charles,

Thank you for talking with me yesterday. I found it very helpful. I appreciated you taking time out of your busy schedule to do this.

With best wishes

Jo Harvey

5 - Cycle Two

After the first round of her ten contacts, Jo has added another twenty contacts. And the process continues. Eventually a contact may say:

"Delighted to give you advice. Did you say that you know about abc? Our human resource people would like to talk to you about an opening we have here. . . "

Often, the opening has not been advertised, and perhaps has not yet been fully defined.

Other ways to network (networking for introverts)

Networking is a sociable activity – you are getting out there and meeting people. Not everyone finds this easy. If you are someone who is more introverted in nature or who finds being with many new people a stressful experience, you may wonder if there are any alternatives to the usual networking events.

There are! You don't have to network face to face. You could also make contact with others via contributions to discussion groups and forums, having a personal web log, or writing an article.

Contributions to discussion groups and forums

There are many discussion groups out there and you can find lists at www.groups.google.com. There are also specific sites such as: http://tinyurl.com/kom47 which comprises discussion groups and mailing lists specialising in specific aspects of medicine, pharmacy, pharmaceutical sciences and health-related issues.

On these sites, you won't want to go straight in and ask for a job. It's more about adding to your contacts list (while helping others on the forum). You need to get a feel for these sites before you comment (known as lurking), but do look for where you can add helpful comments enhancing your reputation. Many sites will allow you to add a signature line where you can add some personal details of yourself with your contact details clearly stated.

Create a personal website or blog

A personal web site, where you comment on current issues facing your industry, can introduce you as an expert on the subject. Blogs can be included in newsfeeds and can quickly get picked up. Someone I know who is a stress management expert commented on the link between diet and stress, based on something she read in the paper and found herself at the top of Google for that particular search term.

Note: You can host a blog using *Type Pad* for $4.95 a month or you can get one for free at *Blogger*.

If you start a blog, you need to keep it up to date, and if it focuses on job hunting rather than raising your profile, be sure to clear it once you have a job. (You don't want your new employer to think you are already looking for another job.)

An alternative to creating your own site is to develop a Linkedin account. You can read more about this in *Chapter 10, Stand Out From the Crowd.*

Writing an article

If you are quite eloquent, you could write an article that appears in a publication read by your target employer group. Many professional associations have journals and newsletters, plus many companies have in-house magazines. To find out about publication details, contact the editor so you are clear on the typical length for such an article, how the article should be submitted, etc.

Writing an article can get you access to people that are otherwise unavailable. When making a cold call to ask about a job, it can be difficult to get through. But phoning someone and saying, "Hello! This is Jo Harvey and I'm writing an article on the challenges in charity marketing in a time of recession. May I please talk with your Chief Executive?" stands a much better chance of success. This could then prove very helpful when you go for interview at a charity marketing department.

Once you have an article printed, arrange for reprints so you can enclose them with your CV or broadcast letters when you contact companies.

Amazon book review

If your job has been made redundant you will have some free time, you could spend some of this on reading relevant business books and write reviews on Amazon. This would be a good example of keeping your knowledge up to date and is a great way to be thought of as knowledgeable. These reviews will also be picked up on search engines and will help to raise your profile.

Remember:

Never	Always
Ask for a job. Your contact may not know about all the vacancies in a company	Show that you are taking responsibility for action, not expecting them to act for you
Sound desperate	Follow up your contact so people never feel the effort is wasted
Put people in the position where they can't help	Make people feel good. They will see they're helping you
Lose control of your own job hunting	Say THANK YOU

Keep in contact after your job search is over

Now that you have taken the time to develop relationships with people in your network, you need to make sure you stay in touch. Contact the people who were unable to help as well and let them know how you have got on and thank them once again for their time. Look for ways to stay in touch at least a couple of times a year and look for ways to pay the person back.

Chapter Six

Fact finding interviews

To find out more about a particular job or career path, it's best to speak directly with those in the field you are considering. Conducting fact finding interviews is the best way to do this.

By the end of this chapter, you will:

- Understand what a fact finding interview is and how it should be conducted.
- Be prepared for your first fact finding interview.
- Be ready to use the technique to help with your job search.

Fact finding interviews - Introduction

If you are considering changing jobs or beginning a new career, the first step is to spend some time online, gathering as much information as you can about your chosen field. You'll find websites with job descriptions, job postings, chat rooms and forums full of information. Such information gathering will also help you clarify your interest in, and suitability for, a particular job.

This online research is a great step towards finding a new job. You can use websites and forums to find out about different jobs, entry requirements and career prospects and also what people say about the company on forums. You can also find out more about the potential industry. There's no point looking to get into a career where there aren't any jobs.

Once you have pared your list down to a couple of jobs, you can move onto fact finding interviews. These can be of real help, but they do take a lot of effort to do them properly. The person you will want to speak with is likely to be someone with a busy schedule so you must be prepared so you don't waste his or her time. Don't take up any more of their time than necessary. Nothing is more infuriating than people asking questions they could have found via web sites. Don't waste their time or yours!

Whilst these are called fact finding interviews, they sometimes result in job offers

Whilst these are called fact finding interviews, they sometimes result in job offers. What can happen is you come across as someone who is already far more knowledgeable than most of the applicants people see at interview and you may impress sufficiently to get a job offer. Of course it's not the purpose of the meeting, but by asking intelligent questions, discussing how you consider your background and experience matches your understanding of the job, you can appear as a very credible candidate.

You will find people to talk with via a "cold call" or through people you know (or are known to people you know). We've already talked in *Chapter Five, Get Networking,* about the need to develop a network of people you know. They may be doing the type of job you'd like to pursue, or they may know someone who does.

These interviews are a chance to really find out more about a particular job. You can move beyond what you have found online and ask more detailed questions from someone who does the job and can tell you about the negatives as well as the positives of the job. You can also use this as a chance to find out about some of the challenges facing a particular industry. Finding out more about these areas will really make a difference at interview and help you stand out from the crowd. Paul used the following approach.

Paul had been working in agricultural sales. His degree was relevant and he could relate to farmers, but he found the job unsatisfying and this was making him anxious. He realised he needed to get another job and his research lead him to consider a career as a land surveyor because it would use his high level of mathematical abilities and also his degree and experience working in agricultural settings. He sent out 10 letters requesting an interview. The 10 letters garnered three meetings and someone attending one of the meetings offered him a job! It worked for Mark too. Mark had been working in a busy administrative office and was so busy, there was never time to think. He also had a difficult boss who would blame him for anything that went wrong, despite them being outside his work sphere. He was interested in becoming a legal executive so he sent out a number of such letters, was able to schedule a meeting, and was offered a job by the first company he approached.

Both Paul and Mark had relevant work experience, which meant they would have been credible candidates if they had applied for an advertised job. But their research, their access to important information, and their opportunity to talk with someone in their chosen fields, allowed them to be considered outside of a normal recruitment process. They did not have to compete with applicants that found the job through advertisements.

Let's now talk you through what you need to do.

Step 1: Identify who to talk with

You can arrange for fact finding interviews by a referral, an introductory letter or a cold call. The previous chapter on networking will help you identify and find people who can help.

If, like Mark, you are interested in becoming a legal executive with a firm within a 20 mile radius of your home, you can identify companies via an internet search or looking in the yellow pages. If you are interested in working in marketing for example, you can find people by contacting companies and asking for the name and contact information of their marketing manager.

Any and all of those you added to your network can be helpful. It's a big plus if an acquaintance or colleague gives you an introduction, as the person you'll be talking with will already know something about you.

Use a reference library

You can also find out details of particular companies at the library. Each county will have at least one county library with a business section where you'll have access to many helpful resources including:

BRAD Directories and Annuals of Current British Directories. These are published annually and contain details on all publications in the British Isles. Current British Directories is published by CBI Research, Beckenham, Kent.

Britain's Privately Owned Companies. Useful source of information about private companies, ranked by sales. Few other directories cover this information. Britain's Privately Owned Companies is published by Jordan & Sons Ltd, Bristol.

Kelly's Business Directory. Includes manufacturers, merchants, wholesalers and companies offering an industrial service. There are over 40,000 companies listed, giving company name, address, telephone number and a brief description. Excellent initial source for a company (and your job search).

Key British Enterprises (KBE). Provides up to date profiles of the top 50,000 firms in the UK. Each entry gives financial data, details of trading names and functions and other data designed to enable the user to make a concise assessment of a company's size, range of activities, including the names of key personnel.

Kompass Register of British Industry and Commerce. This provides details on Britain's leading 42,000 companies. As well as address, telephone number and products/services, Kompass gives names of directors and executives, turnover and the number of employees. You can also access this online at http://www.kompass.com/kinl/index.php.

Other reference books are available including local directories. An increasing number of directories are produced by chambers of commerce, local councils and other local bodies.

Step 2: Questions to ask

Being able to ask questions of someone in a particular industry is a great opportunity so choose your questions carefully. What do you really want to know? What kind of information is most important to you? You may choose to start with some general questions then pinpoint certain areas with more specific questions. The longer you speak with someone, the more detailed you can become. You'll find that the more people you interview, the more you'll know what to ask.

A fact finding interview usually lasts for a maximum of 30 minutes so plan your questions in advance. You should pare down your list to 10 at the most. The following questions will be a good start:

- What do you do during a typical workday or week?
- How much of your day do you spend working with ... (people, computers, sports cars etc.)?
- What kind of challenges or problems do you have to deal with in this job?
- What skills make you good at what you do?
- What do you find most satisfying and most frustrating about your job and field?
- Is it important to be able to pay attention to detail?
- What administrative duties are required of you? How much time do these take?
- What do you see as the future for this kind of work?
- What preparation, training and/or experience would you suggest for someone entering this field?
- Knowing what you know now, how would you have approached this career differently?
- If people say you need to have an MSc, ask if they know anyone who works in this field who doesn't have one.
- What would I need to do to become an attractive candidate for a job in this field?
- Can you suggest any relevant professional associations, journals or publications that I should be using?
- Who else would you recommend or suggest I talk to, to learn more about this career?

- Do you have any other advice for me?
- May I contact you if other questions arise?

Some of these questions may require quite a bit of reflection and thought from the person being interviewed so consider sending the questions in advance.

Step 3: Arrange an appointment

You will have to decide whether your initial contact is by telephone, email or letter. A phone call will work well with someone you know but with busy people, you may not be able to get through. I suggest sending out a short letter, and following it up with a phone call. That way, the person is expecting your call and if they are not available, they may have left a message with their secretary.

Whichever approach you choose:

- Clearly state your purpose. Be brief, concise and explain your interest in the company or field.
- Reinforce that you are not looking for employment. You are seeking advice and information.
- Take responsibility for making contact. Follow up with a call to set up the appointment. It is often best to call at lunchtime or after 5 p.m. when secretaries are not at their desks.
- Email is quicker and cheaper but it is too easy for your email to be deleted. A posted letter has greater impact.

Here is an example letter:

Dear Mr Johnstone,

I have spent a great deal of time researching different careers of interest to me and to determine which will play to my strengths and abilities.

I have already undertaken some research via the Internet and would appreciate meeting with someone who is experienced in this area to find out further information.

Would you be able to give me just 15-20 minutes of your time to gather information and obtain some advice about pursuing a career in land surveying? If you believe a colleague would be more appropriate to speak with, perhaps you could help me contact them.

I will phone on the afternoon of Tuesday, 25th April to discuss a convenient time to meet.

I really appreciate you taking the time to read this letter and look forward to talking with you.

Yours sincerely

Be sure to follow up the letter with a phone call to arrange the appointment. The person you contact will be busy, so ask again for just 15-20 minutes of their time and make sure you don't linger on the phone. Being brief and to the point demonstrates your professionalism. A sample phone script is:

Hello Chris,
This is Jane Robinson. I sent you a letter a couple of days ago where I wrote about my interest in working as a land surveyor.

I've done extensive research online and now need to talk with someone who is able to answer some questions and provide feedback on my approach.

Could we schedule a 15-20 minute meeting either in person or by phone, whichever you prefer?

I'm happy to talk in person or by phone, whichever is most convenient for you.

When you call, be ready to ask your questions on the phone then and there in case they choose to speak to you. That is not ideal, but often people want you to go ahead and ask your questions.

Sometimes people think you are looking for a job. If they ask, reassure them that you are not. Stress that you are just doing research into this particular career.

These sorts of calls can be a bit stressful the first time you do them, so consider doing a trial run with someone you know and have them comment on your approach and style.

You must do the follow up call. If you wait for them to contact you, it just won't happen!

When you make the call, stand up! It keeps your energy high so you sound confident. And breathe! If you haven't spoken to anyone that day, talk out loud to yourself, it will stop you having a dry mouth.

When you ring, you'll probably get through to their PA/assistant, so politely ask to speak to the person you have written to. You can truthfully say that they are expecting your call as you wrote to arrange this. Why not plan out what you will say.

End the call by thanking them and confirm the date and time for your meeting. You can email a note of thanks and confirm the appointment in writing.

Of course you won't get a meeting with everyone you contact. Before the recession, the success rate of my clients was between 30 and 70% but if you are pleasant and not pushy, you will have some success getting appointments. If not, take a good look at your approach. Are you making it too obvious that you are looking for a job?

Step 4: The meeting

When you arrive, don't forget to look in reception to see if any vacancies are posted here. For some types of jobs this is the place where vacancies are listed. In a recession, more companies are advertising this way and it is obviously much cheaper for them than using an agency.

You have done well to get to interview, so make good use of your time. Take along your list of questions and listen carefully to everything they have to say.

Again, make sure the interviewer knows you are seeking advice, NOT a job. If you try to sell yourself as an employee, you have blown it!

Show them that you value their time by being prepared. Show them you are a serious about getting into their field (but not a job with them) by asking about their business, what they do and what it takes to be successful.

Ask for feedback on your CV, qualifications and proposed direction.

Your questions could include finding out the likelihood of any suitable jobs being advertised in the near future and where the jobs would be advertised.

Prepare a list of companies the interviewer may know and ask for advice and for his or her opinion as to whether you would fit in to these organisations. Ask for contacts who could help with advice and suggestions (NOT to request jobs from) and ask for introductions written or personal. Always make sure you have permission from the interviewee to use their name as part of the introduction to the person to whom they refer you.

If you are asked questions, make sure you do not express negative views about previous organisations you have worked for. Ask permission to keep the person you interviewed informed of the progress you make.

You went there for advice. Make sure you get it!!

You could end the meeting with something like:

> *"I've learned a great deal today. Having seen your organisation, I'm interested in talking to more people in this field. I'm especially interested in (any special area that came up during your meeting). Whom do you think I should talk with next?"*

Be sure to phrase it that way. It's positive and assumes that they know someone (as opposed to asking "Can you think of anyone I should talk with next?").

Usually one of three things will happen:

- He/she will pick up the phone and make an appointment for you.
- He/she will give you one or more names and say, "Tell them I sent you."
- He/she will just give you one or more names.

In any of these cases, you are now being referred to someone by a colleague of that person, which is extremely beneficial. As you continue, you will learn more about the career, meet many people, and begin to become known in the career field.

It's very effective. It's networking!

An example of such a referral conversation might be:

*"I really appreciate all of your time and effort today.
Now that I've seen the career closely, I feel that I might
be more effective in a smaller organisation where I will
not be called upon to specialise quite so much. At least
I need to find out. Whom do you think I should talk with
next?"*

After you have been referred, and you have completed that
meeting, write to the person who referred you. He/she
gave you advice, and it's courteous to let him/her know
how it turned out. It is so important to keep in touch,
especially with people you may want to work for some day.

Step 5: Review

The final step is to review what you have learned and
what you will do next time. Consider both the important
information you gathered and how you came across. Then
ask yourself how you can improve for next time.

Keep a summary of what you have found out and add it
to your file. You may like to keep details on:

- Career/job title.
- Source of contact.
- Name.
- Company.
- Position.
- Phone/fax/extension numbers and best times to call.
- Address.
- Meeting summary.
- Reading list.
- Best preparation (experience and education).
- How to start in this field.
- Further contact (name, phone, company, position, how
  do you know each other, can I use your name? etc.)

Through all of this, you may have realised that a particular career path doesn't interest you. Don't be discouraged, this is a good outcome. Finding out now means you won't waste time pursuing a career that will not be fulfilling. You can still follow up and say that having spoken to them you are now more interested in exploring, for example, other career options in the same or a different field. Then define that new direction and ask for advice or referrals.

As you find out more, you should be much clearer on the jobs and industries you have researched. Then you can focus on a specific job or a combination of two interests. For example, if you are interested in both engineering and music, or food and research, find out about careers that integrate both passions.

Chapter Seven

Different ways to get a job

There are a number of ways to get a job. Most people put the greatest effort into searching for jobs they see advertised – either in newspapers or on job sites. But this can be the least effective method of finding employment. You will need to use a variety of methods to have the best chance of success.

If you saw me on The Tonight Programme on ITV1 (November, 2008), you may have heard me talking about the importance of being proactive when searching for a job. The problem with concentrating on jobs that are advertised is it's what everyone else is doing. Companies get swamped with applications and it's very difficult to stand out from the other applicants.

How do companies fill job vacancies?

First of all, they look within their company, and then they ask their professional contacts. If they don't find someone, they will eventually advertise the job in the press, contact a recruitment agency, or post the job on a professional association web site.

You must, of course, still look at the advertised jobs, but don't use this at the expense of alternative methods. You have many options:

Traditional job search - the advertised route

Advantages

- The ad clearly states the requirements of the position.
- You usually get the name of the company so you can do some research before applying.

Disadvantages

- There is a high level of competition as so many people read and respond to the ads.

How to increase your chance of success

- Identify the most relevant papers to research and read, and also look at their online sites. Professional journals will often have jobs available on their web site in advance of the print publication.
- Respond promptly and log the date you do so you can follow up.
- Be selective and spend time on the closest matches of your skills to the position, rather than sending unfocused letters to many.
- Carefully read the ad and ensure your letter and CV closely matches their requirements.
- If you get a reject/regret letter, ask for feedback. Most of the time you won't get it, but occasionally you'll get a reply that will help with future applications.

The hidden job market

According to an article in the *Harvard Business Review,* nearly 80% of job openings are never advertised. You should therefore focus your job search on establishing networks and identifying the hidden job market. This is not just for senior roles. If you want a job in a local company such as a shop or factory, *deliver* your CV appropriately dressed for the business. However, for large chains such as *Boots* or *John Lewis,* you will find that all applications are made centrally so this approach may not work.

Advantages

- More than 70% of people find jobs this way.
- Networking will help you to find out more about the job and other job possibilities.
- The company may or may not have a job vacancy. But companies are always on the lookout for stars and you just might be it!

Disadvantages

- You may need to develop your skills of networking.
- As an introvert, or a shy person, face-to-face networking can be draining.

How to increase your chance of success

- Look for ways you can help others.
- Be on the look out for problems you can help an organisation solve. You can identify these via news reports in the press.
- Write a targeted letter and follow up.
- Research companies to approach using a business library and online research methods.
- Find details of smaller companies in your chosen area through your local chamber of commerce.

Online job search - such as posting your details on a job board e.g., *Monster, Total Jobs*

Advantages

- It's easy to apply from your home computer.
- Details are uploaded daily.
- The ad clearly states the requirements of the position.
- You usually get the name of the company so you can do some research before applying.

Disadvantages

- The competition is high – companies get hundreds of CV's.
- You need to watch out for fake job postings.
- Some advertised jobs don't exist, they have already been filled. The company may just be testing the water to see if there are any applicants, or an agency may be collecting CV's.
- Be careful about how much personal information you include – you need to be mindful of identity fraud.
- You can get sucked into spending hours online. Limit yourself to a maximum amount of time each day.

How to increase your chance of success

- A key word search will be used, so include as many key words as possible, we've covered this in the CV chapter.
- It's easy to waste a lot of time on these sites, so re-search which sites are most appropriate for you and concentrate your time on those.
- Don't just approach the large sites. It's expensive for a company to post on the larger sites. Smaller companies will often use more niche sites.
- Don't wait too long to apply. The job ad might be taken off once they have enough applicants.

Recruitment Companies

Advantages

- If you build a good working relationship with a consultant, they can help you in your efforts.

Disadvantages

- The company is eager to get names and details on their books so they can talk to business clients about their large pool of potential applicants.
- The company gets paid once someone is appointed so they may try to persuade you to take a job which is not right for you.
- You need to commit at least 50 minutes of your time to the registration phase (it could be two hours or more).

How to increase your chance of success

- It's imperative to build a good working relationship with your consultant so they will work for you. Don't hassle them but make sure you stay in touch.
- You can do a direct marketing approach to selected recruiters, clearly spelling out your strengths and what you are seeking.

Networking

Advantages

- Helps you identify potential job opportunities.
- Gets other people help you find job opportunities.

Disadvantages (for some)

- You have to be proactive.

How to increase your chance of success

- Let people know what you are looking for.
- Be helpful to others. What goes around, comes around.

- If you are a professional or senior manager, consider using www.ecademy.com and www.linkedin.com.
- Clearly identify your contacts and prioritise the people you will approach first.
- Document the results of your meeting, be polite and thank people for their help.
- Ask for more referrals.
- Keep people informed on how you are getting on.

Other possible options

Self-employment

Do you have the personal qualities to set up your own business? It's best to first talk to a career coach, especially if you are considering going into business for the first time. If you want to pursue this further you can get helpful advice from Business Link: www.businesslink.gov.uk

Consultancy/ freelance work

If you are able to get some consultancy work or a short term assignment, it might lead to a new career.

Job Centre Plus

Don't forget the job centre, and you can look online as well at www.jobcentreplus.gov.uk

Voluntary work

You probably don't want to work for free, but offering your services to a charity, or helping out at a charity shop can help you develop skills, remain active, meet people and demonstrate your energy, humanity, and "can do" attitude to any and all potential employers.

You may also like to consider part time or freelance working. Instead of thinking of just one job you could aim for two or three part-time jobs. This would mean that you have some income coming in as you start each job, and will increase your feeling of career security. There's always a possibility you may lose one job but not all three. It also gives you a chance to impress a future employer and to network within a new company.

Using a combination of methods

You can use a combination of methods to help in your job search

Research from home tasks:

1. Research jobs on web sites. Upload your CV and provide further details to match with the requirements for the job.

2. Read through the local paper to identify job opportunities. Not just job vacancies, but also companies that are booming in a recession, e.g., discount food or clothing stores. You may be able to get in touch with them before the job ad is listed.

3. Read up on the company and industry to enhance any application.

4. Plan a covering letter that clearly matches up with the needs of a job. *Chapter Nine, The Covering Letter,* talks you through how to write your covering letter.

Talking to people (using networking skills)

1. Be very clear on what you are looking for. If you are too general, people won't know how to help you. Tell them, for example, you are either seeking a retail position or a marketing assistant role, not both.

2. Develop a short talk (about 50 seconds, short and snappy) letting people know what you want to do and why so they can then talk about you to other people. *This is your personal commercial you read about in Chapter Four.*

3. Talk to as many people as you know about what you are looking for.

4. Then seek out people you don't know. You can ask to talk to people who are doing the job you want to do, about how they got into their role, and what advice they can give you. *See Chapter Six, Fact Finding Interviews.*

You will learn in much more detail, in forthcoming chapters how to:

- Reply to job ads.
- Access the hidden job market.

Chapter Eight

Replying to job ads

The most common way to apply for a job is by responding to job advertisements. This chapter explains everything you need to do to increase your chance of getting short-listed. There is a structured way to respond to job ads, and it's easy once you know what to do. Too many people think that they can use a similar application to all companies when you need to specifically focus on what's included in the job ad. If you follow the steps in this chapter, your application form will be much clearer with a greater chance of success.

Step 1: Finding the job ads

Your daily routine will include looking for the advertised jobs in newspapers, journals and via online web sites.

Newspapers and Journals

Many people search for jobs online but newspapers are still a great resource for finding work. Be aware that different newspapers focus on different jobs on different days. For example, you might read *The Guardian* on a Tuesday, looking for academic and teaching jobs, jobs in the not-for-profit sector on a Wednesday, and other job types on Thursday.

Don't forget the regional papers. If you don't know which day jobs are listed, ask a newsagent for advice or access vacancies in local newspapers via www.fish4jobs.co.uk.

If you have a profession or trade, the relevant journal can be a good source of jobs. You can ask for a sample issue to help you decide if it is worth subscribing.

Job sites

Many people I talk to spend hours at their computer looking for a job. I wonder if all of their time is spent actually looking for work as it is easy to get distracted by *eBay, Amazon, Facebook,* or other sites. Discipline is required for online job searching. By all means browse different sites, but shortlist the ones you will visit regularly. Allocate a specific amount of time for your search and remain focused.

Popular sites include:

www.totaljobs.com

http://jobs.guardian.co.uk

www.monster.co.uk

www.jobsite.co.uk

www.fish4jobs.co.uk

Don't just focus on the largest sites, as you may find the smaller, more specialist sites have jobs specifically targeted at your profession or location.

Online job sites

Imagine life before online job sites. You had to find different papers and publications. Now you can find jobs from your home, with online links. Review the different sites and choose the ones that are most likely to be helpful. For example, if you are looking for a job in the not-for-profit sector, looking at the jobs listed on www.jobsgopublic.com and http://jobs.thirdsector.co.uk might be more useful than visiting a larger site.

Caution!

Be careful before posting your details on job sites. Generally, you have to register through providing your personal details and receiving a password. You want to be clear who will have access to this data. On some sites, "employers" can access the site for free or very low cost, hence the need to check on the security of your information.

There are many fake sites which are set up as a means of harvesting emails and personal details and some have names very similar to genuine sites. Before you enter any personal details, do a google search and read what people are saying about the site. Make sure there is a contact number and actual business address for the agency and find out about security of your data.

Check to see if there is a privacy policy explaining what they do with your information. Read it carefully and print out the Privacy Policy and Terms of Use on the date you first used the site. Then monitor it for changes on a regular basis.

Carefully review the site before signing up. You need to check that this site has jobs of interest to you before registering your profile or CV.

Check if you can post more than one version of your CV on the site so you can focus on different strengths for different jobs. Make a note of the version of your CV uploaded to the site.

Can you delete your CV once you have found a job? You don't want your new employer to think you are already looking for a new job. Keep a note of where you post your CVs so you can go back and remove them.

Is the site easy to navigate? You have better things to do with your time than to struggle navigating through a site. You should find it easy to search for job and location. If not, move on to a site which suits you more.

Be sure that you can conceal your identity and are able to protect your contact information. On some sites, you can restrict the amount of personal information you share (a potential employer has to contact you via the site, not directly). It may slow down the process of getting in touch with you but will also show you as someone with a good job to protect and someone who understands internet security.

Some sites allow you to see how many people have looked at your CV so you can see the number of companies that have and haven't contacted you. Use this information to help you review the information you have uploaded.

You can define the jobs you are looking for in terms of key words, salary, location, etc. Most of these job sites offer a service where you will get notified of suitable jobs via email job alerts.

Why not consider having a cyber-safe CV?

- Remove your standard contact details and replace them with a web based email address such as hotmail, yahoo, or Gmail.

• Change your current company name to a more generic company description.

Analysing the ad

As you review web sites or newspapers, you will find some jobs to apply for. Read the job ad carefully and highlight the key requirements so you can compare how well you match up.

There may be more details available via the company web site or by calling for more information. Gather as much information as you can.

Most people don't focus on the detail in the job ad and supporting information and so their CV and letter don't clearly relate to the specifics of a job.

The covering letter/ letter of application must focus on the needs of the company and refer to the detail you get from the job ad and further information. Following this structured approach below will give you the advantage over other applicants.

Here is a typical ad for a retail supervisor in a large department store:

The Job Ad

As a Supervisor you will report directly to a sales manager and will be responsible for the day to day running of a multi million pound turnover department and its sales team within the store which could include: Cosmetics, Accessories, Childrenswear, Menswear, Womenswear and Home. You will drive the highest levels of **customer service** at all times and ensure excellent **product presentation** and availability.

Skills

You will be a **positive, confident and proactive** individual who has a **passion for selling and retail. Strong commercial skills** are preferable with the

ability to make effective decisions. You will have **excellent communication, delegation and time management skills** as well as being a **proven leader** who can **motivate** and **coach** people to achieve. **Numeracy** and **computer literacy skills** are essential.

You can see how I've highlighted the key requirements of the job. The covering letter should then cover these points. You can read more about how to write yours in *Chapter Nine, The Covering Letter.*

Let's start with a simple example to show what's required. List the key requirements in the job ad down the left and how you match up on the right.

Their Needs:	My Experience/Skills
Highest levels of customer service	In previous job, put customer first by offering home deliveries and taking the time to understand what they were looking for and making special orders.
Time management skills	Worked 30 hours a week along side university studies. Never missed a deadline for an essay.
Computer literacy skills	60wpm typing skills, competent with Word and Excel. Able to create web sites using FrontPage.

We'll look at this further in the next chapter.

Don't be put off if you don't match 100% to the job ad. Apply for jobs where you match at least 50% of the requirements. You can spot the areas where the company is likely to compromise as they use words like "preferably," "approximately," and "it's an advantage if . . . " Identify each of the key requirements and then highlight how you match up, both in your covering letter and on your CV. If, for instance, the job description requires someone with great organisational skills, you must highlight on your CV, a job or a project in which you demonstrated your strengths in organisation. If it stresses the need for leadership qualities, think back to previous occasions when you displayed your leadership skills.

Through matching your strengths and experience with the needs of the company you will gain an advantage over other applicants because you will be telling the employer how well you match a job's specifications. This makes it easier to be put on their shortlist. Also think about what other skills or experience you have relating to the job requirements (which may not be specified in the advertisement). They could well be of interest to the prospective employer.

Make sure your CV matches the job ad

Be sure you include extra detail in your CV where appropriate. For example, if the job asks for "five years sales experience in computer or related industry," your previous job as area sales manager becomes six (a specific number) years experience as area sales manager for computers, laptops and printers. Describe your experience with concrete words rather than vague descriptions. For example, it's better to use "managed a team of software engineers" than "responsible for managing, training..."

For a big company, highlight your experience working for large businesses. For a smaller company, show how you can transfer your skills to a niche player, how you can work in a small team, and how you are happy to muck in when there is pressure on time.

Look in shop windows

Also look out for ads you see outside shops/stores. Yesterday as I drove into my nearest town I passed ads for a Simply Food store at a BP garage, an independent garage, a supermarket, assistant manager at a wine store and also an ad for vacancies at all levels in my dentist. Not all jobs are advertised in the press and online.

Applying for jobs

Determine how you should apply. The ad may say to send in your CV or you may need to contact them for further information. You also may be directed to an online form to complete.

If you need to phone for an application form, do just that. You don't need to get into a discussion, just leave your detail while sounding friendly and upbeat.

If you are asked to write or email for an application form, a short note will suffice. Give a reference if there is one or else the job title and the name and date of the relevant publication. You do not need to sell yourself at this point. You may want to take the opportunity to ask the name of the person who will be receiving the completed form, if only to be able to personalise your covering letter. Ask if there is a job description and request it to be sent to you along with any company literature.

If asked to phone to discuss the position or to ring for an informal chat, you are likely to get into a conversation that may contribute to a selection decision. Before phoning, do some careful preparation. Study the advertisement and list how you fulfil the required qualifications and experience. If possible, download any information and read it thoroughly in advance of the call so you come across as someone who has thought through the role and has a good grasp of what the position entails. Questions you can ask include:

- What kind of person are you looking for?
- The organisational culture.
- Reporting lines.

- Types of people you will work with.
- Key priorities.

The time spent on the phone will be a screening discussion. You need to be prepared for interview questions, and with your CV handy when you ring or you may find yourself screened out before the formal selection process begins.

Your application

The advert and supporting information will contain a lot of detail. If you analyse this information carefully, you will have a much better idea of how your skills and experience match the requirements of the job. This means you can write a focused letter matching the information from the advertisement to the skills you know you possess.

You should be able to find out even more information by phoning the company and asking for a copy of the job specification, person specification, etc., if such details have not been sent to you.

Don't rush to respond. Sometimes there is a rapid sift through the applications that appear in the first few days, and longer time is spent on CVs and application forms that arrive later.

Completing application forms

It's much easier to send off your fairly generic CV and covering letter. Completing an application form can take a lot of time. However, a generic CV and letter is unlikely to get you shortlisted, and once you have completed a couple of application forms you will find you have much of the information you need and you can cut and paste information into future applications.

Why do organisations use application forms?

Organisations use application forms for two main reasons: they make it quick and easy to compare applications since the information is presented in a standard way. Recruiters have to 'hunt' for information from CVs. Secondly, an application form can seek answers to specific details which are usually omitted from CVs and covering letters such as health, reasons for leaving jobs, etc.

Application forms are usually from four to eight pages in length. In addition to factual information about yourself, your education, career, health, and interests, there will usually be open-ended questions about reasons for applying for the job and the contribution that you think you can make.

Application forms also can be completed online, in which case you prepare your answers as a text document and cut and paste the information into the form. You can read how to do this at the end of the *Chapter Three, Creating a CV.*

First steps to completing the application form

Read the instructions carefully before you start. Make sure you understand what information is needed and where. If this is a paper form, make a photocopy so you don't spoil the original. Follow all the instructions carefully (e.g., don't use blue ink when it says complete in black). Keep your handwriting consistent and legible.

When you complete an application form, your CV is usually not required, so if they ask you not to send it, don't. Follow their instructions to the letter.

Always keep in mind the particular requirements of the job for which you are applying. That's why an initial analysis is helpful. It means you can highlight previous work experience that relates to the job you are applying for.

It sounds obvious, but put the information in the correct boxes. The layout of forms is not standard and people will regularly fail to put the required details of previous jobs in the right columns. Occasionally you may not have anything to include (e.g., a professional membership). In this case, write N/A (not applicable) rather than leave it blank. Otherwise it looks like you missed the question.

With electronic forms, the gaps may increase as you type. But sometimes the space to write is fixed so think carefully about what to include and exclude. You may be limited to say, 300 words for a particular question. Be aware that it will take time to use the word limit to it's best effect.

When you complete a printed application form, you may be able to insert additional pages. This also means that you can add a typed section rather than to have to hand write it. Clearly mark any additional pages with your name, the position applied for, and the number of the question you are answering.

Some questions will require brief, factual answers. Others will seek a narrative reply. Your responses should be drafted and redrafted before the relevant part of the original application form is finalised. If you are asked to name referees, make sure you ask them before listing their names.

Keep your form neat and tidy and check all your answers carefully before you send it off. Proof read it twice, and preferably get someone else to proof read it.

Additional information section (also known as personal statement)

Usually there will be a section for you to provide further information in support of your application. This is often the section that interviewers read most carefully. Make sure you include information on why you want the job and what makes you the right candidate. Stress your strengths, experience and achievements.

Imagine you are asked at interview "why should we appoint you?" Your answer to that question could be all the things to be brought out in the open ended section.

Strengthen your application by stating a key reason you applied for the job and back it up immediately with an example. If possible, use terms from the advertisement for your key reasons. Continue for two or three key points, substantiating each general statement with an example. This can make your application very persuasive and penetrating.

If there are gaps in your career details (time out for study, family care, travel, etc), give an account of them on your form. Unexplained gaps are quickly spotted by the trained reader and can undermine your application.

The very best way to tackle this section is to use the advert, job description and person specification and use each point as a sub heading with a specific example for each. This same approach can be used for a covering letter when sent with a CV. It's easy once you know how, but for too many people they waffle and include irrelevant detail and never get shortlisted.

Competency based application forms

Competency based application forms may appear complicated but they are a very structured approach to selling yourself. The competences cover the key skills or personal qualities needed for the job. Here are a couple of examples to show you how others have responded to these types of questions.

Please provide an example where you have demonstrated leadership.

"The young people who live in my village were interested in having a village skate park. Although there was discussion, nothing was happening so I volunteered to take charge. I gathered views on the

subject, found out peoples concerns, and then high-lighted the benefits of a skate park for young people, and also discussed possible problems and how we could address them. I encouraged the young people to raise money and also submitted a bid for funding. The skate park is now in place, it's well used and I'm pleased to say there hasn't been any trouble."

Please describe a project or challenging task when you needed to work effectively to deliver a timely outcome.

"As part of my undergraduate degree, I presented a 15,000-word dissertation on U.S. policy in Vietnam in the 1950s. At first, I faced considerable opposition from my academic advisors. I was able to overcome this only through persuasion and thorough preparation of the project, clearly delineating achievable objectives. Considerable self-motivation was required to research the work in Britain, Washington and Dallas and then to analyse the great quantity of archival material collected. Through all this I remained focused on the overall objectives of the study. At the same time it was necessary to regularly evaluate the project, redefining the parameters in the light of the emerging results of my research. I had to carry out the work whilst completing short-term assignments in parallel using my lengthy experience in prioritising tasks. The final text had to be presented in accordance with specific rules and on a tight deadline with strict penalties for being incomplete, over-length or delayed. I was pleased to gain 1st-class marks for this component of my degree."

An alternative approach is to be given one of the core competences and asked to provide a specific example. You should be given instructions for how to respond. For example, one company says "For each scenario you should briefly outline the situation, describe what you actually did, describe what the outcome was and what you gained from the experience." Because the instructions can vary from company to company, pay careful attention to their requirements.

Let's look at a couple of examples:

Describe an effective team of which you are a member. What is your particular contribution to the team? In what way is the team effective?

"I have been a member of a local cricket club in Cheshire for the last two years, which not only is fun but also provides me a chance to keep fit and healthy. I am an important member of the team as I am the main strike bowler and sound middle order batsman with an average of over 20 last season. I was therefore, partially responsible for one of the clubs most successful seasons in its history. In addition to good performances on the field, the club also performed well off the field, as we organised various fundraising events that have benefited both the club and the community. For example, this year we held a fete where I was responsible for running a food stall, which improved my organisational and interpersonal skills."

Describe a situation where you had to persuade someone to do something. How did you go about it? Were you successful?

"During the Duke of Edinburgh's Award scheme I led a group that improved the habitats and facilities of the Country Park at Marbury, Cheshire. It was often necessary to motivate a member of the team to start a new project or work in unfavourable weather conditions. Past experience of captaining the school rifle shooting and tennis teams has shown that the most effective method of persuading someone to do something was to confront them and persuade them of the wisdom of my proposals. There was an instance during the Duke of Edinburgh's Award scheme where a person

did not want to begin the construction of a footpath as it was getting late. As his participation was essential and his negativity could have had a damaging effect on group morale, I drew on past experiences and persuaded him to continue working and the group made excellent progress."

Provide an example of a time when you have motivated and improved the performance of an individual who was struggling to meet their objective or targets. How did you go about motivating or developing the person or team and why did you choose this approach? What challenges did you face when you looked to motivate and improve the individual / teams performance, and how did you overcome these challenges? What was the outcome and how did you measure your success?

"As a new National Sales Manager I noticed that one of my Sales Consultants was struggling to meet her sale targets. Keen to help her improve, I arranged to meet with her to find out what she thought of her performance to enable me to find out how best to help her succeed. She said she was lacking in confidence when talking to the customer and so found it difficult to close a sale, partly down to product knowledge. I tailored a specific programme for her.

Firstly, I ensured she understood the product through reading materials and discussion. We then worked on the practical elements. First step was for her to observe as I "role modelled" what to do. We discussed differences in approach. I helped her to become clear on a process, writing down the different stages of the sales dialogue and then to make some outbound calls with coaching and feedback from me. I praised her good points but also helped her to develop her weaker areas. The main challenge was to work on her self confidence, and through feedback and encouragement, she began to believe in herself.

Occasionally she would fall back in confidence, but by continuing the coaching session on a weekly basis for a month and then moving on to a monthly basis, we were able to keep her confidence high. It is pleasing to see for the most recent month she performed the best in the team against sales target."

These following examples are of a slightly different style but also require you to be specific in the way you respond.

It can help to use the STAR analogy. First describe the **S**ituation, then the **T**ask you had to do. Follow up with the **A**ction you took and then the **R**esult.

See *Chapter Thirteen, Interview Preparation,* for more details.

Motivation

You will need to be intellectually curious, interested in the work, interested in international affairs, gain satisfaction from the nature of the work itself, behave with integrity and honesty in all matters, be a self-starter and be committed to developing skills and abilities. Please give an example where you have demonstrated these abilities.

"While working at Akcent in Prague, I regularly attended teaching workshops presented by more experienced teachers. These workshops were highly interesting as they provided new ideas and methods for teaching English and they were a valuable source of inspiration.

After attending a workshop on using the news as a source of discussion, I organised debate around the theme of immigration in one of my advanced groups. There were two teams; one had to argue against immigration, another in favour of it. I was the judge/moderator of the discussion.

This exercise went well as both teams became extremely involved in the discussion and I was pleased by the quality of their arguments and the English they used."

Rapport/teamwork

You will be required to work as part of a team. You will need good social skills, be able to build relationships quickly and make use of contacts, listen and see situations from different perspectives, be thoughtful to others, be a co-operative team worker, ask for and offer help when needed and be diplomatic.

"Between September 2007 and July 2008, I worked at a language school in Prague. Classes were divided between two co-teachers, who had to work together to coordinate their class's course plan and material. This meant that the two teachers had to quickly form a good working relationship in order to ensure that everything went smoothly.

One of my co-teachers, a native Czech, asked me if I would teach the idioms section of the course, as she didn't feel confident in this area. I agreed to do this, but suggested that she observe the lesson in order to improve her knowledge of idioms. I also offered to go through the idioms with her and help her with any she didn't understand. Before the lesson, I tried out my presentation of idioms on her and asked for suggestions on how to improve it. After observing my lesson, my colleague felt more comfortable with idioms and said she would be happy to teach them next time."

Submitting CVs and applications via email

When submitting a CV or job application by email, you must treat it just like a written approach with a covering letter included. You could put this in the body of the email or you could have the letter as a second attachment. That way you maintain all formatting. In that case, the covering email can be short.

When attaching your CV. Do not call it "CV," how will the recruiter find this again? Much better to name it something like DSmithCV or even better DSmith_electrical_engineer.

Also, review the email address you use. Too many applicants send them with their fun/jokey name they use for communicating with friends such as 2JDandcokes@ yahoo.com or drunkencow@gmail.com. Keep these for your personal contacts. For work, use a more formal email address such as dk.smith@virgin.net.

Please do not use emoticons, like ☺ (happy face) it does not create a business orientated impression and may lead to your message being considered spam.

Don't forget to create a signature line so that all job emails can go out with your contact details automatically included at the end of each mailing.

The follow up letter

If you haven't heard anything after a week you could increase your chances by following up with a letter. For example:

I am writing to ensure you received my CV, posted to you on 3 February 200x and to emphasise my interest in the role of marketing manager.

I am extremely interested with the high quality products and services offered by your company and XXXXX is exactly the kind of company I want to work for.

(Reemphasise some key points from the initial letter).

I look forward to talking with you soon and will call you on Thursday ready to answer any questions you may have.

By taking the time to follow up, you are demonstrating your interest in this job.

Always make a note in your diary for seven days after the closing date to enable you to follow up.

Why you may not get short listed

Sometimes an application can be excellent but people still don't get shortlisted. This could be attributed to factors outside of your control. You may not get short listed because:

- The job is already filled but the company policy is such that they have to go through the motions of an advert.
- Some recruitment agencies place ads to get people on their books.
- Organisational changes may mean there is no longer a need for the job to be filled.
- Other candidates more closely match the employers' requirements.
- Or it could be that the company is so busy that recruitment is at the bottom of their priority list and even though they conducted the interviews, they never get around to making a decision.

All of these reasons are outside your control, so don't blame your CV or covering letter when nothing you could have done differently would have made any difference.

Chapter Nine

The covering letter

Why you need a covering letter

A well-written covering letter will enhance your CV or application and help get you shortlisted. It allows you to explain why you would be a strong candidate, it summarises what you can do for the company and captures and expresses your enthusiasm.

Most of the people I work with have been sending out letters, application forms, and CVs with little attempt to match their skills and experience to the job requirements. Many people send out too brief a covering letter which makes no attempt to illuminate their strengths and explain how they match up with the job, such as:

I am pleased to attach my CV for your vacancy of Marketing Executive. I look forward to hearing from you.

Or else they provide a very comprehensive reply that still isn't targeted to the job. Pete sent the letter below to various companies with just the final paragraph slightly altered.

I am a recent Business and Management graduate from Worcester University gaining a 2:1 classification, which gives me an extensive and invaluable current view point of the Marketing and Promotion and a working knowledge of computer applications such as Word, Excel and PowerPoint. Throughout my academic career I have been focused firmly on the area of Business specialising in Marketing and Management. I think what makes me a unique applicant for this key role is the fact that I do not merely see this position as a 9-5 job, throughout my life I have had a passion for business which has developed my creative and innovative ideas and I am more than willing to go the extra mile in order for the goals to be achieved.

As well as my theoretical knowledge I also have extensive practical business & marketing knowledge gained from my extensive employment history. My most recent employment as Manager at Stars News Limited saw myself instigate the launch of a brand new store, I was fully responsible for the pre-marketing and promotion of the store including media advertisements, canvassing campaign, e-marketing and external marketing of the company. This role also allowed me to gain extensive knowledge of customer promotion and awareness. As Manager I was responsible for a small team of 4 staff and actively encouraged development and involvement of my staff within the company's functions while also achieving accreditations from professional bodies such as the Chartered Manage-

ment Institute & the Chartered Institute of Marketing. During 2005 I set-up my own small internet business which gave me a vast knowledge of e-marketing, target groups and self management. Finally in 2008 I became an accredited volunteer for Victim Support Gloucestershire a role what recognised my excellent communication and interpersonal skills and gave me great awareness of working with confidential/ sensitive material.

I would just like to further express that I feel I would be an excellent addition to Gloucester City Council, I have both the theoretical and practical knowledge needed for this role and have already a great many fresh ideas and exciting innovations that I would like to see put into practice and move Gloucester City Council events into a secure and leading future.

Alongside a not very focused CV, Peter wasn't getting anywhere. The letter isn't focused on a specific job and the big blocks of text lack impact. It's full of statements that sound grand but don't have specific examples to back them up:

- "Vast knowledge" – what kind of knowledge?
- Willing to go that extra mile – so what did he do?
- What makes him unique – he doesn't see this as a 9-5 job, neither does the employer!

So I taught him the process of highlighting the key requirements in the job ad and job description to use as the basis of his letter. Peter's next letter was much better and resulted in an interview. The job was for a supervisor at a large retail store, we saw this job ad in the previous chapter on pages 197 and 198.

The covering letter should address these. Below you can read the letter that Peter sent following some coaching from me.

Bristol - Supervisor - FT
Job Ref: MISSI0296778

I am very interested in the role of Supervisor, and believe I have many of the qualities and experience to enable me to be successful in the role.

Key aspects of my background include:

- **Customer service:** *Demonstrated within my ability to put the customer first, no matter what the current work priority might be. I offered to drop off products at local elderly residents houses if they were unable to visit the store and provided a community atmosphere where customers were actively invited for their input into product selection.*

- **Product presentation:** *A naturally keen eye for presentation, ensured products and faced-up stock were replenished. Identified counter lines & products relating to current media attention in an easily accessible and identifiable presentation making full use of professional POS Material.*

- **Passion for selling and retail:** *With seven years of retail experience, I love to serve customers and to offer great value and exceptional service, thus making a profit.*

- **Strong commercial skills:** *Both practical and theoretical experience, including making use of professional commercial research & planograms. Clear understanding of all areas of the sales process & commercial awareness though experience at Stars News Limited.*

- **Ability to make effective decisions:** *As manager of Stars News Limited, I made many decisions including the introduction of electronic payment processing & national lottery application. Decisions based on effective planning and implementation.*

- **Excellent communication skills:** *Able to communicate with a diverse range of people within my Victim Support and retail work. Can successfully adapt my* communication skills to cater for different audiences, switching between caring and sensitive while volunteering with Victim Support to more commercial and sales focused at Stars News Limited.

- **Excellent delegation skills:** Specific examples include communicating with part time staff at Stars News and introducing a 'Notices Book'. When delegating tasks to staff, I always ensured that it had been fully understood and staff were happy with what's been asked.

- **Excellent time management skills:** Demonstrated in my effective and successful time management between my responsibilities at university and my work at Stars News Limited. Also, throughout my university work, all my assignments and projects where handed in complete and to deadline.

- **Proven leader – motivation and coaching skills:** I believe I possess natural leadership skills through working for Stars News Limited from the age of 16 with four years as manager. My style is non-autocratic, always seeking to take opportunities for input or change. I also took on project leadership roles at university.

- **Numeracy:** My capabilities in numeracy are demonstrated through finance and economic modules at university and dealing with profit and loss and percentage margins within Stars News Ltd.

- **Computer literacy:** I am an avid computer user with practical experience of Windows operating systems and Microsoft Office applications. My word processing skills are excellent.

I trust you will find my details of interest and I look forward to hearing from you in due course.

Yours sincerely,

Peter Maine

Top tips for your covering letter:

- Most of your important information will be contained in your CV, but a covering letter gives you the opportunity to impress. Do not provide too much information – one page should suffice. You want to be short listed, so leave some things to discuss at interview.

- Be careful to personalise your letter so it does not look like a circular or junk mail. The reader must know immediately that you have not have sent this letter to another employer. I still receive the occasional generalised letter. It doesn't impress me.

- Avoid the phrase "I am writing" in your opening paragraph, as this is obvious.

- Consider using the same font and address style for both your CV and your covering letter for a consistent, professional look.

- Tailor your answer carefully to the key words of the advertisement. Provide key examples of your achievements that relate to the key criteria of the position.

- Incorporate into your letter, terminology the employer has used in the ad, written job description, or in a conversation. Don't forget to match THEIR NEEDS to YOUR EXPERIENCE and ABILITIES.

- Address the letter to a specific person. If the advert doesn't say, ring the company and ask who to send the letter to.

- Don't forget to put the job title at the top of the letter and reference number where applicable.

- Your letter should expand on your CV and complement your career summary, which you will adapt for each job you apply for.

- Find relevant achievements in your work history and quote one or two succinctly and colourfully. It's fine if you have also included them on your CV.

- You will have researched the company as part of your preparation, so when explaining why you are interested in the organisation or position, avoid general state-ments like "I am impressed with your products and growth." Write specifically about what products, what growth, and why you are impressed.

- Tailor your letter to a particular company, for example, a firm of solicitors or a computer games company. Decide how formal or casual should you make your language.

- Are you sure about the reasons you want the job? If you are applying to every possible job, your application may not be sufficiently focused on a particular job and will be seen as weak.

- Follow reply instructions. If it says to include a hand-written letter, do so.

- Do not be afraid to phone the recruiter or company to chat about the vacancy.

- Always get a name for the covering letter. If it's not in the advert, use your initiative (and your phone).

- If seeking to change sectors, look for common cultural links between the two work environments such as comparing the fast moving nature of retail with that of information technology.

- Display good judgement by selecting the right, relevant information. Make sure the CV and letter are fully focused on the job.

- Answer the question of "why you?" What makes you worth considering? Emphasise your positive assets such as education and experience, skills, accomplishments, and personal qualities in relation to the employer's needs.

- You may be competing with recent graduates who will work for a much lower salary. So your letter has to emphasise your strengths and experience and how you will get things done much more quickly.

- If you have gaps on your CV, give an explanation of why in the letter.

- Pay attention to details. Type the letter and be sure to use spell check. And read it carefully. Too many people send things out with errors in grammar, style, and punctuation.
- Do not state that you are bored with your present position. It makes the employer wonder if you will get bored with your next job.
- Check to see if you have avoided beginning all your sentences with the word "I"? (Place a greater emphasis on the word "you" where possible).
- Lengthy paragraphs are overwhelming to read. Divide text into shorter chunks when necessary to keep paragraphs short.
- As you send off your CV, whether by email or via the post, you want to adhere to grammatical rules: If you are writing to a named person, end the letter "Yours sincerely." If you have to write Dear Sir or Dear Madam, your letter should end "Yours Faithfully."
- If an advertisement asks you to apply to Michael Black for example, do not start the letter "Dear Michael." it's too familiar (unless you know him personally). Use "Dear Mr. Black" and "Yours sincerely," to close. If you are not sure if a woman should be written to as Mrs, Miss or Ms, contact the company to check how the person prefers to be addressed.
- End the letter with a specific statement of what your next step will be. If you plan to follow up with a telephone call, say so. If you plan to wait for the employer's response, say so as well.
- If there's a closing date, time your posting so that it arrives a few days after the main 'rush' that occurs within 4-7 days of the advertisement's publication (but not after the closing date). Alternatively, you may prefer to be the first to respond.
- Conclude by saying that you look forward to discussing your career with the advertiser.

Too many I's

> *I am writing to apply for the vacancy as sales negotia-tor I saw advertised in the Gloucestershire Echo. I believe I would be a good candidate for this position as I have good interpersonal skills, and have experience of selling through work at both Vodafone and Boots the Chemist Ltd. I am pleased to include my CV for your consideration and I look forward to hearing from you.*

Above is an actual letter drafted by a client of mine. **The word "I" is used 7 times**. The focus should be more on the company, so this letter needs to be rewritten. I've looked at how others do this, and too often it's just a case of changing the work "I" to "my." But this still puts the emphasis on you. For example:

> "**My** 2 years of successful experience in online cus-tomer support with a web site processing 250 orders a day, **my** strong interpersonal skills, and **my** education fit the requirements of the website customer support opening you have posted on *Career Builder*."

I rewrote this:

> *With high levels of customer support experience, gained through working in online customer support, I have the necessary skills for success in this role. For example, an ability to deal with difficult and challenging customers who have a problem, to respond quickly to queries, and to provide the customer with a calm and customer-orientated environment.*

I would expand further based on what else was in the advert. As you can see, this response focuses on the job, with specific helpful experiences to support the application.

You have already looked at Peter's covering letter which resulted in an interview. It's now time for you to have a go. Here's the structure for the letter:

A structure for a covering letter. Never exceed one page!

Your name
Your street address
Your postal town and post code
Your phone numbers, including mobile
Your email address
Date

(Three spaces between the date and the company address).

Name and job role of person you are writing to
Company name

Address 1

Town

Post code

Dear name of person

Opening paragraph: State why you are writing, identify the position for which you would like to be considered, and indicate how you heard of the position. (If you are sending a letter of interest which is not in response to a specific job opening, simply indicate the type of work you are seeking). Be specific. Also, make sure you sound interested and explain what interests you about the job.

Middle paragraph(s): Your goal here is to show how you can be useful to this particular organisation. Describe what strengths you have to offer this employer by showing the relationship between your skills and experience, and the vacancy. You can also describe your previous achievements and how they relate to the vacancy and identify three reasons why you should be called for interview.

Refer the reader to your enclosed CV for additional information.

(You can divide this into a couple of smaller paragraphs rather than have one large, dense paragraph).

Closing paragraph: End your letter by clarifying what will happen next and how they can most easily reach you.

Yours sincerely,

Space for your signature

Type your name beneath your signature

Enclosure: CV

Now review what you have produced. Are you happy with yours? Put it to one side and come back to it in an hour or so and look at it objectively. If you try and apply without a job in mind, it's hard to be specific enough, so if you don't have a job to apply for, base it on a previous application. You can adapt and choose a style that suits you.

Example letter 1

Here is an example letter, with a slightly different format. It picks up on the key requirements from the job ad.

11th June 20xx
Samantha Howe
Legal Aid Board
85 Grays Inn Road
London WC1X 8AA

Dear Samantha,

Business Auditor

I am very interested in the position of business auditor. My skills and abilities are a close match to your requirements.

I've enclosed the completed forms as requested. I have also included details of my skills and attributes against your key headings.

I have extensive experience of audit type work, gained through business excellence assessment which involved working as a member of a seven-person team to gain evidence against the nine areas of the business excellence model. I analysed the information and produced a report. I also undertook audits to measure the effectiveness of operational units against three key areas – customer, employee, and operational.

Analytical

Through MSc and MBA studies, project management and production of reports.

Inspiring

I am seen as an effective team leader through direct team management and also through leadership of a network of occasional tutors, all senior managers, who at the time were all senior in organisational rank to me.

Focused

This was needed to complete my MBA studies. I work best when there are clear goals to be achieved. I am seen as enthusiastic and very much a "half-full" personality.

Fluency

I am noted for my avoidance of technical jargon and my ability to communicate in an easy to understand way.

Visionary

I can think and operate strategically, via MBA studies and senior management roles.

People Focused

I am noted for my empathy. I am a trained counsellor and work sensitively with others while also taking account of business aims.

I look forward to hearing from you.

Example letter 2

The style can vary, all that matters is that it gets you to interview.

Corrie Guilden
March Consulting Group
39 King Street
Wolverhampton WV4 3PX

Dear Ms Guilden,

Ref: AR/116 Financial Controller

Your advertisement in the *Financial Times* for a Financial Controller appears to match both my skills and experience and I should like to apply for the post. As requested, I've enclosed a detailed CV and have highlighted the following attributes:

- Currently Financial Controller of a £35M. turnover paint company.
- Through the introduction of stringent financial disciplines, I effected a saving of £1.8M in last year's account.
- Initiated, sourced, and installed a computerised system for efficient MIS reporting. Previously introduced a computerised stock control and inventory system at *Blank PLC*.
- Fully qualified accountant having spent my initial years with *Spicer & Pegler*.

My current salary package, including benefits, is similar to that proposed in the advertisement. I would be happy to relocate if this is necessary.

I look forward to hearing from you if my details are of interest.

Yours sincerely,

Example letter 3

Dear

I am very interested in the position of Manufacturing Manager (DL574) as advertised in the *The York Times* and enclose my CV.

I have taken the time to list your specific requirements and my applicable skills in these areas (see table below). I hope this will enable you to use your time effectively today.

Please do not hesitate to contact me if there is any further information you require.

I look forward to hearing from you.

Yours sincerely,

Your key criteria	My background
Work with the Manufacturing Director.	Extensive experience of working with board members and managers.
Develop and implement manufacturing strategy.	Involved in planning of company strategy.
Prepare budget and monitor and control performance against it.	Worked with M.D. on setting budgets, tracked them monthly against targets.
A good communicator with considerable management skills.	Liaised with customers and agents to maximise outputs and profits.
Team work / flexible culture.	Strong training focus combined with being a team builder.
Graduate calibre.	HNC in mechanical production engineering plus a range of management development courses.
5 years experience working in a modern manufacturing environment.	In excess of 5 years experience.

All of the above examples are from actual clients I have worked with and all resulted in interviews.

A worked through example

Let's now work through an example of some work I did with Kim. You've already read Kim's diary in the Introduction and seen her before and after CV in Chapter Three.

Step 1: Kim finds a suitable job

She contacted the employer for further information and this was all that was available (sometimes you get more than this to work with).

THE JOB AD

Trainee Case Handler – Job

Job description

This role is based within the Recoveries and Finance team at our Manchester office and will involve being trained to manage your own caseload of recovery cases. Apart from the academic side, practical training will include learning how to open/close files, put on debts, archive and issue court proceedings.

Qualifications/experience

- Good communication skills.
- Client management skills.
- Team player.
- Attention to detail.
- Willing to learn academic part of the law/ prepared to study.
- Proactive.
- Clerical experience.

- Possibly from an admin background or perhaps educated to degree level of equivalent would be helpful.

Step 2: Read the more detailed job description

Usually there will be a detailed job description and person spec. You will want to read this through carefully and highlight any key points you need to refer to in your application.

The role consists principally of **monitoring developments** in the law, **summarising** the effect of new primary & secondary legislation, and **annotating and editing** these and other materials to be included in the department's publications.

We are looking for someone with a **2:1 Law Degree** who may be fresh from university or with some editing experience.

You should possess a **good eye for detail, excellent English written skills.**

We are offering you the opportunity to work with a highly respected publishing group and we can guarantee a challenging, exciting career with excellent training prospects.

Salary will be from £19710 - £23,000 with excellent benefits including 28 days holiday, Pension and much more.

If you are interested in applying for the position please send your CV including a covering letter (essential) detailing your interest in the position and your key skills.

Apply for this position

If you would like to apply for this position, simply fill out your details here, enter your name in our reply box, attach a copy of your CV and click on the button to submit.

I have highlighted key points from the ad to show you what you need to cover in your application.

Step 3: Read through the ad and identify some areas to research further

Research will help you understand more about the company you are going to apply to and give you some pointers of where and how to follow up. In this example, you will want to have at least glanced at the publications and be ready to ask an intelligent question at interview to demonstrate you have taken the time to find out more about the employer.

Step 4: Prepare the letter, making sure to address the key criteria

Your letter, along side your CV, is going to be used for short-listing purposes. One way you can make things easy for the person doing this is to provide examples alongside key criteria. We can also look at this example from Kim:

Trainee Case Handle Reference No: HJ 987

Dear Miss Dixon:

I'm writing in response to your advertisement for a Trainee Case Handler and have pleasure in enclosing my CV for your perusal. I have been working as a Legal Executive where I have developed many of the skills used by a Case Handler. I have detailed below how I meet your required qualifications and experience.

Communication Skills

I have excellent communication skills, dealing professionally with a diverse range of people including estate agents, mortgage brokers, bankers, surveyors and other solicitors. I enjoy building good working relationships and have developed a good rapport with clients who returned to instruct me on further matters.

Client Management Skills

Experienced in working in a professional manner for high profile clients who have recommended me to others. This has resulted in a number of letters of appreciation, available on request. My high level of commitment and integrity results in excellent client care survey comments. I have represented the firm at corporate and client entertaining events. My commitment to an organisation is demonstrated by my willingness to work over and above the call of duty on behalf of my clients to achieve the desired goals.

Team Player

I have deputised for solicitors and partners in three different offices. I assisted locums especially during extremely busy periods when they were only employed part-time to cover my colleague's heavy caseload and on one occasion the locum thanked me with a bouquet of flowers. I have demonstrated flexibility by cancelling my holiday to assist the team and enjoyed good relationships with all the support staff and other departments within the firm.

Proactive with Attention to Detail

Working on my own caseload, I confidently used my initiative to deal with a wide range of legal work including complicated matters where I carried out research to answer enquiries. I enjoy working under pressure and with tight deadlines and I am able to prioritise my work according to internal and external influences using the case management system to diarise and monitor tasks and appointments. I will also regularly review the priorities of my work to meet urgent demands. Working methodically, I proactively dealt with any problems that arose.

Clerical experience

I have experience of using both DPS and Eclipse case management systems and I am also currently studying the European Computer Driving Licence course, passing Module 2. Working as both a paralegal and a fee earner, I have experience of opening and closing files, as well as archiving and managing client accounts.

Due to the downturn in the housing market I have recently been made redundant and I believe this is an exciting opportunity where I can use all my existing skills in a new area of law. I enjoy learning new skills and I have proven ability to change career successfully.

I look forward to hearing from you.

Yours sincerely,

Kim sent the above letter with her revised CV and was shortlisted for the job.

Salary Questions

An advert will sometimes ask about your salary requirements. You should never mention salary unless specifically asked. It may be too high or too low and provide the employer with an excuse to screen you out. Leave discussion on your salary and benefits package until much later in the selection process. However, sometimes a company wants you to be specific, in which case saying "to be discussed at interview" will annoy them, so it's better to give a range, such as 25k to 30k.

You may be considerably underpaid in your current or last job, and if, for example, you are earning 25k and the job you want has a salary range of 35k to 50k, you may be concerned that they will think you are not senior enough for the job.

Salary quotes can be based on many different things, and nowadays some companies will give you a choice of using some of your salary to pay for car, private health-care, etc. So in addition to your basic salary, make sure you add on your bonuses, car, health insurance, gym membership, etc. Collect the monetary value of everything. Then you can truthfully quote your total package.

Chapter Ten

Stand out from the crowd

In a recession, it's an employers market. There are a lot of people chasing each job, so anything you can do to differentiate yourself will help you be the one chosen.

What ever your job: accountant, project manager, media planner, look for ways to make yourself stand out from all the other accountants, project managers, etc.

Think like a celebrity

High profile people such as musicians and actors can be found online and in many cases, you'll find access to information about them from official and unofficial sources. Celebrities encourage this as it increases and enhances their media presence. You can do the same. Create a work-orientated personal web site to enable a potential employer to learn more about you. They are likely to google you anyway, so make sure they will only read positive things about you. This can increase your chances of being hired.

Do you have the right reputation?

Many people forget that information is available about them, as a private individual, online. Such information comes from our professional lives, our memberships in organisations, as copy of a conference talk, or through our involvement in committees, etc. But there is also personal information that we may not want accessed by people outside our circle of friends. These can include details from our social networking sites such as *Facebook, Myspace* and *Bebo* pages; the photos uploaded on *Flickr,* and photos and comments that other people have put on their pages.

You may think this doesn't matter thinking that everything you want a potential employer to know about is included on your CV and application. However, companies now routinely do a search on applicants. In a *Career-builder.com* survey (2006) of 1,150 hiring managers, one in four said they use internet search engines to research potential candidates. According to *Search Engine Watch,* there are 25m to 50m proper name searches performed each day. So you must make sure only positive details are found when a company runs a search for your name.

Key things to do

Google yourself

Have you ever googled yourself? If not, **do it now**, and see what comes up. Just enter your name into the search bar and look for the first four pages to see if there are any links to you. You may find links to your social networking sites or activities you have been a part of.

Now is the time to get rid of the non-business orientated information. I searched for one candidate and found a page about him boasting about his drug taking. This page is from several years ago but still could result in his application hitting the reject pile. Remove anything that may stop you from getting a job, such as unfavorable articles, photos and comments. Also ask your friends to remove such information from their sites.

You may find you have a name shared by others. When I search for myself for example, I also find out about others named Denise Taylor. One rides barrel horses, another is a researcher at university with a focus on wolf conservation, and another is a senior teaching fellow in clinical pharmacy. Searching for your name might bring up more unsavory characters than these so make sure any potential employers are clear on who you really are.

Ditch the digital dirt

If you have anything on the web that you wouldn't be happy being on the front page of your local or national paper, you need to remove it. If it is a page you have access to, remove the text or pictures. If there are like items your friends have on their sites, ask them to remove them as well.

If there are things you can't get removed, you are going to have to get things posted that will bump these lower down on the search engine page. Get started soon!

Improve your presence – create a web site

You can improve your presence by creating your own web site or blog. This allows you to provide further details on your pertinent experience and knowledge of your chosen field.

A work-focused web site could include a number of pages to expand your CV. For example, you could include more detail on your skills and experience, along with copies of presentations you have made, pictures of you at work, any articles you have written, etc. You can also include non work-related activities that could be useful such as community involvement or independent travel.

Improve your presence – create a blog

An alternative to a web site is a blog. Your blog could be integrated into a web site or it could be a stand alone. You can set up a blog for free using *Blogger* or at low cost using *Typepad*. You must keep a blog current, so at least a couple of times a week you need to make a new entry such as comments on articles, daily news and your opinion on work-related topics. You could even document your job search.

Improve your presence – create a Linkedin account

Linkedin is a great way to keep in touch with business acquaintances and also for developing new contacts. It's a way of expanding your network to help with fact finding interviews and to find out about possible opportunities.

With a Linkedin account you can personalise your link such as www.linkedin.com/in/denisetaylor and this can be included on your CV, business card, etc.

Linkedin has groups you can join, to exchange ideas and expand areas of knowledge. You can also answer questions to promote your expertise. It will of course take time, but I think I created mine in about three hours spread over a few sessions. Once you are on Linkedin, don't forget to ask for recommendations from people you have worked with as people will read your recommendations when they visit your page.

Go a bit wider – comment on other sites

Another possibility is to read business books in your field and post reviews on Amazon – it's a good way to show you are keeping up to date with changes in the market place.

In addition, you could read other peoples blogs and make comments. These comments don't have to be long – just one or two paragraphs will do.

Write articles

You could write articles and submit them to article sites such as www.ezinearticles.com. If you do write articles, focus on key words that people will search for. Also give some thought to the title and the header of the article. Would it make you and others want to read it?

Let people know

If you create a blog or web site, be sure to include details on your CV and applications, so that potential employers and networking contacts can read more on you.

Client example:

Judy had a degree in interior design and was working as a waitress. She really wanted to get into journalism and was planning to take a post grad qualification. To increase her chance of success I suggested she write a blog. I also suggested she write about areas of interest and newsworthy items such as fashion trends and reviews of restaurants and films to be included on her own blog or web site and posted to other sites.

The are plenty of other places you can comment, from answering questions on *Yahoo* to responding to discussions forum posts.

A well-designed and positive online presence can really help you in your job search. It really can make a difference – why not get started soon!

Chapter Eleven

The hidden job market

There are different ways to get a job. You can be *reactive* or *proactive*. The reactive approach is to respond to job advertisements.

The proactive approach is to take charge of how your job search develops. This is done by not waiting for jobs to be advertised, but making contact with people and organisations that may be able to help. It's not an easy option. It takes a lot of preparation including understanding yourself, and writing a carefully researched letter where you can identify how your skills, qualities and abilities can be of value to a company. This is what's meant by accessing the hidden job market.

This follows your research phase and identifies where you want to work. Now make contact with people and organisations that can help you get a job.

70% of jobs are found through networking, but only 30% of people use this method

Proactive approaches include networking and speculative letters to potential employers and recruitment consultants.

When people talk of targeting a company directly, what they often mean is to send a copy of their CV with a standard covering letter, hoping there will be some interest. However, this sets you up for failure. And not only is this a waste of time, both for you and the person receiving it, it can have a negative effect on your self esteem. It's hard to stay upbeat when you are being rejected time and time again.

When you take a proactive approach, your letter will highlight a few specific achievements that make the reader want to find out more. Of course, there will still be rejection letters, but with careful preparation and specific targeting, you can reach a success rate of about 4%. This means you need to send out a minimum of 25 letters to get one response.

Too many people use a shot gun approach. It's much better to be a sniper!

It works best when you have some very specific skills and experience to offer. If not, you may prefer to use the fact finding interview approach.

You have already read about networking in Chapter Six. We'll now cover speculative approaches to potential employers, people you know, and recruitment agencies and consultants.

Speculative approaches to potential employers

Writing speculative letters to potential employers to target unadvertised, actual vacancies as well as imminent and spontaneous vacancies, is a very effective means of getting a job. You need to prepare thoroughly. Here are the steps you need to take (each is detailed below):

Step 1: Desk research.

Step 2: Phone research.

Step 3: Prepare your letters.

Step 4: Send out your letters.

Step 5: Follow up with a phone call.

Step 6: At the meeting.

Step 7: Follow up.

Step 1: Desk research

You are clear on your strengths, skills, talents and experience. You now need to identify companies who are likely to have a need for such qualities. These may be from a particular industry sector or with departments that can use your skills and experience.

You can identify companies via suggestions from friends, colleagues, and others in your network. You can also use press articles on companies that have achieved a take over or achieved a new large contract, and research other companies using your local business library or a reference book such as *Kompass.*

In *Chapter Six, Fact Finding Interviews,* you read about all the relevant books you can access from your local business library.

Newspapers

You can find out about a company that may be expanding through reading the business press, reading about who is moving into new premises, etc. You can also see which companies are advertising, maybe not in your field, but if they are taking on employees in one area, there may be other opportunities soon.

As well as seeking a suitable role, job advertisements are a useful source of intelligence for your job search campaign. Scan through all of them in the journals/newspapers which cover suitable jobs for you, but don't just look for jobs you could do, compile a list of approaches you could make by finding out:

- Which companies are recruiting at the moment?
- Which companies are expanding, restructuring, relocating or branching out into new markets?
- Are higher level posts being advertised? If so, it is likely that jobs lower down an organisation might also become available.
- Which recruitment consultants handle jobs of your type or in your market sector industry?
- What salary is being offered for people like you at similar job levels?

Online research

You can find out about companies via online research such as at: http://www.kompass.com/kinl/index.php

This is useful for searching by different criteria. For example, you can search by county, product code, turnover, and numbers of employees, producing a tailor-made list to best suit your needs. It is useful for an initial 'trawl' for your direct approach lists. You can also get a more detailed printout of a specific company.

You can also buy lists of companies from *Business Link*, opting for location, industry and size of company. There are many possible companies, so you will want to define some criteria to narrow your search. Your basic criteria are likely to include:

- Location.
- Industry or type of business.
- Size (whether by employees or turnover).
- Number of sites, etc.

Do take time to clarify these criteria. If not, you'll become swamped in information and have a difficult time choosing the right company for you. For some people, it is unlikely to be worthwhile to contact companies below a certain size. You must choose the criteria that are right for you.

Activity: Define your criteria now.

List the key elements you will look for when you begin your research:

You can refine your search later, or widen your criteria. Your first task is to define criteria so you can focus your search and get ready for your first batch of letters.

Let me introduce you to Tom

Tom is an engineer who wants to continue his career in textile manufacturing. Tom lives in Moreton-in-Marsh and is willing to travel in a radius that includes Bristol, Birmingham and Oxford. When he goes to the library, he practices his relationship building skills with the librarian and she shows him how to use the different business directories. Tom has been to the library three times now and has been capturing details on his laptop. This means he will be able to keep a good record of who he has contacted and can use the data in his letters. An Excel spread sheet will help Tom create mail merge letters.

Step 2: Phone research

After you have identified companies to write to, you need to find out to whom in the company you should address your letter. This will be the man or woman you would expect to report to if you got the job. (If in doubt, choose the more senior of your options on the premise that letters frequently get referred downwards but rarely upwards).

You cannot rely solely on reference books for the names of the people you want, as the book could be 12 months out of date. Web sites are not always up to date either. So make a phone call to get the right name and job title.

Ask yourself, who in the company would be interested in you. If you have a background as a production manager, will you get the most useful reply from the human resources department, or the production director who can foresee the need for a production manager due to forthcoming changes in his department.

If you are more senior, a letter to the managing director may mean that you are invited to attend for an informal chat to discuss possibilities that he or she is only just considering. This puts you ahead of the queue.

You will also need to ensure you take down the details correctly. If you have many companies to contact, perhaps you could outsource this task to a family member.

Let's see how Tom is getting on. He is ringing to check the details are correct.

Good morning. My name is Tom Prinder. I wonder if you could help me. I have to write to your Production Director (or Works Manager/Quality Control Manager etc). Would you give me his name and initials please?

This isn't a question but a request. Expect the information to be supplied and you will receive it. Sound hesitant or unsure and the receptionist may hold back and wonder about your motives.

On the rare occasion when the receptionist is unforth-coming, ask for "PR," who are accustomed to giving out information or contact the sales department. In each case, ask for the department, not the manager. You do not want a conversation at this point so don't be drawn into having one.

Tom has asked to be put through to the sales department:

Good morning. My name is Tom Prinder. I'd appreci-ate your help. I'm writing to your Production Director and your receptionist wasn't able to check on the name and the initials for me. Do, you have a list handy? ... The Production Director...

Step 3: Prepare your letters

In most cases, you cannot send out a standard letter to all companies. If you do, your rate of success will be extremely low. Think hard about the objective of your letter. The letter itself cannot get you a job. What it must do is attract sufficient interest so that someone wants to meet with you.

Your objective is to put your career details in front of decision makers in your chosen sector to secure a meeting or interview with them. Your letter must be convincing and incisive.

It's also very important that you know each company's needs. You can find this out by visiting the company web site and downloading relevant literature. If it's not avail-able there, you can get it from the marketing or public relations department.

Think about the problems faced by the managing direc-tor, the senior researcher, etc., to whom you are writing. How can your combination of experience, training and aptitude help them? How can you make their life easier or more profitable? This is a time-consuming approach, but you will have a much higher success rate if you tailor your letter specifically, rather than taking the mail-shot approach. Write a letter to the individual within the organisation who has operational authority. This may be the managing director, or the head of the section you would like to work in.

When writing, highlight anything that directly relates to contributions you can make. Do your best to make the letter brief and to the point. Your CV will provide a detailed summary of your career – the letter aims only to whet the appetite. You also have the option of not including a CV, but a more detailed letter, highlighting specific, relevant information. If you do this, do not be tempted to attach your CV as this will distract from your letter.

Confirm you will be phoning later to enquire about a meeting. And make sure you follow up as you have promised. If the person is not available, leave a message to say you called. It's proof you kept your word. Arrange a good time and day to ring again.

Your letter may short-circuit not only middle management and the sometimes rather impersonal HR department, but it frequently makes it possible to get to see the managing director or another director of the firm.

It doesn't make any difference whether you are looking for a job that pays £10,000 or £100,000. Get that proactive letter composed!

Four steps to a successful proactive letter

Step 1 is to catch the readers' interest, to make them want to read the rest of your letter. For example:

"As an assistant marketing manager for a leading consumer product, I helped increase sales by 13% through a new marketing policy"

You do not want to start the paragraph with "I." You want to quickly show how you can benefit the organisation.

Step 2 is to make a connection between the first paragraph and its application to their business. It should relate to the company and their needs, not yours. For example:

"Your company may have a need in your marketing operation for someone with my experience."

"Your company may be in need of a sales consultant. If so, you may be interested in what I have achieved in sales"

"If your company needs a manufacturing manager with my background and experience, you may be interested in some of the things I have done."

Step 3 is to give details of relevant achievements. Include some of the bullets you produced for your CV and choose the most relevant for each particular company. Include a number of bullets to highlight your key achievements. **The fourth step** is to mention your educational background including your university, qualifications, other education or training, etc.

The final step is to ask for, or suggest, some action or response. Give an indication of availability for interview. Be proactive by writing "I shall telephone you early next week" rather than "I look forward to hearing from you" as below:

"If you would like to discuss my experience in greater detail, I shall be glad to do so at a personal interview. I will phone you early next week."

Don't be tempted to say, "I would appreciate an opportunity to discuss any openings that you may have in your organisation." First, "I would appreciate" suggests begging. Secondly, "discuss any possible openings" weakens your position. Remember that you are selling yourself in your speciality, not seeking general employment.

Let's catch up with Tom:

Tom Prinder, 1 New Road, East Town, South Shire
ET1 0PP 07931 303366   tom@prinder.co.uk

25th January 200X
Mr. H. Mitchell
Finance Director
Pendleton Paper Products
Cheltenham Business Park
Cheltenham GL52 5HL

Dear Mr. Bradley

Your company has expanded with great success during the last five years and is present in nearly every town centre. Perhaps your IT resources are sometimes over-stretched, and in particular, there may be difficulties from time to time in establishing fool-proof systems at Point of Sale.

I am an IT Specialist with particular experience in the sourcing, development and installation of Point of Sale. In addition, I have addressed the needs of providing effective training for all staff operating such systems, and ensuring that full online support is always available.

My last two assignments were with RETAILCO Ltd and BIZCO, who both needed effective Point of Sale IT equipment to retain customer advantage in the de-manding retail food trade.

A current curriculum vitae is enclosed for your atten-tion. I trust my details are of interest and will contact you in the next couple of days to arrange a time to meet if this would be of interest to you.

Yours sincerely

Tom Prinder

Tom's letter is a suggestion, but not a template. It doesn't include model answers, where you fill in the gaps. This is your marketing document and has to be specific in how it reflects your own experience, skills, abilities and personal qualities. It should sound natural and be easy to read.

It is essential that the letter ends with what you want – to meet with a particular person. Make it easy for them to set up such a meeting with you by providing email and mobile phone numbers.

Studies by the British Direct Mail Association show that a catchy PS can increase response rate. What could you add? Perhaps something like:

P.S. I live close by and could call in and see you at short notice.

Once complete, read it out loud

- Do the phrases come easy, or are the sentences so long that you run out of breath?
- Read it out loud to a friend or colleague and make sure they understand what you are trying to say.

Then put a reminder in your admin system to make sure you do as you have promised.

The purpose of these letters is not to get you a job, but to get an interview

You should aim to send out around 20 letters a week. Be sure to keep sending them out even as you move into a second interview phase. Don't assume anything till you get an offer in writing.

Activity: Draft out a letter now.

It can be hard to get started, so write an introductory paragraph. (You can rewrite all or parts of it later if necessary).

The purpose of the letter is to make the person reading it want to meet you and explore the ways you can benefit their company. Take a hard look at your letter and ask yourself:

- Could it be strengthened?
- Is it too long?
- Can you remove any "I"s and replace them with "you"?
- Is it focused on what you want to do?
- Have you wetted their appetite?
- Have you indicated you could solve some of their challenges such as increased turnover, make savings to the bottom line, and develop new products?

For example, if you are seeking a job as an accountant in a high tech company, make sure all the information you give enhances either your experience as an accountant or your knowledge of the industry. On the other hand, if you are seeking work as a production manager, emphasise production examples. Don't dilute your message by including details not of interest to the one reading the letter.

Focus on the situation. Think about the problems that must be faced by the managing director, marketing manager, etc., to whom you are writing. How can your combination of experience, training and aptitude help them? How can you make their life easier or more profitable?

- Are you describing your accomplishments?
- Have you included a measure of the result?
- Look again at your examples.

You can follow the guidance for writing a cover letter in *Chapter Nine, The Covering Letter*.

Don't forget to check the contents before posting. It is surprising how many people undermine their best efforts by omitting pages or key details. First class post conveys the urgency and importance you attach to your job search.

Step 4: Send out the letters

Unless directed otherwise, always send out the letters by post, not email.

A proactive letter should produce about four interviews for each hundred sent out. Often the percentage will go higher. Remember, you must keep sending letters out. You can't just send out one set of 20 and expect to get a number of responses. It doesn't work that way.

The proactive letter is the most positive, effective, time-saving, and reasonable way to get placed

As a rule, always specifically target companies and customise a letter for each. However, if you want to work as a trainee accountant for example, you can send a similar letter to a number of companies. The example below, from Louise, was sent out to 104 accountancy firms. Her letter is structured around the key competences identified for accountants. This resulted in five meetings and one job offer.

This letter is on the long side, but with careful formatting will still fit on one page. This letter was based on internet research which identified the key skill requirements of accountants.

Dear

Audit/Accounts Trainee

Recent analysis of my future career direction, including tests and discussions with an Occupational Psychologist, have indicated that training to be an accountant is the right next step for me. The reasons I believe I will be successful are:

Business Understanding: Gained through a business studies degree and experience across a range of organisations such as XYZ Company. I have worked through periods of organisational change and so have first hand experience of organisational challenges.

Motivation: Having already demonstrated this through the ability to work full time as well as study for a part time degree. I set myself goals and do not give up.

Communication skills: I am used to producing reports and analysing data and have to explain complex issues to non-experts in an easy to understand way. My counselling qualification is evidence of my overall skills and I am noted for my ability to listen effectively to others.

Numerical skills: I enjoy using numerical data and am comfortable with interpreting figures.

Team skills: I am used to working effectively as a member of a team, and have contributed to effective teams where we each have our own areas of responsibility and knowledge.

Analytical skills: Problem-solving skills is one of my strengths and I take a logical approach to analysing issues.

IT skills: Proficient across the Microsoft Office suite and very comfortable with the Internet, and use of email and in-house packages.

In every organisation I have worked I have been praised for my high level of attention to detail and customer relation skills.

I appreciate that I am not a typical recent graduate, but believe I am a credible applicant due to my business degree and background, and the thought I have given to my future career direction.

I already have gained the following 4 ACCA papers (by exemption) 1.1, 1.2, 1.3 and 2.2.

I have had exposure within a finance environment totalling approximately nine months. This consisted of a placement within XYZ Credit Control department and a temporary assignment within Ambassador Financial Assurance.

I trust you find my details of interest and will telephone you in a few days to arrange a time to meet.

Yours sincerely

Louise Lawson (Enc: Curriculum Vitae)

Step 6: Follow up with a phone call

If you do not hear from the company within three working days, you should consider telephoning. Your aim is to speak to the recipient's secretary with the hope of scheduling a meeting.

Remember to:

- Call from a quiet location. Be pleasant. It may be a good idea to smile as you speak.
- Speak loudly and clearly.
- Do not use slang such as "uh-huh", "right on", "cool" etc.
- Listen carefully. If the person seems distracted, offer to call back at another time.
- Keep the call short.
- Have your CV and letter in hand.

Find out to whom you are speaking and at what level, i.e., receptionist, secretary, someone who has just picked up the phone, etc. They will either:

- Try to put you off.
- Engage you in meaningless conversation.
- Not know anything about your letter.
- Know something about you from your letter.
- Direct you to the respective department.
- Suggest you contact Personnel for advice.

I suggest you use a series of postcards, each covering a particular point. On the back of each, prepare how you will respond to objections.

Card 1: Introduction to the gatekeeper.

Card 2: Introduction to decision maker.

Card 3: Your reason for calling.

Card 4: Your main skills and achievements.

Card 5: A request for an interview.

Card 6: Close and confirm next steps.

Have a script if it helps you feel prepared and keeps you to the point. A well-written script will:

- Give you more confidence.
- Give a business-like structure to your message.
- Act as a prompt, not a crutch.

Getting past the gatekeeper

The person you speak to may be a receptionist, assistant, or private secretary who is skilled in the art of screening calls and diverting them from their hard-pressed boss.

Don't tell the gatekeeper the purpose of your call – simply say you have written to xxx and are following up with a personal call. If he or she is unavailable, find out when it would be a good time to ring.

Once you are through to the relevant department, you should then say something along the following lines:

"I wrote to Mr .... on ...., you/he/she should have received the letter yesterday, suggesting a meeting and I am telephoning to arrange a suitable time."

If you are finding it difficult to get through, you could ring before or after work when the secretary is not there as the phone is usually switched to their direct line. Be ready with your script because they may answer and you need to appear confident and professional.

You must be persistent. You will not necessarily get to talk to the person straight away, so leave a polite message and call back when you said you will.

Please don't expect a high number of people agreeing to meet with you. This is not a personal insult but a part of job searching and the nature of the recruitment process.

Back up admin

- Keep a list of phone calls made and outcomes such as sending on your CV.
- Note arrangements to phone back.

Getting a meeting

Tom got three meetings out of 50 letters – a 6% success rate. There are a number of reasons people will agree to meet with you:

- The post has not yet been announced or passed on to a recruitment consultant to be filled.
- A vacancy has been announced, but your letter has interested the company and once they have seen you, you have successfully jumped the early part of the recruitment process.
- Either your skills interest the organisation because they are looking at new projects which require these, or your meetings have in turn led to the managing director looking at new projects requiring your particular abilities.
- The vacancy would have been filled by an internal candidate had you not written to the company at that time.

Step 7: At the Meeting

When you get to see the person, take a look at the meeting from their perspective. They will possibly begin in one of the following ways:

- What can I do for you?
- Why do you want to see me?
- Let me start by saying we have no vacancies at present, nevertheless I am interested in what you have to say.
- What can you do for me?

You must be prepared to think on your feet. Show respect for the person who has given you their time. *Chapter Six, Fact Finding Interviews,* will provide some useful additional support.

Step 8: Follow up

Always send a thank you note to the person you have seen and follow up as appropriate. For example, you could send a relevant and interesting article to keep your "name in the frame" and to indicate your interest and initiative.

Approaching recruitment agencies and consultants

Speculative letters to recruitment agencies who handle assignments in your sector are another good method of finding jobs. You will target any actual vacancies (advertised or unadvertised), which they may be handling, as well as putting your name on their lists in case of an imminent vacancy.

In a recession, recruitment agencies will be swamped with people wanting to get on their books alongside a significant drop in vacancies. If you create a good relationship with an agency, you are more likely to be considered.

What the agencies do

Recruitment agencies seek staff at all levels and often hold details on their own databases. Often they will ask you to complete an application form so they have the data in a standard format. They are paid by the employer, sometimes for providing them with a shortlist of potential candidates, sometimes only for a successful candidate.

They obtain candidates by coming to an agreement on a job description and employment specifications and advertise for the client under their own name. They may also approach people whose skills match a particular position and encourage them to apply.

These consultants are in business to place people and to satisfy their client-companies' recruitment needs. They earn their fee by supplying suitable candidates to their clients. To them, you are therefore a commodity. If they can make a profit out of you, they are interested. If they cannot, they may not be. By understanding and accepting this, you will not have unrealistic expectations of them.

When you meet with a recruitment consultant, you need to present yourself and behave as if you are meeting a potential employer. Make sure you are honest, professional, well presented and polite. You must be familiar with your CV and be ready for a screening interview as they will want to get to know you and make sure you present well.

As more than one agency can be in contact with a particular employer, ask the recruitment consultant to seek your permission before your details are passed on. Otherwise, a potential employer could receive your details from several agencies which may dilute their interest in you. You can call the agency once a week to check on progress but no more or it seems like harassment.

Making an approach

Dependent on your experience and background, you may approach local or national agencies. Lists of agencies and consultants are available in *Executive Grapevine,* available from the county library. Identify those which are most appropriate. Make a call to introduce yourself and seek confirmation that they are interested in your skills and experience. They may prefer a one-page summary without your full CV and want to meet candidates before accepting them.

Take care with your letters to consultants. They may not find you suitable for one position but could well have another likely to be on the market in the near future.

I've included a couple of letters which resulted in meetings with recruitment consultants. Read these through carefully so you understand the style and can adapt this to create your own letter. You will see that they both contain specific detail to interest the consultant. Jack doesn't include his CV as this would dilute the power of the letter. It can be forwarded on – this gives it a second chance to get in front of the consultant. Lance's letter is less detailed and his CV is attached. Either approach can work – keep track of which provides greater success for you.

Example letter 1.

Jack is an engineer looking for a new challenge:

Jack White, 10 Elm Tree Close, West Town, South Shire WT41 9KL
07931 303366   jackwhite21@hotmail.com

Marie Williamson-Jones
Head of PFI/PPP & Major Projects, SSI Inc.

3 February 2009

Dear Ms. Williamson-Jones

As head of division in one of the foremost search and selection agencies, I am writing to you to ascertain what steps I may take in order to secure a move into a senior level of management within the PFI/PPP arena.

I have listed below the areas of my achievements and experience which I consider are most relevant:

- 37 years of age and currently employed as Principal Engineer in one of the top 5 UK Engineering Consultancies, engineering qualifications to Degree level and a Chartered Engineer, Postgraduate Diploma in Business/Management and Administration (DBA).

My public and private commercial sector experience includes:

- Successfully managed operational budgets of £1.5 million per annum, including substantial human and financial operational resources within complex sites and environments.
- Commercial design and project management of construction engineering schemes up to £11 million, on time and to budget, in commercial/industrial/hospital environments.
- Initiated and implemented key management processes, i.e., QA systems, Intranet implementation and experience in the IT environment.
- Successfully initiated and implemented change management techniques, e.g., restructuring and integrating two engineering departments to achieve a flatter structure, reducing costs and introduce empowerment, and introducing process improvements utilising innovative modern maintenance management techniques.
- Well-developed communication skills, able to liaise effectively with client management, staff, contractors and consultants at all levels. Strong customer focus, results-driven and highly motivated with a proactive and pragmatic approach to developing and managing services and projects to optimise resources, reduce costs and improve customer service.

I will call your office within the next few days to discuss my experience in greater detail.

Yours truly,

Jack White

Example letter 2

Lance wants to gain another project management job:

Lance Lewis
6 Bodwyn Gardens, Cardiff, CF14 2PW
Tel: 07935 444567   E-mail: lewis@yahoo.com

Geraldine Moore
Thompson Butler Associates
Minister Chambers
Church Street
Southwell
Nottingham
NG25 0HD

Dear Ms. Moore,

RE: PROJECT MANAGEMENT OPPORTUNITIES

I would like to be considered for any suitable project management vacancies that you may currently be trying to fill on behalf of a client. Accordingly, I have attached a copy of my CV for your review.

For 16 years, I was involved in substantial project management for BT. This included most recently a successful £7 million project involving the move of 550 BT people with "down-time" kept to an absolute minimum. I am also experienced in the facilities management of a number of diverse sites, including all aspects of security and safety.

I have been a successful team leader and have gained broad experience in contract negotiation, including tender adjudications for contracts up to £5 million. Apart from managing the overall facilities strategy for my unit, I was also responsible for arranging contractual rates for over 100 software contractors from agencies in both UK and India.

Throughout 16 years with BT, I worked successfully with managers at all levels and developed particular strength in the areas of both verbal and written communication. My role as project manager involved me constantly in problem solving to ensure projects were completed to agreed timescales, cost and quality targets.

I look forward to the possibility of discussing suitable opportunities with you and will call you on Thursday afternoon to take this forward.

Yours sincerely,

Lance Lewis

Most agencies and consultants will reply to your application in one of the following ways:

An immediate standard reply if they cannot use you. Your details will probably be kept on file for a few weeks or months and may be used to match against future assignments. But don't count on this.

An early phone call will be made to arrange a meeting to discuss a vacancy. Often such a call will come in the evening.

A delaying letter will be sent stating that due to heavy response to their advertising, they are working through the replies. (They could be considering your application but putting you "on hold" to see what other candidates are like).

Preparation for telephone call

Once the letter has been sent, you should prepare for your follow up telephone call to arrange the appointment. *Chapter Twelve, The Phone Interview,* will provide useful information.

Head hunters

Head hunters have a brief to 'go and find' a suitable candidate for a particular (senior) role. They do not keep a 'bank' of CVs (nor, in fact do many consultancies in recruitment, search and selection) and may not appreciate being bombarded with information. If you know a head hunter who has approached you in the past, it is worth a phone call to advise them of your availability and ask if they have anything which requires your background, skills and experience. If they do not, they may be prepared to network with fellow head hunters on your behalf.

It is unlikely that contacting a head hunter directly will prove fruitful, but if you do choose to use this approach, make sure you choose one that specialises in your specific area. You can find this out by checking *Executive Grapevine* at a business library.

Knocking on doors

With office based jobs, it's less likely you can just turn up, but for manufacturing, retail and trade positions, and companies with high street offices, you could follow the steps below.

1. Print out 30 or more copies of your CV on high quality paper. Fold in half and put each in an A5 envelope.
2. Actually go and visit stores and HR departments of larger stores and business units to physically hand over your CV. Do this in the early part of the day when it's quiet. Avoid trying to make contact if the sales staff are busy with customers.
3. As you go into the store, have a quick look around so you can make meaningful comments.
4. Make sure to dress smartly to create a good impression.
5. Ask to speak to the manager. Tell them how interested you are in the store/industry. Refer to what you already

know about the company and/or what you have noticed as you look around.

6. Hand over your CV.

7. Listen carefully to any cues they may give you. If they say they may be recruiting people in the future, ask if you should get back in touch with them in a couple of weeks.

8. This is a very important method and can't be done just on one day. It requires doing a blitz of different areas in your travel to work radius. This should be done several times a week.

Chapter Twelve

The phone interview

Many companies conduct telephone interviews as the first stage of being short listed. This chapter guides you through the process of preparing for an interview and teaches you how to conduct yourself on the phone.

By the end of this chapter you will:

- Understand why companies use telephone interviewing.
- Be well prepared and ready if you get the call.
- Have completed a trial run with a coach or a friend.

The phone interview

The phone interview can be one of the most difficult interviews to handle. It is used by head hunters, executive search agencies and by the HR department of larger companies.

When I was involved in running large recruitment campaigns, we used phone interviews as a way of sifting through the people who could probably do the job to finding those we definitely wanted to see. This left us with only the best possible candidates to interview. It also gave a good impression of our company as people liked the way we had a rigorous selection process.

We would phone the person in advance to schedule a time for the call. This meant that the interviewer could plan their diary and the applicant could take some time to prepare. They would have been sent details of the job and the competences being assessed, which helped them in their preparation.

Other companies take a different approach. My clients tell me about being put on the spot by a recruiter who rang and expected them to be interview ready without notice. I advise my clients to say it is not convenient, and they have to leave for an appointment in five minutes, but would be very happy to schedule a time for the interview. Doing the same keeps you in control and makes sure you will be in a "peak state" for the phone interview.

> *The advantage of the phone interview is that you can readily refer to a lot of data. The disadvantage is you cannot assess the body language of the interviewer*

Other clients have said that they have rung a number for more information following seeing a job ad that appeals and then found themselves in a phone interview on the spot! You need to be prepared in case this happens to you.

The preparation you can do

As you start applying for jobs, you should expect to get some phone interviews so be prepared. Take time to be prepared mentally so you sound energetic and upbeat. If you live with other people such as family or flat mates, make sure they know what to do should they answer the phone.

Review the questions that you might be asked and prepare your answers. You don't want to sound scripted, but it doesn't hurt to have notes that you can easily refer to. Have your CV, letter, and any details on the job available. If you know when the call will be, you can spread these papers out and have a pen and paper handy. Make sure you don't have too many as you don't want to spend your time looking for the right sheet of paper while someone is waiting for your response. You may like to have details on your skills, abilities and other strengths on separate index cards with examples on the reverse.

For a phone interview, keep in mind there can be noise in you house (chatter, TV, or music), so make sure you have a quiet room to concentrate on the call and you can fully hear a question. Make sure that everyone knows how to properly answer the phone and take messages, and keep paper and pencils close to the telephone.

Your voice is key, so be aware of how you sound. Record yourself talking and listen. Do you sound enthusiastic? Are you articulate? Do you speak clearly? Remember, the person on the other end of the phone won't pick up on your smiles and nods so you need to convey interest with carefully chosen words and appropriate voice inflections.

The call

Like other interviews, the outcome of a phone interview is often determined in the first five minutes.

- When you receive the call, stay on your feet. Most people project themselves much better over the phone when they're standing up. Try it with a friend or family member and see if they notice the difference.
- Avoid distractions. Background noise may irritate both you and the interviewer. Have a quiet room you can go to so that neither you nor the caller is going to be distracted.

- The call usually starts with confirming factual information and then asking more specific questions, often related to key competences and characteristics of the job. Often a CV or application form gives the impression that someone has the experience to do the job, but it doesn't stand up to questioning by the interviewer. Fill in any information the caller may need as they may not have your CV in front of them.

- Smiling can be heard in the voice. It also makes you feel more positive and self confident. You need to sound bright and positive.

- Speak clearly. The telephone artificially speeds up sound, so speak slightly slower than usual. The telephone electronically depresses the sound of your voice, so put some variety into your speech.

Typical questions

The first question you may be asked is "Is it ok if I record your responses?" You will, of course, say yes! If it is being recorded, they may stop and check recording levels so be patient.

You may be asked for a brief overview of your career. Say exactly the same things you would at a face to face interview. This is covered in *Chapter Thirteen, Interview Preparation.* Prepare and practice this until it comes naturally to you.

Some recruitment consultants will use a short psychometric test, often giving you four options and you have to choose the one which is most and least like you. Don't try and second guess what they are looking for. Just come across as a positive version of you!

You may be asked for specific examples against the competences. These are the areas you would prepare for at a face-to-face interview, so get your preparation done ahead of time.

Finally, there may be general questions. These tend to fall into two specific categories:

1. Apparently difficult, such as "Why does one need managers"? They are really looking to see how you tackle a difficult question rather than searching for a specific answer.

2. Apparently easy, such as "How do you spend your normal working day?" This is trickier because they will be looking for specific content in terms of organisational ability and efficient time management.

So how are you feeling now?

It might be helpful to do a practice interview with a friend as this can help take away some of the fear of the phone interview. Often, when we are nervous, we waffle. You want to avoid this and be more logical in how you present your information. And you want to speak clearly so asking a friend to listen to you practice your responses could help your prepare (and thus calm your nerves). My clients are often quite nervous about this, so we do a couple of practice sessions, the first with me being kind and supportive, the second with me being much more direct and matter of fact.

Making and receiving phone calls

When making a call

- Plan what you intend to say. Have a clear plan on paper of whom you are going to telephone, the purpose of your call, and make sure you know something about the company.

- Make sure you will not be disturbed. Tell your family that you need to be left quiet when on the phone.

- Keep a copy of your CV, a notebook and a pencil by the phone.

- Smile as you speak! It does show through (as does a frown).

- Stand as it is much easier to sound enthusiastic when you stand up than when you slouch.
- Speak more slowly and as clearly as you can. Vary the tone of your voice – it will add emphasis and vitality.
- Confirm any details before you hang up. Did you take the date or telephone number down correctly?
- Did you get the caller's name and job title?
- Have an answering service or machine so you don't miss a call. Keep your message clear and professional.
- Write down the points you want to make before you call.
- Be polite to everyone.
- Say clearly who you are and who you want to speak to.

When receiving calls

- Receive all calls in a positive and cheerful way.
- If you are not ready for an unexpected call, say you will call them back, and take time to get yourself in a positive frame of mind.
- Ask the name of the person who has called you before you start to discuss things.
- If someone else answers the phone, ask them to make a note of:
  - o Who has called.
  - o The time they called.
  - o Their phone number.
  - o Any messages.
  - o When you will call them back.

When returning calls

When leaving a voice mail for someone to return your telephone call, try to have the correct pronunciation of their name and make sure you state the following clearly:

- Your name.
- Your telephone number.

- Your message.
- The best time to reach you.
- Your name again.
- Your telephone number again.

Then hang up gently.

You are likely to get voice messages, so personalise your mobile phone message so people know they have got through to you. Make sure your message is polite, direct, and businesslike and can be understood clearly.

"Hello, this is (phone number). I am sorry I am not available to take your call right now.

Please leave your name, telephone number, a brief message, and the best time to reach you. I will get back to you as soon as possible."

Chapter Thirteen

Interview preparation

1. Introduction

Your CV can get you shortlisted, but you need to be able to perform well at interview to get the job.

There are different styles of interviewing and different approaches taken. Although you expect the person interviewing you will be a well-trained professional, be aware that many of those interviewing job applicants have little or no training. As you prepare for your interview, be prepared for both.

Alongside my career coaching practice, I still undertake recruitment assignments as I want to be up to date on changes in how companies interview. Plus, I want to be able to offer the best possible advice to the clients I work with.

It's best to undertake a practice interview with a skilled interviewer. But you can still develop your skills through having a friend coach you through an interview, and by recording it you can watch or listen to it again and further develop your skills.

What is an interview?

Never forget the interview is a two way process. It's not just the company wanting to be clear about whether you can do the job, what differentiates you from others, how long it will take you to master the job, if you'll display initiative, or fit in with other employees. It's a chance for you to make sure it's the right job for you and whether you would want to work for this company.

Different types of interviews

When Peter said "I've been asked for an interview," I replied, "What sort?" After asking him a couple of questions, I identified his interview as an initial meeting with a recruitment consultant. Peter hadn't appreciated the need for formality and that it was going to be much more than a chat. He needed to prepare himself well, to the same extent as if he were going for an interview with a company. Interviews can be with one person or a panel and the style can be unstructured or competency based.

A screening interview is usually with a recruitment consultant and is often a short interview to establish whether your previous experience and competence appears to fit their requirements. You need to provide good, clear, factual answers.

Sometimes a panel of managers will interview you. This could be two or three or as many as ten. Answer the questioner and also look at others from time to time, noting any reactions. See if you can identify who holds the power and who may have the casting vote.

Some interviewers have no clear plan. They assess a prospective employee by means of a gut reaction and ask questions based on that. You need to be prepared for off the wall questions and learn how to anticipate upcoming questions so you can clearly make your points no matter how much a question might throw you off balance.

On rare occasions, you may be placed in a stress interview. Tough, even offensive questions may be asked. Interviewers may criticise or question your judgement, integrity, or continually interrupt you. Try to keep your nerve. Taking some deep breaths can help keep you calm. If the organisation interviewing you uses this technique, you may want to consider if it's the right organisation for you.

Kim spoke to me about the experience she had with one interviewer. Having met the HR manager, she went into the interviewer with her potential line manager who asked questions such as:

"Do you actually need to work?" Would he ask this question of a man?

"There are partners here that I wouldn't walk within a five mile radius of. " This was his comment when I said I wanted to work for a professional firm.

"Whilst your CV looks good there are some bad points. For example, you've had a lot of jobs and how do I know that you won't leave after the housing market picks up?"

He had not read my CV properly. I informed him that I had only worked for two employers and that I had different roles working for those employers and so on and so on.

After the awful interview he said, "Well, I have finished beating you up now" and handed me back to the personnel manager who apologised for his interview style saying that they had a number of staff leave after a short time! No wonder!

Competency based interviewing

This type of interview is becoming more and more common and you need to be prepared to give specific answers to specific questions. The interviewer is likely to have a set list of questions that will be asked of all candidates. Some interviewers will ask further questions if you haven't provided sufficient detail but others will not give you the chance to respond a second time.

This style of interview puts less emphasis on first impressions and more weight on the specific examples you provide. It's format is based on the premise that the best guide to future behaviour is past behaviour. It is a reasonably effective method of predicting future job performance, although it assumes that all candidates have the specific experiences required.

The interviewer is likely to seek examples against problem solving, communication, motivation, interpersonal skills, adaptability, etc., so think through examples. Typical questions include:

- Can you recall a situation where you had to demonstrate your skills in problem solving? What was the problem and how did you tackle it?
- We all need to communicate clearly. Please give me an example when you have needed to do this.
- Please give me an example of when you have had to quickly build relationships with others.

Using the STAR approach in interviews

Most questions centre on your past or current attitudes, and your work, academic, or service experiences. When talking about these subjects, choose specific examples to illustrate your answers. Describe the **S**ituation you were in, the **T**ask you were asked to accomplish, the **A**ctions you took and why, and the **R**esults of your actions. This will help the interviewer follow your "story" and see your accomplishments.

Here's an example of a response that uses this method to address an employer's question.

SITUATION: I didn't handle the transition to university well and failed my first year exams.

TASK: I knew that if I wanted to succeed, I had to develop better study habits and manage my time better.

ACTION: I created a calendar and marked the due dates for all of my assignments and tests. Then I set aside certain hours each day for studying, allowing more for exam times.

RESULT: My essays were in on time, and I took notes regularly to make things easier for exams. Because I was separating study time from social time, I would work hard and then relax, which has helped my time management.

Some companies will expect you to take part in a number of interviews. At a second interview, whilst the company will be interested in what you have done, there will be much more focus on what you can offer the company. You must show warmth, energy, commitment and competence. You will be expected to have a quick grasp of the issues and talk with confidence.

Interview preparation

General preparation

Start your preparation now. You don't need to wait until you get the interview. It helps to be well prepared as you could get a call for an interview at any time. And a call from a recruiter to "come in for a chat," needs as careful preparation as a selection interview with the "Ideal Company."

There are seven main areas of preparation:

1. Your response to the question – "tell me about yourself?"

2. Understanding your strengths.

3. Talking to your referees.

4. Researching the company.

5. Being up to date on the industry you are applying to.

6. Finding out who will be interviewing you.

7. If you have a medical condition, deciding how to respond to questions.

You can then prepare for the main interview questions.

1: Your response to the question – "tell me about yourself"

The first question is often "tell me a bit about yourself" or "talk me through your career to date." Too many candidates give a rambling life story, whereas a quick summary of key points is more appropriate.

You need to be able to provide a succinct and concise summary of you, your experience and achievements in less than three minutes. Take time to make it clear, concise and interesting. Here's a common structure:

The 2-3 minute profile

Step 1:

You need to prepare an introductory sentence to get the listener used to the tone of your voice.

"As you are aware ..."

"Thanks for giving me the opportunity of an interview ..."

Step 2:

Provide a short summary of yourself and your achievements. This may differ depending on the particular job you are applying for.

Step 3:

This is where you provide a brief chronology of your previous employment, concentrating on achievements and skills gained. You should spend most time on your most recent career and your key achievements and less on the past. Focus on the key aspects of the job you are applying for.

Step 4:

Conclude with a strong statement emphasising your abilities, and a question such as:

"Would you like me to elaborate on any part of this?"

Practice until it comes natural. On no account read from notes at interview.

2: Understanding your strengths

You must know the top five reasons why you will be a great candidate. Think of what you have achieved and re-read the achievement bullets you have on your CV.

Write out a question you could ask at interview which would allow you to use a particular achievement as an illustration. Do this for each of your achievements so you can use it to ask a question. For example,

"Is there a need to simplify processes? I'm asking as when I was in my last job I introduced processing mapping which resulted in savings of time and increased effectiveness."

Review your career so you can highlight less obvious strengths that are relevant to this situation. You want to provide examples of why you will be perfect for the job. You are likely to be asked if you are well organised, so be prepared with a particular response such as how you switched 200 people from one hotel to another in 30 minutes.

3: Talk to your referees

You will need to supply references. If you were dismissed from your last job, check what your last employer will say in answer to enquiries about the reason for job termination. If necessary, negotiate an agreed statement. Many interviewees say one thing and their last employer another. Make sure what you both say is congruent. Don't forget to keep them updated on the jobs you are applying for.

4: Research the company

Too many candidates fail to research the company they are applying for. One of the best ways to research a company is via their web site and a Google search. You will gain a competitive edge if you can demonstrate your knowledge of the industry you are applying for, not just knowledge of the role you have applied for.

5: Be up to date on the industry you are applying to

A common question on which many candidates stumble is: "Where do you think your industry is heading?" Particularly in management and professional positions, you need to be able to show that you keep abreast with your discipline and follow current changes in the industry. Have a well thought out response to this question. Make it a habit to read professional magazines and the business pages of newspapers.

6: Find out who will be interviewing you

This will help you find out if it is to be a one to one interview or a panel interview. You can then look people up on the company web site and also Google them to see about their particular interests.

7: If you have a medical condition, decide how to respond to questions

If you have a medical condition, consider and practise how you would respond to questions about your health. You might reply, for example, that you are perfectly happy to undergo a medical examination by the company's medical officer.

Getting ready to answer questions

Interview questions are likely to cover your work experience, training, education and you as an individual to determine how closely you match the specification and whether you will fit into the organisational culture. You may also be asked about your outside interests and present circumstances.

If you want the job, you will want to prepare yourself so you can solve the interviewer's problem – finding the right person for the job. You need to concentrate on meeting their expectations, overcoming their objections, and demonstrating that you have the attributes, skills, experience and characteristics they seek. Make sure you can explain any gaps in your CV or answer any questions about the information on your CV.

Although you can't predict what questions you will be asked, certain questions come up quite frequently. These are listed below, with guidance on how to answer them.

Questions

Tell me about yourself?

(We covered this on page 278.)

Why have you applied for this job? or Why do you want to work here?

The obvious answer is they have a vacancy and you want a job, but this isn't what an employer wants to here. They want you to show enthusiasm and conviction. You need to explain how well you match up to the job. Emphasise what you can contribute, rather than how the job will benefit you.

Your response will be based on what you have learned about the company so show that you have fully researched the company. Explain what you have found and why it interests you. Perhaps you could refer to the company's reputation and that being a part of their work environment would help to bring out your best.

A really strong answer would be:

"Based on the research I've done, this company is a market leader. I was very impressed by the information I read on the web site about how you have gained a large contract and are also doing voluntary work with a local school. And I like the way that the company gives something back. I was also impressed by the history of the company and how people work together on voluntary activities. This is exactly the sort of company I've been looking for. One that seeks highly motivated people who are keen to work well with others and help the company become even more successful."

What do you know about us?

This question is very common. Employers want applicants who have had the initiative, courtesy and enthusiasm to find out something about the organisation. What you know is not as important as that you know something! You can, for example, refer to the annual report and notice that the company is moving into Europe and ask about the implications of such a move.

They could also ask you some more specific questions:

What does our organisation do?

What do you think of our web site?

Who do you think are our major competitors?

What or who do you think is the main threat to our business?

What do you think of our product/service?

What do you think are the main issues for our business over the next few years?

Why does this job interest you? Or why should we offer you this job?

You must talk about what you can offer the company, not the benefits you are seeking.

In advance, think through why you want the job and what you can offer the company. This makes you much stronger at interview as you are talking from the heart rather than just giving the interviewer what you think they want to hear.

Why do you want to be a ... mechanical engineer/chemist/ store assistant manager, etc?

Every profession has a unique element so you should tailor your response to what is key about a role. As an example, for a nurse, it could be helping people, for sales, it could be competition and financial reward.

What are your strengths?

Tailor your answer to the interviewer's ideal candidate. For example, if you are applying for a sales position, you might describe one of your strengths (if it's true) as "I've made a study of personality types and I've learned to quickly classify people in terms of the kinds of approaches that will most likely secure a sale." Be prepared, in this case, to back up your claim if the interviewer suddenly asks: "How would you classify me?"

What is your biggest weakness?

This question can sometimes be asked as "How would your colleagues answer if we asked them about your faults?"

This question is being asked to see if you are arrogant. It would be best not to say "I really don't think I have any weaknesses" but rather describe one and how you are working to overcome it.

"I knew as a psychologist, my business knowledge was weak, so I took some business management qualification to bridge the gap."

Or how you turn a negative into a positive:

"My biggest weakness is that sometimes I work too hard, my life can get out of balance"

"My colleagues have told me that I can be too focused on my work and I have to remind myself to lighten up."

Don't be tempted to offer a real weakness, nor to be funny such as saying "fast cars and loose women."

What would your last boss say were the areas you needed to improve?

This is a variation on you having to identify your development needs. You could talk about one or two and what you have done about them. For example, "My boss identified my lack of broader business knowledge, so I am opting to take a management diploma and shadow people in other parts of the organisation."

Why should I hire you over the other people I have interviewed?

The interviewer expects you to be confident in answering this question so be assertive and proud of your efforts. Say something like:

"With my four years experience in the financial sector and a track record of simplifying processes and thus saving time and money, I believe I would be a great addition to your team."

This gives insight into how a person thinks. They want you to show you have put thought into this **decision and looked into the future.**

"I chose marketing because I enjoy working with others and I am motivated by success. Marketing allows me to capitalise on my unique blend of creativity, hard work and ability to learn."

Be able to answer questions about your education such as:

Why did you choose your degree subject? (Often asked of a recent graduate)

You do not want to say it was because it was the only degree offered to you via clearing, or that your parents thought it was a good idea. Give particular reasons and do so confidently.

What are your interests?

Make sure your interests are in line with the job. Some suggest to take a look around the room. If you see pictures of golf players and a golf ball paperweight, you could mention being passionate about golf. But don't lie – if you don't play golf, don't say you do. It's best to think in advance and have a balance of team and individual pursuits and perhaps showing leadership in a voluntary organisation.

What are your short and long-term goals?

This should be inline with the job you are applying for. If you want to be a solicitor, a job as a legal executive is a step along the way. But if you want to be a doctor, why are you applying for a job as a sales executive? You could say:

"My short term goal is to join a company where I will be challenged and have room to grow. One of my longer term goals is to grow with the company and move into management."

"Can you give me an example of team work and leadership?"

Give an example of working effectively in a team and also a time when you took the lead. But don't let people think that you can only work with others. Give an example of working effectively alone as well.

Do you prefer working on your own or in a team?

If you know this is a team or individual job you can base your answer on that. It's probably best not to show a preference but to say that you enjoy both.

What was your greatest challenge and how did you overcome it?

Have an example ready which moved you outside your normal comfort zone or into a new area, but keep it focused on the job!

Why are you looking to leave your current job? Or why are you contemplating leaving your company?

You must have a reason. For example, you could say "I'm at a stage in my career where I want a job that is more challenging and rewarding." Or you could say that the company you are working for is not stable or the journey to work is too long. You could say you are seeking a greater challenge or a better chance of promotion. Never be critical about your current company nor say your leaving is due to difficult people. They may wonder what it is about you that is difficult. So think about an answer that is close to the truth and will be acceptable.

In a recession, companies expect some of their applicants to be unemployed but you can make this sound a bit more upbeat such as: "I managed to survive two rounds of redundancy, but by the third round, an additional 20% of people were let go, including me."

What major problems did you encounter in your last job?

Whatever you say, make sure the problem was overcome.

You don't have any experience of marketing, do you?

If it was a problem you wouldn't have been short-listed. So don't say "No, I don't." Instead, talk about how you want to broaden your experience, how you are adaptable and quick to learn, etc.

Why did you stay so long with one company?

They were a good company and you were continuing to develop yourself.

You seem to have done a lot of job hopping. Why?

You had to move to other companies to progress your career but you would much prefer to develop it in one company.

We were looking for someone a little younger? Do you think this will be a problem?

Again, if this was a problem you wouldn't have been short listed. They want to find out if you see age as a problem. Say how fit and healthy you are and how well you get on with people younger than yourself.

If you could choose any job what would it be? or What is your ideal job?

Do not start discussing your fantasies. The job you have always wanted is the one you have applied for.

What would you describe as your greatest achievement?

Be prepared to give an achievement that is relevant to the job you are applying for.

Are you ambitious?

You don't want to be content to stand still, but you don't want to be seen as climbing over everyone to get to the top. You could say that you are ambitious to do well, but job satisfaction is key.

Are you applying for other jobs?

Let them know you are in discussions with other companies. They will be reassured that other companies are interested in you.

What was the main weakness of your last boss?

Do not be tempted to say anything detrimental. People expect loyalty: "I have the highest respect for my manager. He has supported and challenged me so I am now in a position to apply for a greater challenge."

Would you be prepared to relocate?

You need to have thought this through in advance so you can answer honestly.

How would you describe your management style?

If you are a manager or supervisor, this should be easy for you. Think this area through in advance of the interview.

How do you prioritise when you are given too many tasks to accomplish?

This question is asking about the way you plan and prioritise your time. Whilst you want to be seen as someone who is flexible, you will also want to show how you will manage your time by differentiating between what is important and urgent.

What salary are you seeking?

You want to keep this vague so you can move into the negotiation phase when you are offered the job. However, part of your initial research should be to understand the typical range for the job you are applying for. You could put the question back to them.

- *"How much does the job pay?"*
- *"I'm sure we can come to some agreement where my skills and experience are fairly paid.*
- *This company pays a fair salary, doesn't it?"*

If they ask:

What would be your reaction if we offered you the job but at £x p.a (less than you hoped for).

You need to be realistic on your options, and weigh a drop in salary with having a regular income. It may be best to say that you would be very willing to discuss this once they are sure that you are the best person for the job.

Give me an example of when your work has been criticised. How did you respond?

Make sure you describe an idea that was criticised, not your work. As examples: you suggested a new approach to your boss who told you exactly what was wrong with the idea. You listened carefully and realised he had some valid points. You went away, reviewed your work and came back with a revised suggestion which was better received.

What do you see as having been your greatest strengths as an employee? What have been your best achievements?

You already know your strengths, so refer to those, making sure they link in with what the new employer will want.

What would be the area you feel least confident about if we offered you a job?

You are being tested on your self confidence. Expand on your strengths and what you can bring to the company and how you are looking forward to this new role.

How would your colleagues answer if we asked them about your faults?

This is another way of getting you to describe your weaknesses. See earlier question.

How would your last boss describe you?

This is another question to allow you to describe your strengths. So think of something specific such as "my boss told me I was a great team player, willing to get involved and someone the team could rely on."

What are your strengths and weaknesses?

You might like to present your strengths modestly with phrases such as, "At my last appraisal my manager commented that..." or "I was asking a client for some feedback the other day and they were kind enough to say..."

You can also present your weaknesses positively. For example, "I can get impatient with people who put up obstacles so I've learned to listen more carefully," or "I've found they often have a valid point, they just haven't expressed it well." It's often better to provide an example from the past so that you describe the weakness (such as finding it difficult to delegate in a first management role) and then how you overcame it.

How would you describe your health? How many days sick leave have you had in the last two years?

Do not be tempted to lie, they can check this with your last employer. If it has been due to a serious illness, explain how you are now fully recovered and have not had a day off sick since xxx.

Would you accept this job if I offered it to you?

Of course! Answer yes without hesitation. You can save the negotiations for later.

Are you considering other jobs at this time?

Just say yes, and leave it at that.

How does this opportunity compare?

From what I've heard so far, it compares favourably and I'd like to know more.

What other companies are you looking at?

Appreciate the need for confidentiality in this area.

Where do you see yourself in five years time?

The company wants to know that you plan to stay for a while so stress your strengths and how you can use them in this job. Express that as long as you can develop and grow, you see yourself staying for quite some time.

Aren't you over qualified for this position?

Tell them they you see lots of challenges in this opportunity and that you will find the work interesting. Remind them of why you have applied for the job.

A practice interview

Since you know the questions you are going to be asked, practicing these questions will help. But also be ready for some quite esoteric questions! I continue to be amazed at some of the questions my clients have been asked. Weird questions include "If you were an animal, what sort would you be?" What are they after and how should you respond? A panda might be considered too soft, a lion too aggressive, a snake … I think I'd like to be a cheetah!

Are there any questions you are afraid of being asked? You need to write these down and practice them!

To make it easy, visit the web site and download the mock interview handout. You can then hand this over to someone who takes on the role of interviewer. Ideally, record it so you can play it back. I know it's awful for most of us to watch ourselves, but it does enable us to pick up on some of our annoying habits.

Action: Download the mock interview handout from the web site: www.howtogetajobinarecession.com.

Rehearse but don't memorise

Rehearsing before an interview is an appropriate way to prepare yourself for the questions you'll be asked. Think ahead, anticipate the questions and write a winning answer. Rehearse your answers and time them. Never talk for more than two minutes straight and don't try to memorise answers word for word. You may come across as stiff and unable to function off the cuff. To help remember the answers, you could use a few key words as mnemonics.

Appearance

You never get a second chance to make a first impression.

You only have one opportunity to make a good first impression! So take care with your appearance and dress.

How you dress reveals a great deal about your self-image, your values and your attitudes. So wear clothes appropriate to the occupation, organisation and occasion. What might be acceptable in one organisation may not be suitable in another. People only notice when you don't look the part or when your dress or appearance distracts them. Remember that if you look and feel good your confidence will be enhanced, and that will transmit to your interviewer!

We are a very appearance-driven culture. If you can find out in advance how people within the organisation typically dress, you can put together the right look. Try on your interview outfit and think about how accessories, your hair, and general physical grooming will contribute to the effect. Work on this as carefully as you worked on your CV.

First impressions

People make judgements based on how we look. Which would you choose: a pilot who wears jeans and a stained T-shirt or a pilot in a well pressed uniform?

To be well-dressed, you must wear clothes that complement you physically and are appropriate for the occasion. For some jobs it will help to be stylishly dressed.

Your choice of clothing should help you achieve an image that will reflect your personality, career path and position. The most important thing is to be comfortable. If you have put on some weight, don't squeeze into a too tight suit, you will spend more time focusing on how it cuts into your waist than on listening to the interviewer.

Make sure your clothes are clean and well pressed. I once interviewed someone who looked like he was in his gardening clothes. Whilst I tried not to let it affect my judgement, I did notice it. Have a careful look at your clothes to make sure there aren't any loose threads or buttons. Experts suggest that wearing darker clothes can look more business like, but if you know that a certain colour suits you, then wear it, particularly if you are female. If you have a new outfit, wear it beforehand to check that it is comfortable and wash any shirts to avoid the risk of irritation.

Be smart. Wear clothes to suit the company culture. An open neck shirt and chinos may be OK for some companies, but if in doubt, opt for a suit. It is unlikely that you will ever look too smart, although if you are going for a job as a carpenter, for example, you will be better in smart casual dress than over the top smart.

Keep jewellery to a minimum. By all means wear your wedding ring and engagement ring, but don't wear too many rings. For men, a wedding ring or signet ring is enough. Earrings are fine but remove any other piercing unless you are confident it's acceptable. Make sure your wristwatch is in keeping with your overall appearance and your watch face and strap are clean.

Avoid wearing too much perfume or aftershave. This is not a date! While you may think you smell wonderful, your particular fragrance may be overpowering to the interviewer.

Take care if you eat or drink anything en route. You don't want to arrive with a stain on your clothes.

Do make sure your shoes are clean, polished and in good repair. No scuffed toes, or shoes that need reheeling.

Do make sure your hands and nails are clean. If you have chipped nail polish or bite your nails, remove the polish.

Socks, tights and hankies. Women need to take a spare pair of tights in case they get snagged or laddered; men need to think about the socks they wear. Do they stay up? Lots of white leg can be distracting. Make sure you have a handkerchief or some tissues in case you sneeze or if you spill your drink, you can use your handkerchief to mop up the mess.

Glasses. Make sure your glasses are clean, and free of dust and grease. Take your contacts and lens solution or your spare glasses.

Hair. Make sure your hair doesn't flop into your eyes or over your face. If you have dyed hair, make sure your roots don't show. Also, take a hairbrush or comb to avoid the windswept look.

Wear discreet make-up. Do not over apply lipstick, blusher, eye make-up or powder.

If you smoke, or live with someone who does, make sure your clothes don't smell of smoke. Give them a good airing. If you must smoke beforehand, make sure you have some mints with you. The odour of cigarette smoke is offensive to most non-smokers.

Importance of body language

I can't stress strongly enough the importance of body language during an interview. Whether you do it consciously or subconsciously, your body language plays a big part in the relationship building process. Here are some tips to help you improve your body language during your next interview.

Eye contact

Have you ever spoken with someone who won't look you directly in the eyes? You probably won't feel a connection with the person and might wonder if they're even interested in speaking with you. You need to maintain good eye contact and look people in the eye in a friendly manner. It's OK to look away for a few seconds, especially when you may need to think about a response to a tough question. However, only look away for a few seconds then return your focus to the interviewer. If you feel uncomfortable holding eye contact with people, look at their forehead, just above their nose.

Posture

Slouching down in your chair suggests laziness, lack of interest, and a lack of confidence. Being too rigid and tense will convey inflexibility and nervousness. Be comfortable. Keep your shoulders up and back. Put both of your feet on the floor. It's all right to lean slightly towards the interviewer.

Don't lean on the interviewers' desk. You're invading that person's personal space, and by making them uncomfortable, it won't help you create a good impression. Be careful not to create defensive barriers between yourself and your interviewer(s). Don't leave your briefcase on your knees, or keep your arms folded or your legs crossed. It may feel natural to you, but it does create a defensive barrier between you and your interviewer(s).

Gestures

Gestures, such as use of hands, eyebrows, etc., can enhance your message if they are not over done. Raising your eyebrows at something interesting or exciting and using your hands to express a point and relay a story, all add to your presentation. However, if these things are overdone, they will distract others and take away from your message.

Don't fidget. Be aware of any nervous habits that you have. Don't tap the desk, play with your hair, bite your fingernails or touch your face constantly. These will be noticed by the interviewer, will serve as distractions, and are indications of a low level of confidence.

The more natural you can appear, the better chance you have of creating a good impression. Don't stress about all of the things that you're supposed to be doing or not doing. Practice before you go into the interview so that you aren't focusing on your physical mannerisms and missing out on what you're being asked. If you have the equipment, record a video of your practice interview you can see how you come across.

Developing rapport

Notice the tone of voice the interviewer uses. If they are very business like, do not be overly cheerful, but if they have a friendly tone, be cheerful and enthusiastic.

Match the pitch, rate and volume of the interviewer. If they speak slowly and softly, with a low pitch, don't talk in a loud and rapid manner as you will overwhelm them.

Problem interviewers

No matter how well you prepare, you may still meet with problem interviewers, so here's some suggestions for how to deal with such an interviewer:

The interviewer asks only closed questions

Closed questions demand a yes or no answer. For example, "Do you have experience with Excel? It's a closed question so treat it like an open one and if the answer is yes give some further details. If the answer is no, you could follow up with how you are quick to learn or describe something similar that you have learned.

The interviewer monopolises the interview

Try not to encourage the interviewer by your non-verbal language or supportive comments. When the interviewer draws breath, you might say firmly, "I'd like to respond to what you've been saying" and keep going. Without being discourteous, you can also sometimes tactfully ignore the cues that the interviewer wants to speak again.

You are faced with a very inexperienced interviewer

There are few good interviewers. Most of those you meet will not have been trained. Do not become irked if the interviewer has no plan, but use your own preparation to help the interviewer out. If questions seem unclear or complex, try to handle the points one at a time. Sometimes you can answer one question, suggesting another one at the same time. For example, `Yes, I made considerable savings at XYZ CO and that paved the way for my remarkable turnaround at ABC plc.

If the interviewer runs out of questions, keep the dialogue going by introducing new material. Two useful responses for this are:

When talking about my experience at ...was it clear that...

When I was describing what I did at ... I should have added...

Another way to help out a nervous or muddled interviewer is to think what an ideal candidate would say to an anxious interviewer. This can help you to reframe the situation, focusing on what is important – the job, the criteria, responsibilities, etc. Referring the person to your CV can also help recapture relevance and direction. At the end of the day, you will want to reassure the interviewer that you are the frontrunner for the job.

Dirty Tricks

You may occasionally meet an interviewer who delights in making you feel uncomfortable. They will do things such as:

- Ask you to sit in the glare of the sun. Ask if you can reposition yourself so you are not affected by it, or ask if the blind or curtain can be closed.

- Ask you to sit on a chair that is much lower than the interviewer's chair. You just have to accept this and not allow it to make you feel uncomfortable.
- Give you a choice of chairs, take whichever seems the most comfortable and convenient.
- Ask you to take the other chair, just do it!
- Ask you what magazines were outside, or how many chairs were in the waiting room, just answer as best you can, or admit to not noticing.
- Ask you to shock the interviewer. I've read of extreme examples such as throwing a chair out of a window, but I can't think of many people who would be comfortable doing that!

Try not to be discomfited or intimidated by these strategies. Do your best at interview and use the style and content of the interview to assess the organisation. And stay focused!

Think yourself to success at interview

It's important to practice interview questions and sort out your interview clothes. But it's just as important to take the time to develop a positive attitude toward your interview.

Does your inner voice say things like, "I probably won't get this, other people will be more qualified than me, I hate group discussions, find it hard to make an impact ..."

These sort of thoughts are likely to raise your anxiety level. You may find it better if you tell yourself:

- This is going to be a really interesting interview.
- I'm looking forward to talking about my experience with XYZ.
- I want to learn more about the company.
- I will be fine regardless if I get the job or not.

This will help you be calmer and enable you to focus on your strengths. It can be easy for negative thoughts to come into your head during the interview:

- I'm too old/too young for the job.
- I rambled through that answer.
- What if I don't get the job?

But this distracts you from doing your best, so as these thoughts come into your head, ignore them! Take deep breaths and stay calm.

Do a mental rehearsal, remembering the last successful interview you had. What did it feel like, what did you see? Capture only the positive feelings as it will help you to feel more confident if you carry your positive attitude to interview. (NLP practitioners will anchor this by getting you to squeeze two fingers together as you remember these positive thoughts and feelings. Then in the interview, squeezing these two fingers again will recapture those positive thoughts and feelings).

Be confident and expect to do your best. Remind yourself of times you have done really well in the past

It will help to have a list of your strengths and positive qualities. Read the list to remind you of your greatest qualities and accomplishments. Read this just before you go into the interview, then put your notes carefully away.

Dealing with the stress of the interview

Interviews can be stressful. Most of us are only interviewed infrequently and can become worried and concerned about a forthcoming interview. Careful preparation will help, as will putting the interview into perspective. The worst that can happen is that you don't get the job, but you will have gained more experience. If you are out of work and money is tight, you may feel as if your life depends on getting the job. But there is a danger in coming across as desperate. It helps to do some practice interviews with an experienced interviewer who can give you feedback. If that's not possible, ask someone to ask you interview questions.

If you think you will be stressed at interview, look at ways to calm yourself down. One of the best ways is to regulate your breathing. Breathe in through your nostrils and exhale quietly through your mouth. This helps you to relax. Practice such breathing in advance of the interview situation.

As you wait for the interview, if you notice yourself clenching your hands, feeling tense in your stomach or if your hands are feeling sweaty, stop focussing in the present and remind yourself about a pleasant memory to help you relax.

Handling the salary question

We have already looked at how to respond to this in your application, but it can also come up at interview. Let's look at some of the questions you could be asked:

"How much are you earning in your current position?"

This is usually asked to cap your salary ambitions. Ask to learn more about the position before you get into detailed salary discussions. If asked a second time, have ready your research into the salary of the offered position and similar positions. If your current position either doesn't provide a meaningful comparison or is comparatively low, then briefly spell out the reasons why this figure should not guide current discussions.

"What are your salary requirements?"

Summarise the requirements of the position as you understand them and then ask the interviewer for the normal salary range in his/her company for that type of position.

"What are your salary expectations?"

You can ask what the normal salary range for this position is (assuming you haven't already uncovered this information). If asked again, distinguish yourself from the masses by stating, "I am much more interested in doing (type of work) for (organisation's name) than I am in the size of the initial offer." If asked yet again, a final response can be "I will consider any reasonable offer."

"How much did you earn on your last job?"

Tell the interviewer that you would prefer learning more about the current position before you discuss compensation, and that you are confident you will be able to reach a mutual agreement about salary at that time.

"The salary range for this position is £22,000 to £27,000, is that what you were expecting?"

Tell the interviewer that it does come near what you were expecting, and then offer a range which places the top of the employer's range into the bottom of your range (i.e., I was thinking in terms of £27,000 to £32,000). Remember, be sure that the range you suggest is consistent with what you learned about the market rate for that position.

"The salary is £2000 per month."

Try not to look excited or disappointed. Simply repeat the salary, look up as though you were thinking about it, and pause. Don't worry about the silence. Give the employer an opportunity to increase the offer. If the interviewer does not change the offer, try the response suggested above.

Over to you ... questions to ask at the end of the interview

At the end of the interview, you will be asked if you have any questions. So many of the people I interview mumble about everything having been covered. It makes for a weak ending. The best candidates open their briefcase and pull out a pad with a few questions listed and choose three or four to ask, such as:

"Can you tell me more about the company?"

You should already know quite a bit from your research, so better to ask something specific, again demonstrating what you have found out such as services, employees, financial position or other aspects.

"Since the job was advertised, have your requirements been amended?"

This is a good question to help you to sell yourself by solving some of their newly defined problems.

"How does this job contribute to the success, efficiency and profitability of the organisation?"

An excellent question, showing strategic thought. In some jobs though, the interviewer may not know the answer so beware of appearing too smart!

"Before leaving today, would I be able to look around?"

It shows enthusiasm and even if they say no, nothing has been lost.

"If I were to join the company, where might you see me in 3-5 years time?"

They are likely to have asked you where you see yourself, so find out if they see the job as part of a career path. You can follow this up as appropriate.

"What would you see as my priorities in this job?"

This helps you to find out if there are any major problems. You may also find out there is a specific task that you can do easily, and give examples from your past.

"If I was to be offered the job, what preparation could I do?"

This demonstrates your enthusiasm, interest and helps them to visualise you in the role.

"I am very interested in this job and believe I can do it well; what concerns do you have about me as a candidate?"

The interviewer may not like to commit themselves, but if they do, offer reassurance. For example, if they were to say, "we were looking for someone older," you can emphasise the wide experience you have gained and give examples of your ability to relate to older people.

"Imagine that I excel in this position. Is there room for progression?"

Better to ask now then to find out later there are no real prospects. But things can change. Years ago, when I applied for a job as a Post Office counter clerk, I was told there would be no opportunities to promotion, but a move to a regional centre resulted in less than a year, getting a junior management position.

"I'm really impressed with your company, its products / services and everyone that I have had the opportunity to meet. I'm confident I could do a great job in the position we've discussed. When can I expect to hear back from you?"

Try to get a specific time period to enable you to follow up if you haven't heard anything.

A perfect close

Make sure you deliver a one-minute closing statement. It must be short and to the point and 60 seconds is the absolute maximum. You must know the top five reasons why you will be a great candidate and be able to weave these into the discussion. This is your chance to summarise your qualifications for the position, your top skills, experience, and accomplishments so the interviewer is really clear on why they should hire you.

Thank the interviewer, and be sure to ask about the next step or stage. Failure to do this may leave the interviewer in some doubt as to whether you wish to proceed.

If you realise that the job isn't a great fit, make sure you still leave a good impression. You may be considered for another vacancy.

Make sure you say goodbye to the receptionist / secretary as you leave.

Chapter Fourteen

The interview - you're shortlisted!

Introduction

When you get the letter asking you to attend an interview, it may tell you:

- The nature of the interview.
- Whether there will be any psychometric tests.
- Who will interview you, with name and position.
- If you will be given a tour of the company.
- Who you will meet.

If you don't get this information, ring and request it.

Larger organisations will often send an information pack with an invitation to interview. This should contain the annual report, job description, company details and a map. It may also contain details of the conditions of employment. Be proactive and ask for it if it isn't sent. The job description is important to allow you to be well prepared – make sure you receive it.

Confirm the interview place, time, day and date:

- In case of a mistake.
- As a courtesy.
- As another opportunity to record a good impression.

If you have any special needs or disabilities, forewarn the organisation.

Your suitability for the job

Make sure you do some initial research to help with your application form – both about the company and your suitability to do the job. Re-read the advertisement, application form and letters and assess what you have to offer – your relevant strengths, experience and skills. Memorise five or six key points. You can't assume that the interviewers have read everything in detail so be ready to provide important information that is overlooked.

Your preparation should include a thorough analysis of your motives and interest in the specific job. Taking into account what you know about the job role, think through your responses to the following questions:

- What qualifications do I have, what jobs or assignments have I done, and what achievements do I have which fit with what I know of the position?
- What other unique selling points do I have in relation to this appointment?
- What are the areas where I do not seem to fit the job description and where I might be questioned?
- How will I deal with these questions?
- Will this be the right job for me?

- Why am I interested in this position?
- Why am I interested in this organisation?

Your knowledge of the company

Many interviewers will ask the question, "What do you know about us?" Employers want applicants who have had the initiative, courtesy and enthusiasm to find out something about their organisation. It matters less what specific information you found, than you took the time to research the company. The more senior the position you seek, the more important the research becomes.

Typical areas to research include:

- The organisation's recent history, competitors and market performance.
- Any developments at industry levels, which may have affected the company.
- Range of products, goods or services.
- Markets and market shares at home and overseas.
- Business purpose and aims (mission statement).
- Future strategy.
- Stated or inferred opportunities, problems or developments the company is facing.

You can find out more from the company website, business sites such as www.ft.com, and through a search for the company name through Google or similar search engine. Read what is being said in the business press and study public views on open sites.

You will gain a competitive edge if you can demonstrate your knowledge of the industry you are applying for, not just knowledge of the role you have applied for.

Key guidance for the interview

Preparation – final check. I need to …

- Obtain a copy of the job description and person spec.
- Research the company web site and read up as much as you can on the company and the person/people who will be interviewing while considering their current and future business issues.
- Find out the names and position(s) of the interviewer(s).
- Re-read the job advertisement.
- Review your CV and career history and be ready to answer questions and go into more detail on any topic.
- Practice interview questions.
- Prepare questions to ask (it's fine to have them written down).
- Produce a concise statement to explain why your previous employment ended or why you want to leave.
- Drive to the interview location in advance so you know where it is and where you can park.
- Plan what to wear. Make sure your clothes are clean and you feel comfortable wearing them.

On the day

- Have something to eat beforehand. Sometimes interviews are delayed and you may find that there has been no opportunity even to obtain a snack.
- Dress professionally, clean and neat.
- Make sure you know where to go and how you are going to get there.
- Allow extra time for the journey going wrong.
- If you chew gum, remove it before you get out of the car.
- Take a mint to freshen your breath.
- Be confident and expect to do well.
- If you know your hands can get clammy, use antiperspirant spray.
- Aim to arrive with time to spare, so that you can be as relaxed as possible.

What to take

- A briefcase or folder. In this you can keep:
  - ○ Copies of all correspondence received.
  - ○ Spare copies of your CV.
  - ○ Notebook with your questions listed.
  - ○ A good quality pen.
  - ○ Something to read in case you are kept waiting.

Also, wear a watch so you know the time.

The journey to interview

The importance of being on time to the interview cannot be overstated! It is crucial for you to find out the exact location of the interview. If possible, drive to the interview site a day or so before at the time you will drive there on the day of the interview. This way, you can adequately estimate how long it will take. Ask yourself if you can get to the building via another route and allow for any contingency that could occur along the way (such as road construction, traffic, or public events).

When you arrive:

Be punctual. Don't just be on time. Be ten minutes early. Use this time to re-check your grooming and comb your hair.

Be appropriately dressed. Dress as you would on the job. The interviewer does not expect a welder in a three-piece suit or a sales manager in jeans.

Switch off your mobile phone. You don't want to have the embarrassment of it going off when you are with the interviewer.

Be friendly but not over familiar. When speaking with receptionists and secretaries, remember that they may later be asked by the interviewers to comment informally on the way candidates have conducted themselves outside the interview proper.

Visit the toilet. Not just for natural reasons but walking to and from the toilet will often take you past working areas of the office from which you can indirectly glean a great deal of information about a company, e.g., cleanliness, atmosphere, friendliness, efficiency, etc. While you are there, check how you look. Is your tie straight? Shirt tucked in? Nothing stuck in your teeth? Lipstick freshly applied? I've lost count of the people I have interviewed with windswept hair and a wayward tie.

Be prepared to shake hands. Make sure your hands are dry and a firm handshake reflects your confidence level. Your handshake should never be too firm, nor should it be limp like a fish. If the interviewer does not extend his or her hand to you before or after the interview (this is rare), you can either make the first gesture by extending your hand or not shake hands at all. Do not hesitate, however, to initiate the handshake.

Do not accept a drink within five minutes of your interview time. You don't want to be burdened with a hot drink just as your interviewer arrives.

Keep calm and keep your cool even if you are kept waiting. It can help to take a book or magazine to look at.

Leave your overcoat, briefcase, umbrella, etc., in reception. So you don't need to worry where to put them.

Be in a positive frame of mind. You may or may not feel confident but for the interview, you must portray a positive image. There's some research that says smiling can help make you feel happy. So put on a big grin in the car (or in the toilet) and keep your eyes smiling afterwards.

At the interview

Stand out! Be Confident! Enjoy it!

Remember: no interview is a formality

Whatever anyone says, go into every interview prepared for a rigorous questioning session, even if you have been told something like, "We'd like you to see so-and-so, it's just a formality." Remember 'so-and-so' can still pull the plug at any time.

Remember: 'You only have one chance to make a first impression'

Many interviewers make up their minds about a candidate within seconds of meeting them. This is known as the 'halo effect'. When we observe one good thing about someone, we assume all kinds of other good things about the person. It's not fair, but we do it anyway. For example, if you are well dressed, many interviewers will assume you are probably responsible in other ways (even if in truth, you are a bit of a mess).

The importance of a first impression lies in the fact that, once it is made, the interviewer subconsciously wishes to have that initial favourable impression confirmed by the subsequent discussion. The opposite is the 'horns effect'. If you start off badly, perhaps by the way you are dressed, your clammy hands or tripping up as you go into the interview room, you'll have an uphill struggle for the rest of the interview.

Don't sit until you are invited to do so. If you are placed in an awkward position, ask, "Would you mind if I moved my chair?" and move it immediately.

Take a few deep breaths, relax and be natural. This is your opportunity to show the interviewer that you are the person they are looking for. Sit well back in your chair, in an upright but comfortable position. If you use your hands when talking be aware of it and don't over do it. Make friendly eye contact with the person asking questions, but don't stare.

Be friendly, confident and articulate. This means standing, sitting and walking with good posture and confidence. Grasp the interviewer's hand in a firm and decisive handshake. Call the interviewer by his or her name, saying how pleased you are to be there.

Demonstrate you like the person. Expect to get on with your interviewer, and show you do through your verbal and non verbal behaviour. Don't let preconceived notions about them show in your face or how you speak.

Speak loudly and clearly enough to be heard. Make sure you stress your good points, showing how well informed you are about the company. Keep your attitude businesslike and respectful. Sell yourself by giving solid reasons why you want to work for the company and how you can help them. Make sure you recount things in an interesting and positive way so that the interviewer will remember you.

Listen closely as the interviewer introduces themselves. You will want to address them by name at some point during the interview.

If you feel uncomfortable holding eye contact with people, look at their forehead, just above their nose. If there is more than one interviewer, make sure you also involve them by addressing the next part of your answer to them. For panel interviews, address the main body of an answer to the questioner, but then hold eye contact with other panel members in order to involve them.

Be natural, relaxed and enthusiastic. Remember you are already more than half-way to the job. You are only there at interview because selectors consider you *can* do the job. Be yourself and be sincere. Unless you're a professional actor/actress, most employers will be able to see through any "mask" you're trying to project. Be self-assured, but not over-confident, over-bearing, or arrogant. Show your passion. If there are two equally qualified candidates, the passionate one will most likely get the job.

Think before you talk. Take a few seconds to collect and organise your thoughts, and then answer each
question simply and directly. If you do not understand the
question or the motivation behind the question, ask for
clarification. Use jargon or technical terms only if you fully
understand them and if they will help show your knowledge of a subject. You should always add this statement
to the end of every question asked by the employer, no
matter what the question is: "Now I need to answer that
question in a way that will show how I can be of value to
this employer." If you start to ramble, interrupt yourself by
coughing or pausing. This will give you time to collect your
thoughts and you can say "Sorry, I'm rambling, can I start
that answer again?"

**Mentally tick off, as you cover them at interview,
the five or six key reasons why you should be considered for the job.** Find opportunities to raise any topics
which have not been covered. You might be asked whether
you would like to add anything or you might make the
point yourself: *"Would it be helpful if I mentioned something else relevant to this job?"* Take every opportunity to
explain your achievements and abilities within the context
of the job description.

Never hesitate to ask the interviewer to repeat the
question if you haven't fully heard or understood it. You
can also use the technique of restating the question in
different words to check your understanding.

Let the interviewer control the interview, but always be
prepared to take the initiative. Have a strategy for handling interviewers who monopolise the talking, or ask only
closed ('Yes/No') questions. Be prepared for the deliberate
question which the interviewers know you cannot answer
(common in the work place). Such questions are useful to
interviewers as much to see how you will cope as for the
content of your reply.

When the interviewers start asking the "How would you handle...?" questions, pretend that you are not being interviewed for a job. Instead, imagine that you are a respected consultant helping a new client with a problem. Adopt a probing approach so that you can understand their situation in sufficient detail before providing an answer. Relate that answer to their business objectives rather than to theories or models (unless specifically asked to do so.)

Similarly, when they ask about your past achievements, relate them to issues your employer was trying to address and the business (organisational) benefits they gained. This way, you will be giving very useful examples and by not trying to 'perform', and you will be more relaxed.

Remember:

Keep on your toes. Everyone feels nervous before an interview; this is quite natural. Butterflies in the stomach are caused by the same surge of adrenaline that an athlete gets before an important race. It's the body's way of tuning up your faculties for peak performance. Channel this energy by keeping super-alert and notice the interviewer(s) body language for clues on how much detail you should be giving them. For example, are they attentive or bored?

Build rapport. The interview is often less about your factual knowledge and more about what are you like to work with. Hence building rapport may be more important than impressing with expertise.

Think! Give careful consideration to all your answers. Don't be afraid to pause and think before replying to a question and don't hesitate to say you don't know if that is the case. Giving questions their due consideration is also a good way to avoid interrupting the interviewer – though in an animated conversation with someone of similar mind, you may find words tumbling out.

Be natural. Wanting to give your best doesn't mean that you have to be unnatural. High anxiety about the outcome can lead to candidates either trying too hard or coming over as dull and stilted. Aim to strike a balance between being (a) comfortable and relaxed and (b) alert and incisive. Above all, show your interest by your natural enthusiasm for that winning future combination – you and the job.

Be positive: Handle mistakes properly. Don't criticise previous employers as you'll project a negative image. On the other hand, if you have made a mistake in your career, it is not a disaster to admit it, but make sure you convey clearly the lessons it taught you. Admitting the odd mistake also gives you credibility when you start to talk about the positive things in your career.

If things go wrong

It may have been a long time since your last interview. Be prepared for anything! Plan now for what you will do if the worst happens. Such as:

You arrive late: The situation is perhaps retrievable if you apologise and offer to come back another time. No matter how late you are, do not park in the chairman's parking space and rush into the building. Your interviewer, looking out of the window could see you as unreliable and flustered before you even say a word!

You are kept waiting for a long time: Do not complain, check regularly with reception, and if offered a replacement interviewer, accept it.

Other candidates are in the room: Read the newspaper you brought with you or, if available, the company literature on display. It avoids getting involved in a discussion.

You can't remember the interviewer's name: This is unforgivable. Ask the receptionist. On no account should you admit your oversight.

You spill your tea or coffee: If you have interview nerves, don't accept a drink. Should you find yourself in such a dilemma, however, do clean it up.

The interview is regularly interrupted: Offer to leave the room or to come back at another time.

Your mind goes blank: This usually occurs when people are extremely nervous. If it happens, take a couple of deep breaths, (which will calm you down by getting oxygen to your brain), and try to get your perspective again. If nervous, you can stall for time saying something like, "I couldn't quite hear you exactly, could you repeat that?" Or you could tell the truth and say "I'm sorry, my mind has gone blank." You could then explain that you are prone to nerves in interviews and your disarming honesty may save the day (unless you are applying for a job that requires you to keep your nerves such as a fire-fighter).

You are asked a question you don't know the answer to: If the question is a factual one and you don't know, then admit this with a smile and explain that this particular question is outside of your experience. If the question is a theoretical one, ask for a few moments to collect your thoughts so that you can give a considered answer. Preface any answer with "I'm not sure if this is exactly what you are asking, but..."

You are interviewed in a noisy and crowded room: This is a sign of an inexperienced interviewer who may be trying to suggest that he is so important that he cannot leave the centre of his powerhouse. In most cases, you will just have to put up with it and concentrate hard to keep out the interruptions. You could drop them a line afterwards, underlining a couple of points which you think may not have come across well because of the background noise.

The question doesn't make sense: Ask them to repeat or rephrase the questions. If you give a good answer in the end, they will probably forget a little bit of clumsiness along the way. But if you get hold of the wrong end of the stick to start with, your interviewers are more likely to assume that you are a bit dim.

If you get some bad news on the day of the interview: Getting upset, whatever the cause, in an interview will be very bad for your chances. If you feel under par, you could drop a line afterwards explaining what happened. But the best solution in this situation may be to ring beforehand, explain the situation over the phone and see if another appointment can be found.

You don't like your interviewer: Don't let it put you off if you really want the job. Try to "like" them as much as possible during the interview because feelings such as these can communicate themselves through body language. After the interview, you may like to reflect if you would want to join the company, particularly if you will be working closely with the interviewer.

You know your interviewer: Don't let this worry you. If it is a one-to-one, the interviewer may need to consider their position and the onus would be on them to do something about it. If there is more than one person interviewing you, your contact is under less pressure.

Post interview evaluation

Once you are out of the building, and in your car, at the train station, etc., jot down a few notes, outlining the main points discussed. Also ask yourself the following questions:

- What was the interviewer's full name and title?
- What was the receptionist/secretary's name?
- Who else from the company did you meet?
- Exactly what does the job entail?
- Did they mention salary? What was said?

As soon as you can, complete a review of how you think you came across. It will be invaluable to refer to if you get a second interview and you can also use it to monitor your performance before your next interview. Be honest with yourself, noting what you did well, and where improvements are needed. Talk through the result of your review with a friend and re-practise your revised answers to difficult questions.

Ask yourself:

- Was I in the right frame of mind?
- Was my eye contact right, did I smile?
- How adequately did I prepare myself for the interview?
- Was there anything I should have known about the company that I did not?
- How effective was my role in the interview?
- Having seen the people in the company, how appropriately was I dressed?
- Which questions did I handle well?
- Which questions did I handle poorly?
- How thorough were my answers?
- How well did I emphasise how my skills will benefit this position?
- How well did I ask questions? What could I have done differently?
- Was the interviewer interested and involved in what I was saying?
- Did I answer the questions in a way that stressed the most important aspects, my ability, my willingness and my suitability?
- Did I present an accurate and favourable picture of myself?
- Did I look my best?
- Were there any questions I could not answer to my satisfaction?

- Was I relaxed and in control of myself?
- Did I appear confident and show genuine enthusiasm?
- Did I talk too much?
- Did I give answers which didn't seem to satisfy the interviewer?
- Was I able to discuss my strengths and weaknesses?
- Did I show that I was listening to the interviewer?
- Did I say why I wanted to work for the organisation?
- Did I seem interested and enthusiastic about the job?
- Did the interview flow or was it stilted?
- Did I find out all I needed to?
- Would I like to work for that organisation?
- What additional research do I need to do before a subsequent interview?
- Where there any areas I could have prepared better?
- Does it still sound fresh, despite having to regularly repeat it?
- Did I ask some good questions at the end?

Note: The above is available as a form to complete via a low cost eBook you can download from the web site.

Contacting the recruitment agency

If you have been put forward by a recruitment agency, call them as soon as you can to let them know how you got on and to confirm your interest in the job. They will almost certainly feed this straight back to the interviewer and it will be viewed positively.

Follow up with a thank you letter

Typically, only about 25% of applicants write a follow up letter to thank the interviewer for their time. If the interviewer is still deciding between you and another applicant, this may just tip the balance in your favour.

A follow up letter gives you an opportunity to reinforce your strengths, and demonstrates your written communication skills. A hand-written letter shows your interest. You took the time to write it, and it doesn't come across looking like a form letter you send out to every person you meet. You could email, but a hand-written letter stands out. But speed of delivery is very important. If you can't get the letter there for the next day, it's better to send it by email.

Your thank you letter can address areas of weakness, reservations or concerns that were mentioned during the interview. You can also reiterate your strengths and explain why you are the person for the job. Mention how your strengths and past work history (with examples) can over compensate for any areas of weakness.

Don't forget timing – two weeks is too late. You want your letter there within 48 hours.

You could also send a thank you note to the assistant, thanking them for making you feel comfortable.

Structure of a thank you letter

Paragraph 1
Thank you for interviewing me for the position of xxx on (date)

Paragraph 2
Restate what you have to offer to the company.

After discussing the responsibilities of the job, I am sure that I have the skills and experience to perform well in this position. Mention again what you can bring to the job.

Paragraph 3
Thank the interviewer. Say how you may be contacted.

Thank you again for taking the time to meet with me. If you need additional information, I can be reached at xxx in the daytime and at xxx in the evenings.

If your interview did not go well or if you want to add something that was not covered in the interview, you can use the thank you letter as a follow-up marketing tool. Include a paragraph that makes your point and encourages the employer to reconsider your potential. A sample letter is below:

Thank you for the opportunity to interview with you last Tuesday for the position of Business Development Manager. During the interview you asked why I would be a good candidate and I could only give you a vague response. I have spent a good deal of time since then evaluating my strengths in relation to your needs. After serious consideration I can comfortably state that I am a good candidate because _____.

If you would like to discuss in more depth my background in relation to your needs, please call. Otherwise, I look forward to hearing from you and I hope your response will be positive. I am very interested in working for you at XYZ plc. I would like to have the opportunity to discuss job possibilities in more detail.

Second interviews

For most employers, the first interview is a screening interview.

When you get the letter or phone call for a second interview, and you are not interested in the organisation, decline the invitation, thanking them for their interest. If the suggested date is impossible, call the employer to arrange for a more convenient day. Confirm your acceptance in writing.

You will need to do some extra research. **The more knowledgeable you are in advance, the more effective you will be.** Remember that everyone you meet from division head to support staff is evaluating you just as you are evaluating them. Don't forget to review your notes from the first interview.

Waiting

The interview was wonderful (you thought) and the interviewer said she would get in touch with you (you think you remember), but that was four weeks ago and you wonder if you will ever hear anything. Don't despair or panic. It is probable that the interview process is still going on, so wait. When several jobs are available, the assessment process can take several weeks and final decisions are not made until everyone is able to get together for a review meeting.

If it is probable that the interview process is over, a telephone call asking about your status in the search is appropriate.

You get a regret letter

If you get a regret letter: "We regret to inform you . . .," it could be for one of five reasons:

- **There was not a good match between you and the job.** In this case, the rejection letter is a positive outcome. You would not have liked that job anyway.
- **Your do not have the right background for this job.** You may not yet be ready for this job. If this is, for example, a marketing manager, think of applying for a marketing executive job or gathering more experience.
- **There was a good match but you simply did not interview well.** You need to spend time on interview practice.
- **The applicant pool was extremely competitive.** There may have been more than one person who was capable of doing the job. The final decision may have been based on factors outside your control. The person who got the job may have been an internal candidate or had something extra to offer.
- **There is no job available.** This could be because the head office wants to fill the vacancy but the local branch has no intention of filling it or the job has already been

offered to someone, and the ad was to "go through the motions."

Whatever you think is the reason you didn't get the job, contact the company and seek feedback from them.

Finally, even if you do not get an offer, you can still write one last letter. The person who has been offered the job may turn it down and this could lead to an offer for you. Plus, it will definitely leave a favourable impression.

A reply to the regret letter

Send a letter thanking them for taking the time to consider you for the position and wish the new employee every success. Say that you would be happy to be considered for the position should it become vacant in the future. Quite regularly, a new employee leaves quite quickly as it hasn't worked out for them and this would bring you to the top of the list when a new person is being considered.

Thank you for your kind call to tell me that the Business Improvement Manager vacancy has been filled. Although I was not selected for the position, I want to wish you and the new manager well as you begin to work together.

Once again, thank you for the consideration you have given my application for this position. As your personnel needs change in the future, I hope you will keep me in mind and contact me.

You could also ask for feedback on how you missed out so you can give some attention to the reason you were not chosen.

You've got the job!

If you get a job offer, you will want to consider whether it is the right job for you, and then to negotiate the salary and benefits package. We'll cover this in more detail in the next chapter.

Of course, you may decide to turn an offer down. If you do, do so quickly and send a letter which keeps the possibility of you getting in touch again in the future.

Thank you for offering me a position as a Marketing Executive with Guardian Consulting. I found our discussions during the interview process helpful to learn more about the details of this position. I appreciated the time you allowed me to consider your offer.

Throughout the interview process, I confirmed my initial impressions of Guardian Consulting as an outstanding organisation. After considerable thought about my career goals, I have chosen to accept the offer from an employer based closer to my family.

At this time, I must respectfully decline your kind offer. This was a difficult decision for me, although I believe it is the appropriate one at this time in my career.

I want to thank you for the time and consideration you have given my application. It was a pleasure meeting you and learning more about Guardian Consulting.

Chapter Fifteen

Psychometric testing

M any companies seek to make the selection of candidates more rigorous. Ability tests are often used to reduce the number of applicants to form a short list. Sometimes psychometric tests are often the first part of an assessment centre. There are two main types: tests of ability and personality questionnaires.

Ability tests include verbal reasoning, critical thinking, numerical reasoning, spatial skills. Each of these has a right and wrong answer.

Personality questionnaires include: Saville's Wave; 16pf5 and the OPQ (Occupational Personality Questionnaire). They seek to understand the sort of person you are and your responses will be followed up with a detailed interview with a psychologist or psychometrician.

Can you prepare for tests?

It's difficult to prepare for a test when you don't know the content of the questions. However, you can practice technique which will make you feel more confident. There are numerous books containing practice material and it's also possible to access example tests through the Internet. A number of sites are listed in *Chapter Twenty One, Useful Resources*.

For numerical tests, you will often need to be able to calculate percentages and deal with ratios. You may want to practice doing these calculations to ensure you can do them on the day of the test.

Will I get details on tests when I apply for a job?

If you apply for a job and you are invited to a test session, you should receive details on the tests and some practice information. If not, ask, as it's good practice for employers to provide it.

Can I fail a test?

Tests are not thought of as pass/fail as the scores are usually presented as percentiles. So a score at the 60th percentile for example does not mean a score of 60%. It means you scored better than 60% of a comparable group.

You cannot "fail" a personality questionnaire and you should always be given an opportunity to discuss your results with a qualified member of staff. This will enable you to provide examples to support the responses you gave.

Preparation for an ability testing session

There are things you can do to improve your performance in psychometric tests, such as:

- Reading newspapers, reports, business journals to improve your verbal skills for verbal tests.
- Reading financial reports in newspapers, studying tables of data, doing number calculations and puzzles without a calculator may help numerical skills.

- Checking results in the paper could improve checking skills.
- Solving crosswords may help verbal problem solving.
- Looking at objects in various ways and angles could develop spatial skills.
- Looking at flow charts and diagrams should improve diagramming skills.

There are also many books with sample tests you can practice in advance. This can be very helpful even though they might not be exactly the same tests as you will be taking. Such practice can help you prepare.

The night before the test

The best thing to do is get a good nights sleep and try to relax.

During the ability testing session

- Keep as calm as you can. Remember that a certain amount of anxiety is perfectly normal.
- Make sure that you are comfortable. Loosen your collar and tie (if appropriate) and kick off your shoes if you want.
- Listen carefully to the administrator's instructions. Ask questions if you need to.
- If you can't see or hear things properly, tell the administrator.
- Read the test instructions carefully and do not assume that you know what to do.
- Put your answers in the right place on the answer sheet! (It's easy to make mistakes in the heat of the moment.)
- Record you answers in the correct way. For example, do not tick boxes if you're expected to strike through them with short pencil lines.
- Read the questions properly before you attempt to answer them.

- Don't agonise over a question you can't answer – move on to the next one.
- Don't waste time double checking questions with easy or obvious answers.
- Don't waste time looking for 'trick' questions, as there won't be any.
- If you can't work out an answer, make an informed guess.
- Work as quickly as you can, but don't race or you will make avoidable mistakes.
- Remember that the more questions you answer the greater your chances of getting a higher mark.
- With some questions, a good approach can be to eliminate the wrong answers to arrive at the correct one. It's often better to guess, rather than to leave a question unanswered, but do check to make sure you will not be penalised for incorrect answers.
- Keep an eye on the time. If you have time left at the end of a test go back and check your answers.
- Don't stick to a certain amount of time for each question. Many tests are designed so that the questions get harder, and you'll need more time as you progress.
- Look around occasionally and take some deep breaths, it will help you relax.
- Don't be put off if the questions seem difficult, they may well be just as difficult for everybody else.
- Avoid extreme reactions. Take the test confidently and purposefully and avoid being too blasé because some tests will discriminate between the able and the extremely able.
- Some tests will place greater emphasis on accuracy and others on the number of questions attempted – always ask for clarification before you begin.
- Don't be alarmed if other people appear to be working more quickly. It doesn't mean that they are getting the answers right!

Personality testing is a bit different. There will be no right or wrong answers and you will not have to worry about how to deal with complex tasks. Instead, you will be asked questions and the results will be used to determine the sort of person you are.

It can be tempting to want to portray yourself in the most positive light, but tests come with scales that will pick up if you are overly lenient or critical in your responses. You may also decide to pretend that you are, for example, more outgoing than you actually are or more strategic. The assessment will be followed by a discussion and if you don't have the examples to support what you say, it can put a cloud of "who is he/she really" over the whole results.

Chapter Sixteen

How to pass assessment centres

When you apply for a job, the potential employer's decision may be based on more than an interview. You may need to take part in an assessment centre. This is a much more detailed and time-consuming way of deciding the right person for the job.

An assessment centre consists of a number of different exercises and interviews. Some people excel at interviews, but not everyone. Being able to undertake different exercises gives you greater opportunities to demonstrate your strengths and abilities.

Before the centre, you need to prepare

Read the company literature

You should be sent details of the competences that are to be used in the assessment centre. These will all be assessed. So if, for example, strategic understanding is one of the competences measured in the test, you will want to make sure you think strategically. If a certain competence doesn't come naturally to you, take some time to prepare, both for questioning and written work.

Ask for a copy of the timetable, if not supplied, so you understand what the day will consist of.

Make sure you know where the venue is and arrive in plenty of time, allowing time for delays in transport. Get a good nights sleep the night before, and take your reading glasses with you. Alongside your CV and copy of the application form, take a set of highlighter pens. If there will be written work, a highlighter is a great way of emphasising key words and facts.

On the day

On arrival, you will meet the centre manager who should talk you through the day. You will also meet your fellow candidates. In most cases, this will be a competitive assessment centre, but you should be pleasant and make general conversation. Some candidates may want to play "mind games" and talk up their experience and background. Don't be taken in and over awed by what other people say. It's your performance on the day that counts.

Assessment centres will sometimes start with a group introduction and move onto a group exercise, whereas more senior assessments may keep candidates apart. Generally, a time table will allow time for breaks. But sometimes you are given all the day's activities to do at the beginning and it's up to you to manage your time. If this is the case, listen carefully for any clues the centre manager may give you. Be aware that you might be called for an interview part way through a task. Some centres do this to see how well you cope with this sort of interruption.

The group exercise

Group exercises are used to see how you relate to others. Usually, you will be given information to read in advance, and then join with others for the discussion. Everyone has an objective of achieving a personal task, but you also need to consider the overall group and not alienate others. Generally, there is no right answer in a group exercise, how you reach an answer while working in your group is more important.

You must speak up and speak clearly so the assessors can hear you. No matter how shy you are, and how much you prefer to think about things before speaking, in a group exercise you must speak up so the assessors have something to assess. Someone in the group needs to structure the task and the time, so if no one else takes on this role, you may volunteer. However, don't volunteer to keep track of the time unless you are sure you will!

It always helps to address people by name. All the people in your group should be wearing name badges, but if not, as everyone introduced themselves at the beginning, note their name (possibly using a diagram which you can refer to). As you are likely to be assessed on your ability to get on with others, refrain from talking too much. You may like to encourage contributions from a quieter person to show your awareness of the importance of teamwork.

Keep track of the time so you can suggest when it would be good to move on. Make sure to save some time at the end for summarising.

In tray exercise

You will be given a number of documents and will need to make a judgement on what to do within the time allowed. The scenario is usually that your boss is unavailable, it's your first day, and you need to go through a series of papers in a limited amount of time before a meeting. There is often a connection between documents, so read them through quickly. You may want to delegate tasks to other people. If you do, provide clear instructions. Be sure to say thank you and refer to people by name.

The written exercise

Some organisations may give you a lot of material and a short amount of time to grasp the key points and respond to a task. Review this information, quickly make sense of it, then produce a report. Read through the instructions carefully. If you are asked to refer to specific criteria, make sure you do. If it asks for a recommendation, make one and justify your choice. Written skills are likely to be assessed so take care about spelling, grammar and layout. The use of paragraphs, headers and sub headings can help the reader. Often, you will notice numerical data in the material available and doing calculations is likely to impress the assessor.

Presentations

Some assessment centres send material in advance so you can prepare your presentation beforehand. In this case, a very high standard is expected as you will have time to prepare visual aids and practice your talk. Other centres give you a limited amount of time to prepare on the day and thus, you do not have to reach such a high standard (but you still need to appear competent).

When presenting, make eye contact with the assessor(s) and have a clear start and end to your thoughts. This will provide a positive impression and make it clear to the assessors that they can move into the questioning phase. After your presentation, you will be asked questions. Expect to be challenged on what you have said and when questioned, take a moment or two to think through how best to reply. A measured response that is focused on the question is more effective than a rambling reply.

Interviews

The key is to be prepared. You will be aware of the competences, so think of examples that demonstrate yours. If you know you are going to be asked questions about relationships, think through examples in both your working and non work life. For example, think about when you have worked successfully with others, when there have been tension and conflicts and then think through how you dealt (or will deal) with these.

Often you will be asked questions to ascertain resilience. Think about pressure situations, how you dealt with them, and what you learned from them. Don't think you have to come across as superman or superwoman – it can be valuable to discuss what may have gone wrong and what you have learned from specific situations.

Different companies can have slightly different definitions of the same competency, so carefully read the information that is provided. Break down the details and think through examples of each aspect.

Don't forget to re-read *Chapter Thirteen, Interview Preparation* and *Chapter Fourteen, The Interview – You're Shortisted!* to remind you about interviews.

Treat each exercise separately

We're not always the best judge of our own performance. The best way to approach assessment centres is to treat each element independently, whether you think you have done fantastically well, or very badly. Then leave the exercise and move onto the next one in a positive manner.

I once interviewed someone who spent 10 minutes telling me what a hash they had made of their written exercise. In my interview, they struggled to keep focused and I think their thoughts on the previous exercise were still prominent in their mind. Later, I found out their written script was fine, but they did poorly in my session, and they were not offered a job.

Conclusion

Assessment centres can be stressful, but they are also a good opportunity for you to demonstrate your strengths in a number of areas. As well as the company learning quite a lot about you, you will also learn more about the job you are seeking. If an assessment centre exercise asks you to analyse complex data, this is likely to be a component of the job.

Most organisations will provide you with some feedback on your performance, sometimes verbal and at other times, a full report. Sometimes it is sent to everyone, sometimes you need to request it, so make sure you contact the company. It is good practice for companies to do this, and you can review the feedback to help you in the future.

Chapter Seventeen

Staying motivated

No matter how positive a person you are, it may prove challenging to stay motivated in the current economic climate. With news of companies closing down every day and more and more people seeking a job, you may wonder if there will ever be a job for you. What the newspapers ignore are the number of jobs that are still being advertised each day. There are jobs out there and staying motivated will help you find one that suits you.

"Whether you think you can or you can't, you're right"
– Henry Ford

Here are some things that can help:

Remind yourself of previous successes

Remember the time you won a race, created a great report, made a presentation that convinced your boss to go ahead with a project or give you a rise? Now is the time to remind yourself of previous successes. You might like to buy a small notebook and write down successes as you remember them. You've been successful in a job search before and you will again.

Take some time to have fun

Job search doesn't have to be a 12-hour-a-day job, spending four hours directly on your job search allows you time to develop some research and interview skills and still leave time for friends and relaxation.

Be helpful – volunteer

If you do have spare time, why not do some voluntary work? This could be using the skills you already have to benefit others, or it may be an opportunity to develop some new skills. In many volunteer positions, you will be dealing with people who have problems and thus make you more grateful for what you have. It can also mean that you may meet people with the power to offer you a job. At the very least, you will definitely meet new people who you can add to your network. And remember, volunteer work looks great on a CV and many prospective employers think highly of a person who is involved with volunteer activities.

Remind yourself that it's not all within your control

You can have a great CV, interview well, and look great, but still find yourself unemployed and waiting for a job offer. With the recession, there are many people in exactly your position. So keep doing the best you can and don't take your lack of a job offer too personally.

Think of the upside

You will have more free time, so use some of it to do something you have never had time to do before such as learning the tin whistle or getting fitter with a daily run.

Plus, if you never really enjoyed your last job, it does give you time to find a job you love (or at least like better than the last one).

Don't let negative thoughts get you down

It's easy to feel down when a job offer does not appear. You may find yourself lamenting that "I have to complete this form," or "I've got to revise my CV." But don't make it sound like it's such a chore. Gather yourself and try to think positively and set out to enjoy the task.

It's too easy to let negative thoughts come into our heads. You know, the things like:

- I'm too young or too old.
- I can't afford it.
- I'm scared.
- I don't know where to start.
- I don't have enough time.
- People will think I'm mad.
- People will be jealous if I succeed.
- What if I fail?
- I'm not smart enough.
- I don't have the energy to do this.

But why not turn them around? For example:

"I'm not too young/old, but I'm the perfect age to get started..

Instead of worrying about not knowing where to start, say:

 "I'm ready to get started" and let your subconscious work on this. **Use external help if needed such as from a coach or friend.**

If you expect to be unsuccessful at interview, then you are likely to come across that way. And you'll be seen as someone who can't confidently discuss the great examples of their experience. On the other hand, if you think you are going to be successful and have planned how to respond to questions, you stand a much better chance.

Dealing with rejection

You will get set backs and knock backs. No matter how great your application you may still not get to interview. Some companies have literally hundreds of applications and have no time to review them all. In those cases, it is literally a matter of luck if your CV is reviewed at all!

You may think you have a great CV, but if it is not getting you to interview, it's not doing its job. So keep track of your rejection letters, and if necessary, seek an independent job search coach to provide feedback and guidance to help you improve.

In the same sense, you may think you interview well, but carrying out a full interview with an experienced interviewer who coaches you is worth the investment. The relevant chapters in this book tells you how to conduct yourself at interview, and your practice sessions with a friend may help you improve, but you may still benefit from exploring other subtleties with an experienced interviewer.

Visualise yourself succeeding

Why not imagine yourself being successful in your job search? It can be a very powerful technique. Think of how you will dress and what the workplace will be like. Imagine yourself at your desk and on the phone, talking with customers or in the field delivering goods and services.

Maybe the image isn't clear at the moment, but try and picture yourself carrying out your ideal job – what will you be wearing? How will you be feeling? What will you be doing?

Successful athletes dream about winning. They visualise themselves achieving their goal. You can do the same! Each evening when you go to bed, make a movie in your head of being in your ideal job. What do you see? What can you hear? What can you taste or smell? Notice how great you feel! Run this movie through your head again – make it bigger, brighter, and sharper.

You might get there sooner than you think!

Chapter Eighteen

Before you say yes

If you are unemployed, and the recession brings about concerns about when you will get another job, you may want to say yes to any job offer. But wait. Make sure that it's the right job for you. After examining things, you may still go ahead and take it, but you will do so with more realistic expectations.

Just because you get an offer doesn't mean you should say yes. Your interview can be a good indicator of how you are going to be treated in the job. Kim was extremely pleased to be shortlisted for a job with a professional law firm with impressive offices. The interview with the HR manager went well but when she met her potential boss, it was awful.

If you were treated badly at interview (like we read about with Kim in *Chapter Thirteen, Interview Preparation*) or you hear people making negative comments about the company, think twice before saying yes. One of the worst things you can do is take a job and within a couple of weeks realise you made the wrong choice. You then have to spend time learning the current new job, leaving even less time for a new job search. Or you may resign and have a problem explaining your leaving so quickly to a new employer.

So, before you say yes:

Send a letter to show your enthusiasm for the job

This letter should summarise your strengths, outline your key accomplishments and personal contributions. Remind them why they have chosen you. If the employer's compensation package is included in the letter, say how excited you are and that you would like a couple of days to discuss things with your partner. This gives you a chance to weigh the pros and cons of this job, and to get in touch with any other companies to which you have applied to check how your applications are progressing.

Make sure it hits all the right buttons

Check the job offer against your key criteria. How well does it match up?

Gill was one of a number of clients who was seduced into thinking the job was perfect for her. She was going to be marketing manager for an international company and would be meeting with colleagues from around the world on a regular basis. The job was quite a stretch for her but she convinced herself she was up to the challenge. After all, the pay was going to be 30% more than she was currently making and she was being offered a BMW as a company car. Who wouldn't take such a job?

Gill contacted me and she came across as very excited and positive about this new job. She looked at me a bit strange when I asked her what was really important to her in her new job, then she listed all the benefits she would gain – the car, the travel, the status.

How important is that I asked? Again she looked at me a bit surprised. I could tell she was confused as to why I was asking these questions so I explained the importance of career satisfaction to overall well being and that it would help if we took some time to define what characteristics would bring her satisfaction at work.

I did the following exercise with her. She was to rate the importance of each on a scale of 1-10.

- **Security.** If you have been made redundant, you may be looking for a job with a secure company.
- **Salary.** How well can I live on the salary that has been offered? Is it commission only? Does it include profit share?
- **Work content.** Does the job sound interesting and challenging?
- **Working environment.** Will I look forward to going to work each day?
- **Travel time.** Will I be happy to do this in deepest winter? How far will I have to commute and realistically how long will the journey take?
- **Benefits.** Is the package acceptable? What does it consist of? Could I get more?
- **Promotion prospects.** Will I have an opportunity to move forward in this company? Will it help my future career prospects with another company?
- **Security.** Is the company likely to go out of business?
- **Friendly atmosphere.** Do I fit in with the company culture?
- **Prestigious company.** How well respected in the community is the company?

- **Contributes to defined career path.** How well does this job fit in with my long-range career goals?
- **Hours.** Will I mind working the hours required for success in this job? Will I be happy to work unsociable hours? How important is it for me to spend time with my family?
- **Colleagues and client group**. Will I want to work with people like this?
- **Do I really want this job?** Does the work interest me?

When you get a job offer, answering these questions enables you to take a much more objective view of decision making. These questions also allow you to choose between options, weighing each against the other.

For Gill, comparing this job offer and her ideal job, working as a charity fundraiser, didn't match up. So why was she considering it? Because she was letting the money and overseas travel influence her even though they were not high on her list of important aspects of career satisfaction.

Your challenge: be clear about what you want from a job so you can make an informed decision when offered a position.

Before saying yes, ask yourself

- Will this job make good use of my abilities, skills and talents?
- Does it suit my personality?
- Am I happy that I will be paid fairly for the work I'll do?
- Does the working environment suit my values and personal preferences?
- Will it give me a chance to develop and grow?
- Does my manager have the right approach to bring out the best in me?
- What impact will taking this job have on my personal and family life?

- Are the expectations on me realistic and achievable?
- Why specifically do I want to take this job?

Finalise the details

Before saying yes, make sure you also know the answers to these questions:

Job title

- To whom do I report. Can I meet the person?
- Who will report to me?
- Am I clear on the duties expected of me? Do I have a full copy of the job description?
- Are the limits of my authority clearly defined?

Hours of work

- What are the hours of work?
- What are the sick pay entitlements?
- What are the holiday entitlements?
- Will any pre-booked holidays be honoured?
- How long will it take me to get to work and back each day, at rush hour, and how much will this cost?

Meet people in the company

Arrange to talk with other employees to get an inside perspective. This could be your new manager and colleagues, or recent graduates of a management training course.

Saying no

Some people will think it foolish to turn down a job, especially in the current economic climate, but if it isn't providing what is important to you, you are being asked to work too many hours (that creates an hourly wage that is very low), or you're not sure you'll enjoy the work as much as you'd like, you may be better off waiting for a job that is more appealing.

But make sure you have considered everything the job offers, including the salary. For you, it may be better to get 75% of what you ideally want than continue for another six months being unemployed.

If you do decide to turn the job down, do so politely. Show your appreciation for their interest and express regret that you cannot accept the offer. Remember, you may be considering employment with these people in a few years, and you want to leave the door open for future possibilities.

Chapter Nineteen

Salary negotiation

The best time to negotiate salary is once you have been offered the job. So wait till you get an offer.

Some employers will ask about salary quite early on in an interview as it's a reason to screen you out. The don't want to proceed with an applicant they believe will turn them down due to the salary being too low. But also be aware that if you ask for too little, you may get the job, but at a lower salary than they were willing to pay. This can result in a loss of thousands of pounds over a number of years.

Think about what you may lose if you settle. Imagine two of you are offered a job paying £25k. You accept, but the other person negotiates their pay to £28k. Then let's say you both continue to get pay rises of 3% per year. The amount you could lose over time is substantial.

During an interview, you may be asked your current salary. Never lie, as when you hand over your P45, a lie will be obvious and you could well lose the job. And make sure to include all the benefits you receive beyond your basic salary.

You can only win at salary negotiation if you are prepared to walk away

Your preparation

- Work out the minimum you will work for (never tell this to anyone).
- Identify your dream salary.
- Check what salary is listed in the advert.
- Find out what other companies pay for similar skills and experience. Look online and talk to people who may know.

There is scope to compromise. Think about what else is being offered such as a pension, bonus, car, and health care and how much these are worth to you. Would you be willing to compromise? For example, if you don't get enough salary, can you increase your potential bonus?

The negotiation

Go into the negotiation from a "win-win" perspective. "I really want this job and I really want to work with you, so let's see if we can work this out."

Make sure you are negotiating with the person who has the authority to make a decision, otherwise it's a waste of time.

The company may ask you how much you want. Rather than being specific, it's better to say something like:

"I'm really interested in working with your company and I'm sure whatever you offer is going to be a reflection of the job and my skills and abilities."

"I'm glad you are bringing up salary, I want to discuss this, but first of all, can we see if I am right for the job and the value I can bring."

"I'd like to earn what other people of my calibre are earning here. What is the salary range of the job?"

The company may look at your salary history but it may not reflect the values you are seeking in the new job. Many of us are underpaid for the work we have done, or a new job is much more challenging than a previous job. As an explanation of why you are seeking a salary above that listed on your salary history, you could perhaps say how salaries were frozen, how you got paid to attend university part time, how your fees were paid, etc.

Through discussion you will reach the point where a figure is quoted

There is a difference between being one of a number of people who can do a job, and being someone with the right combination of skills and experience. Don't bargain yourself out of a job if you are in the first category.

- Don't say what you want, wait for them to make the offer.
- Be silent, be reflective, take notes but don't rush to say yes.
- A silence could bring you an extra £10 per week, or £500 per year or even more.
- If you are being paid at an hourly rate, it may be easier to negotiate. For example, 30p an hour doesn't sound like a lot to the employer, so they might agree to this. On a 30-hour a week job this could bring you in an extra £468 per year. Over the course of a year it could be a useful increase in salary.

If it is a great deal, ask questions to clarify benefits and also ask about redundancy payments. You can get a clause in your contract offering you six months pay for example, if your are made redundant in the first two years.

Repeat what they say and then pause. You could follow with:

"It does seem on the low side for what the job involves and what I can bring to the job."

. . . and then wait. After they respond, remind them how much value you bring to the job and what you can do for the company.

If the offer is a bit less then you want, bring up additional benefits that may well increase your overall package.

If you are unhappy with the offer, you could say, "Is this the best you can do?" Maintain eye contact as you ask. If they don't respond with an increase, you may then decide to turn the job down.

When you have got the best offer you can

- Finalise the salary before you move on to discuss benefits.
- Be positive about the job, even if the salary isn't as much as you really want.
- Say how you are excited about working for the company but would like a little time to consider things.
- Seek advice and find out whether the proposed salary is fair or not.

Benefits

Alongside the actual salary, there are also benefits such as private health care, pension contribution, bonus, annual leave, relocation expenses, profit share, and working a four-day week. Benefits can include full pay whilst off sick rather than the statutory minimum, pension contribution, private health care and profit share. It can also include relocation expenses such as legal fees, estate agency fees, temporary accommodation, and costs for new carpets, curtains, etc.

Find out if you are entitled to holidays in your first year and if you could negotiate for an extra week's holiday.

There may be an on site gym or reduced membership at a local health club.

If you have to travel for business, what will your mileage allowance be? The guide rule is 40 pence per mile. If you are paid a measly 15 pence per mile, you will end up with out of pocket costs.

What benefits are important to you? Sometimes you can't negotiate on salary, but you can get a better benefit package.

For example, one of my clients, Lindsay, knew she might not get her ideal salary with her new company, a small, not-for-profit company, so I suggested she offer to work for a lower salary on a four-day week allowing her to maintain some freelance work. They agreed and everyone was happy.

Decide if you do want the job

Is the job worth a slightly lower salary? Is there a possibility of an increase in salary after six months? Keep in mind, that it may also be a job where you will learn a lot, work on very interesting assignments, or a job that will enhance your CV.

Once you do accept the job, confirm in writing and spell out exactly what was agreed:

I look forward to us working together. For clarity, I have set down what we agreed yesterday. If I am incorrect in any way, please let me know. Otherwise I'll assume we are in agreement.

Chapter Twenty

The first 90 days

Congratulations! You have been successful in the interview process and are looking forward to a new job!

However, starting something new can be scary, even if the choice to move was yours. This chapter will make it easier for you to make a successful transition.

Before you start

Much of your success during the first 90 days in a new job begins with the groundwork carried out before you report for work on the first day.

Do your homework

Take the time to learn all you can about your new company. Ask for a copy of the company's most recent annual report and read it thoroughly. Read about its products and services and/or business strategies, anything that will allow you to gain a little extra knowledge. Jot down key questions you want to get answered.

Start with a clean sheet

Just as you research the company, do an in-depth personal inventory of your own skills, behaviours and attitudes. Think about previous jobs and experiences and what worked for you, what didn't, and why. You have an ideal opportunity to build the new and improved professional you. Write down the personal characteristics you'd like to improve, then develop a strategy to maximise your strengths and minimise your weaknesses. For instance, if you were never prepared for meetings, write down ways to improve your performance. If you were always late on assignments, develop a routine that will keep you on time.

Be aware you may get sick!

The stress of a major change (such as a new job) can lower your immune system. A new job can mean a new environment of viruses and bacteria your body hasn't built resistance to. So eat healthy foods and get plenty of sleep to help your body, both before and after you start your new job.

Don't expect everything to be perfect

Understand that the reality of any situation rarely lives up to what was reported, or your expectations. Expect some things to be better than advertised, some worse, some the same. That way when you find out, for example, about the need to travel to meetings into the city on a weekly basis, or your need to take your turn at looking after your boss' child when she comes in after school you will be better able to cope.

Expect there to be a crisis at home

It's Murphy's' law – you will get toothache, or the car will break down, or you will need to get the washing machine fixed. What you can do is make sure the house is clean and you are straight on the mending and ironing before you start.

Be on time

Even if it's a new job in the same company, the location may differ, so do a trial run of how long it will take to get there in the rush hour, and allow some contingency time. Make sure you know when and where you are to report to on your first day and who you are going to meet.

Initial considerations

What image do you want to portray?

We all have an image, whether created consciously or not. Before your first day, consider what 'image' is appropriate to your job. It helps to fit in on the first day. Don't let your clothes attract more attention than your ideas. Think about your behaviour, what could be offensive? Drinking alcohol at lunchtime? Using swear words? Monitor your behaviour so you can see what you may want to change.

Define your future

This is your chance to be the person you want to be. If you want to be seen as friendly, act in a friendly way. If you want to be seen as effective and efficient, don't take too many tea breaks and be sure to return from lunch promptly.

Don't be too keen on making a good impression

There is a lot to take in with a new job, so pace yourself. Remember that you are learning a new job, building relationships and settling into a new team. All of this will take time. The temptation might be to work like mad to prove yourself worthy of your new role but you will do better if you take the time to reflect, focus and prioritise. You don't want to have to slow down at a later point as it may look like you have lost your enthusiasm. Plus, you don't want to create expectations of yourself or work at a pace that is unreasonable.

Wait before making suggestions for change

You'll probably have lots of ideas to make a difference and want to let the company know they made the right choice in recruiting you. But don't try to change everything at once or offer a stream of suggestions that borders on arrogance. Before you suggest making changes, try to understand why things are done the way they are. This will help when you do make a suggestion as people will notice that you took the time to understand the current procedure. Remember, don't try and make too many changes at once, choose a small, achievable goal first.

Keep balance

Don't forget the other priorities in your life – your family, your health, your hobbies, your friends. If all facets of your life are not in alignment, there's no way you will find fulfilment in your job. Remember, you work to live – you don't live to work.

Keep a notebook

Always carry a notepad or pocket organiser with you. Get in a routine of writing down thoughts, ideas, and information from others. (Before you forget, buy one now!)

Be seen as a hard worker

Work hard. If a colleague takes long lunch breaks and spends most of the day talking with their friends on the phone, don't be inclined to do the same. They may already be on a warning for their behaviour.

Your first day

On day one, you will need to show certain paperwork, so take with you:

- Bank details.
- National insurance number.
- P45 (if you have worked before).

Be positive and enthusiastic. Portray your best side so people have a good first impression of you.

Notice the dress code

You will want to dress right for the workplace. If you are smartly dressed, and everyone is dressed informally, make sure it is acceptable.

Get to know your colleagues

Find out about their likes and dislikes. Let others know that you're interested in how they do things and take a good look at their work style. Don't form close relationships too quickly as someone perceived as a trouble maker may seek to get you into their camp.

Be friendly

Make sure to say "Hello!" or "Good Morning!" and smile to everyone when you arrive at work. Do not share too much personal information about your social life or how stressed you feel in the job no matter how much you are inclined to do so.

Give your new colleagues the benefit of the doubt if you don't feel at ease with them right away. Think how long it takes, for example, stepfamilies, soccer teams, or construction workers to get used to each other. The dynamics can be similar for a new worker. On one level, your new work team will welcome you. On another level, they may worry about how they will have to change because of you. Be patient and give them the benefit of doubt.

Look to fit in and be helpful

For example, offer to make the coffee, wash the mugs, or take the post to the post room. Make sure you know how to use the office equipment and take the initiative to unjam the copier or sort the mail, before bothering others.

Find out arrangements for lunch and coffee breaks

Are lunch breaks at set times or is there flexibility? If you bring your lunch, great! It will save both time and money, but going to the company cafeteria will help you to meet people. If you like to take a brisk walk for part of your lunch break to clear your mind, ask someone to join you.

Learning how to work in a new job is often harder than knowing a technical skill. It's all about working in a new work culture. A work culture is the combination of behaviours and rules that run the company, organisation, or department. Some of these may be in writing but most will be unwritten. Because of this, they will take time to learn so be patient and observant.

Your job

If you do not already have a job description, ask for one, and then try to define as clearly as you can the boundaries of your job. In this effort, you are not seeking to establish the minimum acceptable benchmarks, but frontiers within which you can make your best contribution. Do this constructively and as soon as you can. The first month is ideal. Waiting six months is too late.

Ask a lot of questions and don't be shy. It will demonstrate your interest in the job. You can ask as many questions as you want at the beginning. But help others by grouping questions together and not asking a question every few minutes.

Find out:

- The way the company works, and your boss and close team members in particular.
- The limits of your authority.
- The parameters and main objectives of your job.
- The kind of feedback you will receive from superiors.
- The limits of your responsibilities personnel, products, services, etc.
- The way your job meshes into any quality system in use. If the organisation has received ISO 9000 status or a similar quality accreditation what impact does this have on your work.
- The resources you will have.
- The priorities in the job and the proportion of your time you should be giving to each.
- The main problem areas and the 'uniqueness' of the job.
- Your objectives. Sit down with your new boss and make sure you understand what he or she wants from you, when they want it and how they want it.
- The expectations of your colleagues.
- How to communicate with your boss. Can you just walk in or do you need to set an appointment? Who needs to be kept informed?
- Who do you need to copy in on memos and invite to meetings?
- How involved does your boss want to be?

Find out how you are doing

Schedule periodic meetings with your supervisor to get answers to your questions and use these meetings to check on how you're doing. Ask for specifics. Find out how you can improve.

Understand the network of people by viewing relationships across the organisation and beyond. Understand how to manage internal politics, recognise the key influencers, gatekeepers, and the allies who will help you achieve your goals. Draw a hub-and-spoke diagram with you in the centre and identify the important relationships you need to cultivate.

Make sure you know the length and terms of your probation period. It's natural to feel anxious about this but you don't have to wait until the end of the period to get feedback on your work. Go ahead and set up some talks with your boss. Point out what you've accomplished so far. And ask about each area of your job. What is going well? What could be improved – and how.

Chapter Twenty One

Useful resources

All hyperlinks in this chapter are also available on the website: www.howtogetajobinarecession.com

Introduction

Alongside buying newspapers, you can also keep up with the news via the newspaper web sites. A comprehensive list is available at
www.amazingpeople.co.uk/researchzone.htm

If your job is made redundant, read up on your entitlements at www.berr.gov.uk. The short link to the specific page you want is http://tinyurl.com/5sgrdq

The following pages provide resources that coincide with the different sections of this book.

Part Two

Getting ready, being organised

Copies of all the forms used in this chapter are available as a low cost downloadable PDF eBook from www.howtogetajobinarecession.com

What do you want to do?

Values: If you would like to work through an extensive values exercise using a a pack of values cards please visit www.amazingpeople.co.uk/valuescards.htm

Jobs Explorer

To find out more about different jobs use the "explore type of jobs" links at www.prospects.ac.uk – here is the direct link http://tinyurl.com/2l7kn or use the job profiles at http://careersadvice.direct.gov.uk, here is the direct link: http://tinyurl.com/22uege

Read more about different careers at Careers TV: www.careerstv.eu

Career assessments

Highlands Ability Battery: This is based on the work of Johnson O'Connor - www.jocrf.org

The Highlands Company main web site is at www.highland-sco.com and if you are interested in taking it, you may like to visit www.highlandsuk.com or http://tinyurl.com/dlw8uc

Other assessments: Details on the Highlands Ability Battery, MBTI and Strong Interest Inventory are available at www.personalassessments.co.uk

You can take free tests at a number of sites including the BBC – what am I like, http://tinyurl.com/6l4n2

The Keirsey Temperament Sorter which is similar to the MBTI can be taken for free at www.keirsey.com (although you need to pay for a comprehensive report).

Wondering if you would make it through selection to be a pilot? You can take a practice test from www.qantas.com.au here: http://tinyurl.com/6lljt6 or www.aviac.com/demo

Creating your CV

If you would like a review of your CV, contact Denise at: denise@amazingpeople.co.uk

Get networking

Diane Darling shows you how to "work a room" at: http://tinyurl.com/crpo8k

Online networking is available via:

- www.linkedin.com
- www.ryze.com
- www.ecademy.com

If you arrange to meet someone, you could opt to meet halfway, in terms of distance or time and this link will identify places to meet: www.meethalfway.com

Fact finding interviews

To find out more about different companies you can research via a business library or look online using the Kompass Register of British Industries and Commerce available at www.kompass.com/kinl/index.php

Stand out from the crowd

An excellent book to read more on this topic is *Career Distinction*, *Stand Out by Building Your Brand* by William Arruda and Kirsten Dixson published by *Wiley*. You can also find out about your online identity by using the tool available here: www.onlineidcalculator.com/index.php

Psychometric testing

You can practice a variety of tests using the links available from test publishers

SHL: www.shldirect.com

ASE: www.ase-solutions.co.uk with the direct link at: http://tinyurl.com/b795kw

Saville Consulting: from Saville Consulting the direct link is: http://tinyurl.com/cl7cfh

PSL/Kenexa: www.psl.co.uk/practice

Kogan Page: www.profilingforsuccess.com/kogan-page

Test your verbal knowledge at: http://tinyurl.com/d8o2v6

You can access a range of practice tests at low cost here: www.aptitudetestsonline.co.uk

Axiom Software, abstract reasoning test at: www.axiomsoftware.com/products discovery-abstract.php?uc=9,396

Test examples for finance jobs: http://students.efinancialcareers.co.uk/numerical_test.htm

Considering work as a computer programmer? You can test yo aptitude here: www.psychometrics-uk.com/bapt.html

This site was created by two Bristol University students to provide free practice tests: www.assessmentday.co.uk

More practice tests are available at: http://space.businessballs.com/paulnewton/index.htm

This site has some free and some paid for practice tests and further information:www.psychometric-success.com

If you are applying to a company they will often have a page with details on their tests, for example from HSBC: www.jobs.hsbc.co.uk/graduates useful-tools/psychometric-test.aspx

What they are saying about this book

This book was written following my work as the career coach on ITV's Tonight Programme: *How Safe is Your Job?*

"I see you got Paul a job in a little over a week – pity we can't replicate you. It would save a lot of government excuses about unemployment." -- **Dave Raddings, Assistant Producer ITV**

"This book provides the weary job seeker with the renewed vigour required to bag that dream job. Denise Taylor provides a step-by-step guide ensuring no stone is left unturned during the job hunt. I would recommend it to anyone who is searching for work during these tough economic conditions." -- **Lucie Mitchell, Editor, HRZone.co.uk**

"As a very experienced careers counsellor, Denise provides inspiration and structured practical advice for anyone seeking their next career move. An expert in her field, she not only provides the exercises for people to be able to assess who they are and what they can offer, but she also covers key practicalities of effective job search. These range from CV and interview technique, to effectively using contacts which is how most new jobs are found. Her tips on the importance of studying and understanding the job market and selecting the right sectors and organisations to target is particularly useful, especially in recessionary times. This is a great up to date book for job seekers at all levels, and also for those advising them." -- **Tony Charles is a career counsellor, writer and broadcaster and owns Wales' leading career management consultancy, Tony Charles Associates Limited**

"Being up to date, this book is the closest signpost I've seen so far to assist current jobseekers in finding their way through the recession turmoil of 2009. Spelling out job search processes step by step, Denise Taylor doesn't fall into the trap of making assumptions about prior knowledge on the part of the reader; this is a warts-and-all guide to finding a job. It is essentially a workbook – designed to encourage the serious job seeker to lift his or her head above the parapet and face reality. It needs time, energy and commitment, and for those serious about applying themselves to find work, it could be the only guide they will need." -- **Claire Coldwell, Career Coach, Ad astra Career Management Limited and author of Take Charge! - focused and inspirational advice for career changers**

"There are lots of job search books about and in the current economic climate you can expect many more to appear in the near future. What makes Denise Taylor's "How to Get a Job in a Recession" stand out from the crowd is that it is so easy to use. Written in a chatty, friendly style, it eases the reader painlessly into the business of finding work in a way that makes it seem fun instead of daunting. The author's experience of helping job seekers shows in the case studies she draws on for examples and the realistic, practical advice she gives." -- **Simon Levack, Author of the *Aztec Mysteries* and former Lawyer**

"Denise's advice is all about staying positive and focused. That's the secret to success in all areas of business – whether you're in a job or forced to look for a new one. That's what we help our clients do – you can too, with the help of this book." -- **Steve Hinton, Executive Chairman, QED Consulting www.qedconsulting.co.uk**

"What Denise Taylor proposes is based on practical experience and her advice works just like she promises it will. Anyone can follow her advice and, by following it, can optimise their career potential going forward. At Career Consultants, we continually refer to Denise Taylor's guidance to ensure we are providing our clients with the best and most comprehensive career advice available." -- **Keith O'Malley, Career Consultants, Dublin**

"Anyone who's been job hunting for a couple months will feel completely overwhelmed by the whole process. All of a sudden you're at home, facing a computer with little or no guidance about what to do first. Most books seem to be telling people the same basic things. This is the first guide I have read that takes you step by step through exactly what you need to do in order to find that all elusive job. Also, it gives you realistic views and figures regarding what is going on in the job searching world, including the amount of time and effort that you need to put in. It really is simple to follow and will make you much more focused and optimistic. Well done Denise! A valuable guide to those looking for a brighter future." -- **Wayne Parrott, Partnership Director, Royal Mail**

"I have been job hunting for a couple months and felt completely overwhelmed by the whole process. All of a sudden I was at home, facing my computer with not much guidance about what to do first. Most books that I got seemed to be telling the same basic things. This is the first guide that takes you step by step to exactly what you need to do in order to help you find a job. Also, it gives you realistic views and figures regarding what is going on in the job searching world, including the amount of time and effort that you need to put in. It is really simple to read and has made me so much more focused now and optimistic. Thanks Denise!" -- **Tatyana, PhD Graduate/ Chemist**

"Despite the economic downturn, the good news is that organisations will always need good people - like you. Whether your interest is getting back into the workplace or navigating a change of career direction, "How to Get a Job in a Recession" is especially timely. Denises's approach is refreshingly realistic, comprehensive and practical. By following this structured and user-friendly book, Denise will guide you through a job search campaign ensuring you stand out...for all the right reasons!" -- **Pauline Drissell, Independent Career Coach**

"This book is essential reading for anyone job hunting in our present economic climate. It covers every aspect of getting the right job for you in a clear cut, practical, motivational way. Denise's expertise just shines through." -- **Carol Crowther EFT Advanced Practitioner and Trainer www.eft-reiki.co.uk**

"Denise is an amazing career coach who has transformed my career and can transform your career. She has put down all her knowledge and experience in this very practical book." -- **Des, Director of a Blue Chip Company**

"*I was inspired just by the introduction to this book. Denise is truly providing a service in what is a desperate affair in the job market. Much of what I have read I am applying in my daily life. I agree that redundancy does not mean it's all over, and volunteering is an opportunity, which, providing you have some spare time, (short term) has immense benefits where you can introduce yourself into the environment that you are interested in, also, you learn new skills, and the possibility of job opportunities. Thank you Denise for all your help and encouragement, and writing a book has also encouraged me to pursue my dreams in writing children books.*" -- **Pauline Peace, Career Changer**

"*An inspiring, direct and simple book that covers every area of applying for the right job for you at the right time. It makes you feel that you are not the only person in your situation and that your goals can be achieved with the right approach and determination. Thank you Denise.*"
-- **Jessica Parsons, National Test Services**

"*Working in a challenging, fast paced environment I was in need of some guidance, to have confidence in my own style, values and strengths, particularly when working with my executive team colleagues. Using the techniques outlined in this book Denise helped me to understand and apply my strengths, to be confident in my own abilities to deal with those challenges. If you are able to understand all this, plus know what it is you love, are good at and how to apply yourself, the rest is up to you, Denise helped me to get there and her book can help you.*" -- **Sue Groom, Services Director for a large social landlord**

"*During a time of economic turmoil the need for professional advice and support in getting a job has never been greater. This book gives you practical support to help you maximise your potential, from an award winning career coach. Denise is a valued member of the Institute of Career Guidance and a regular contributor to our events and publications."*   -- **Paul Hebron, Institute of Career Guidance**

"Denise's knowledge and experience has been amazing and an enormous help. This book is a must-read for anyone wanting a new job, whether it to be in a new career or the next rung on the ladder."   -- **Jose, Health Trainer**

"Denise provides a step-by-step guide to help in your job search and with a career direction, her depth of experience means this book is invaluable to anyone on a job hunt, it's packed full of great advice and helps you to focus on what you should be doing." -- **David Aldrich, Team Leader, SELEX Communications**

"This is the survival guide of the year. With the economic situation declining and more redundancies reported in the news, looking for a job is becoming harder and more competitive. This book is a fantastic and practical step by step guide to be able to stand out from the crowd. Helping you to improve your job search, CV and covering letter; making a painstaking search job much more bearable and successful! Good luck." -- **Emily Spicer, Graduate**

"The advice in this book has helped me to prepare and really focus on interviewer's questions. You really know what makes a difference in the world of recruitment and selection. You truly are an Amazing Person." -- **Debbie, Chief Executive, Charity**

"This book is a toolkit containing every possible careers tool for every opportunity, but, just as importantly, it will also get you thinking about what kind of career you want to build and why. It is like having your own personal careers consultant." -- **Alison Rostron, public sector manager**

"After months of applying unsuccessfully for jobs which were similar to my current role, I realised I needed to figure out what I wanted to do. After working with Denise, I

realised I was applying for the wrong jobs! Using my net-works and working through the questions in the book, I found the job I was best suited for and applied for it. The CV, covering letter and interviews tips were invaluable, and I'm now looking forward to starting my new job. Thanks Denise!" -- **Alison Chappell, senior manager, charity**

"A logical and thorough approach are combined with Denise's warmth and encouraging advice to create a book that will be invaluable in any job search. All aspects of a job search are thoroughly discussed with invaluable tips and advice from Denise along the way." -- **Kay, Finance Manager, large plc**

"Denise is energetic and engaging in person... and her style comes across in this book. Listen carefully to her advice - it worked for me!" -- **Lindsay Travis, Sustain-ability Analyst**

"What do you choose? Doom, gloom and submission to the situation of a recession or positive action to get the job of your dreams? If you choose the latter then Denise's book will give you a step by step guide of what you need to do to get to where you want to be in the world of work no mat-ter what the financial situation is in the world!" -- **Irene Cowling, Life Coach and Trainer**

"Denise's advice is always geared around you, so you always feel that you are getting a tailored view on the right job for you and for the right reasons. She brings her years and breadth of experience in careers coaching and analysis to bear on your problem, which soon seems much less intimidating than when you made that first call. Putting you at your ease, she allows you to be honest with yourself, whilst always aiming for that next step. One thing is for sure - you will always get excellent advice from Denise." -- ***Ben Eckersley, Contract Performance Manager, NHS***

About the author

Denise Taylor is an award-winning career coach.

With a combination of educational credentials and vast industry expertise, Denise is renowned for helping clients get results. She has specialised in career development for over 20 years, and has published extensively in this area. Her specialist knowledge is backed up with diplomas in Performance Coaching and Counselling, and Masters degrees in Occupational Psychology (focused on career development) and Business Administration (MBA). She is also a Registered Guidance Practitioner.

Following a career which saw her rise from Post Office counter clerk to assistant director in less than 14 years, Denise set up *Amazing People* in 1999. Working predominately with individuals, Denise helps students, graduates and career changers understand who they are and how to become successful in their job search.

Denise is also a sought-after consultant and advises companies as diverse as charities, energy companies and the Civil Service, helping them make accurate recruitment decisions and to provide support in times of redundancy. This means the advice in this book is very comprehensive and well-rounded as Denise also trains interviewers and recruiters.

In November 2007, Denise won a National Career Award (sponsored by *The Independent Newspaper*) for The Gold Career Programme, which focuses on those seeking clarity on their career future.

Denise was the featured career coach on the *Tonight* programme, *How Safe is Your Job?*, November 2008, and is regularly featured on national radio including *BBC Radio 4 Nice Work, Radio Gloucestershire* and *City Talk Radio*. Articles by Denise have appeared in a variety of magazines including *Top Santé, The Apprentice, Prospects Graduate,* and the online site *HR Zone*. Denise has spoken at a number of professional events and conferences including The Open University Business School, The Association for Counselling at Work and the Institute of Career Guidance.

Outside of work, Denise enjoys living in the countryside, is passionate about music and believes in following personal passions, hence learning to DJ.

Denise maintains a number of web sites:

www.amazingpeople.co.uk

www.personalassessments.co.uk

www.jobsearchsupport.com

www.highlandsuk.com

www.howtogetajobinarecession.com

www.denisetaylor.co.uk

Denise can help you on a one to one basis with:

- **Career programmes** including the award winning Gold Career Programme.

- **In-depth psychometric testing** including the Highlands Ability Battery, Myers Briggs Type Indicator or Strong Interest Inventory.

- **CV review** – from a short review of your completed CV to a bespoke rewrite.

- **Interview coaching** – to get you in a peak state for an important interview.

- **Career review** – to enhance your career prospects.

Group programmes and seminars also are available.
To be kept informed, join Denise's mailing list at:
amazingpeople-402298@autocontactor.com

If you are interested in working one to one with Denise, finding out more about group telephone seminars or having Denise speak at an event, please get in touch.

denise@amazingpeople.co.uk or call 01684 772 888.

AWARD WINNING CAREER COACHING

Lightning Source UK Ltd.
Milton Keynes UK
02 September 2010
159342UK00001B/120/P